The Parent's
Answer Book

The Parent's Answer Book

Over 101 Most-Asked Questions About Your Child's Well-Being

Gerald Deskin, Ph.D.
Greg Steckler, M.A.

Fairview Press   *Minneapolis*

Published by Fairview Press, 2450 Riverside Avenue South, Minneapolis, MN 55454.

Library of Congress Cataloging-in-Publication Data

Deskin, Gerald, 1929-
        The parent's answer book : over 101 most-asked questions about your child's well-being
/ Gerald Deskin, Greg Steckler.
                    p.   cm.
        Includes index.
        ISBN 0-925190-79-9
        1. Child development—Miscellanea. 2. Adolescence—Miscellanea. 3. Children—
Health and hygiene—Miscellanea. 4. Teenagers—Health and hygiene—Miscellanea. 5. Child
rearing—Miscellanea.
I. Steckler, Greg, 1949-   . II. Title.
HQ767.9.D465   1995
305.23'1—dc20   95-33156
                                                                                                        CIP

First Printing: October 1995

Printed in the United States of America
99 98 97 96 95   7 6 5 4 3 2 1

Cover design: Circus Design

Publisher's Note: Fairview Press publishes books and other materials related to the subjects of physical health, mental health, and family and social issues. Its publications, including *The Parent's Answer Book,* do not necessarily reflect the philosophy of Fairview Hospital and Healthcare Services or their treatment programs.

For a free current catalog of Fairview Press titles, please call this toll-free number: 1-800-544-8207.

Contents

SOCIAL DEVELOPMENT   147
How Do You Know

EMOTIONAL DEVELOPMENT   153
How Do You Know

FAMILY DEVELOPMENT

How do you know what time your child should go to bed?

What is sleep and why do we need it?
We all need sleep. Sleep repairs cell damage, gives muscles time to rest, relaxes the mind, and generally brings the body back to maximal functioning. When we have adequate sleep we awake with a feeling of well being. Without enough sleep we may wake up feeling grouchy and irritable.

Most children need eight to ten hours of sleep a day. Some children sleep more or less than that, depending on individual needs. The best measure of a child's need for sleep is whether the child feels rested the next day.

Children who have been sick, overly stressed, or who are going through a growth spurt may need additional sleep. This is particularly noticeable in adolescence, when a child may need twelve or more hours of sleep each day. Young children who have scheduled nap times at school or day care may need less sleep in the evening.

Why the conflict between parent and child? There are two determining factors for setting a bedtime. The first is the child's physical need for sleep, and the second is the parent's need for the child to have a predictable schedule. Parents go to work and children go to school at scheduled times. Throughout the day, there are usually a variety of activities that have to be performed within certain times.

As parents, we all have somewhat different lifestyles. Some parents come home from work at 6:00 PM and some come home later. A parent who comes home late may want a child to wait up so they can be together. Some parents stay awake late and feel it is normal for children to stay awake until a later hour, while others go to bed early.

How much sleep does your child need? The general rule is eight hours of sleep, plus or minus an amount that is determined by the age of the child and the quality of his or her behavior the next day.

How do you solve the problem when your child will not go to sleep? You want your child to go to sleep, but he or she doesn't want to go to sleep, saying he or she doesn't feel sleepy. How do you solve the problem?

From birth to two years of age children will often find their own sleep times. However, by putting the child down between 7:00 PM to 9:00 PM and not picking him or her up until 6:00 AM to 8:00 AM (except for infants who need a late-night feeding) you can help the child develop the habit of sleeping during those hours. If you begin to decrease numbers of naps during the day, this also will encourage the all-night sleeping.

From two to five years of age many children learn how to go to sleep at regular times. Some learn early and some take longer. If the child has difficulty going to sleep on a regular basis you might try the following techniques:

1. Eliminate napping during the day.
2. Eliminate highly stimulating activities within a half hour before bed.
3. Eliminate sugary foods or drinks within an hour before bed.
4. Give the child a warm bath just before bed.
5. Read to the child or listen to a story on tape to put the child in a more relaxed mood.
6. Listen to soft, quiet music.
7. Sit with the child until he or she falls asleep.
8. Offer the child some reward for going to sleep "on time" during consecutive nights.

For this age group, patience, practice, and consistency will eventually get the child to sleep at regular times. If the child falls asleep and then wakes up two or three hours later, take the child back into bed and sit with him or her until he or she falls asleep. This may result in a few sleepless nights for you, but if you are consistent, it may only last a few weeks.

For children six to twelve years of age anytime from 7:30 PM to 10:00 PM is an average bedtime. Most often these children have to wake up between 6:00 AM and 7:30 AM to get to school on time. By this age, most children have developed the habit of going to bed at a regular time. A child who refuses to go to bed at a certain time is probably asking to be treated as an older child. If you think the child's bedtime is appropriate, set bedtime earlier by the amount of time he or she stayed up past bedtime the previous night.

For children thirteen to sixteen years of age bedtimes range from 9:00 PM to 11:00 PM depending on the needs and activities of the child. The child who continually goes to sleep at progressively later times should be made aware that the sleeping cycle can be shifted. For example, a child who starts going to bed at 2:00 AM or 3:00 AM may sleep until 12:00 PM. This is the beginning of a habit that may not serve the child well.

For children in middle and late adolescence, bedtimes can usually be addressed from the perspective of the child's mental, emotional, and physical well-being. Let the child know that he or she can only "burn the candle from both ends" for a limited time. The consequences of sleep deprivation are sickness and poorer performances—academically, socially, and physically. Remind the child of being courteous toward other members of the family who may need a quiet environment to sleep. A child who stays up late has to be aware of the noise and light factors for those sleeping.

Recommendations: Sleeping medication is not advisable for children.

How do you know if your child should sleep in your bed?

The "family bed." There is some controversy about whether children should sleep with their parents on a regular basis. Proponents of the "family bed" believe that it is natural for children to sleep with their parents and that they should do this until the child wants his or her own space. Often this may not occur until preadolescence or adolescence. Proponents of the family bed believe that children get needed comfort, security, nurturance, and closeness met on a very specific and individual basis. They also believe that when the child eventually separates he or she does so when most ready.

Acceptance of the family bed is greater in European, Asian, South American, and African cultures than in British and American cultures.

Opponents of the family bed hold a range of opinions—from the child never sleeping in the parents' bed to the child sleeping in the parents' bed for the first year or so, then gradually moving the child into his or her own bed, and finally his or her own room.

What is common practice? When a child is born, it is not unusual for parents to keep the child in a crib in the bedroom for the first few months. After maybe six months or so, the child may get into a regular sleeping and feeding pattern. At this time, many parents begin to feel more comfortable letting the child sleep in his or her crib in his or her own bedroom.

Why is it important for children to sleep in their own beds? First, children learn to separate from parents while overcoming their anxiety about separation. Second, they learn a sense of independence. Third, parents need their own bed and their own privacy to maintain their rest and sexual intimacy.

When is it all right for children to sleep with their parents? There are several situations when it may be very appropriate for children to sleep with their parents:

- Children can sleep with one or both parents on rare occasions as a special treat.
- Children may sleep with their parents, on occasion, if they are ill.
- Children may sleep with their parents if they have been particularly frightened, or if some trauma has occurred in the family. However, this privilege should not be overused. It is easy for children to make permanent what is initially meant to be temporary.

When does a child's sleeping in your bed become excessive?

- When there is no apparent reason for the child to be sleeping in the parent's bed. That is, the child is no longer sick, frightened, or in need of special comforting.
- When the parent or child begins to feel uncomfortable with the arrangement.

Is there a danger for children sleeping in their parents' bed? Perhaps the only danger is that some children may become overly dependent. By allowing a child to sleep with them longer than necessary, parents may reinforce the message to a fearful child that he or she is not capable of handling his or her own anxiety or that there really is something to be afraid of by separating. While sleeping with parents may relieve tension temporarily it may actually make the child more fearful and dependent in the long run.

Recommendations: At times, a child may be allowed to sleep in his or her parents' bed—but only for one evening or a short period of time. Children should not be allowed to do this as a way of coming between the parents. Parents must be aware of the reason(s) a child is not sleeping in his or her own bed. If there is a crisis and a child needs special support and consideration, a child should be allowed to sleep with his or her parents until the crisis has passed.

How do you know what TV shows and movies are appropriate for your child?

How do stories, movies, and television affect us all? Human history is time-binding. That is, long before television and radio, humans communicated important information to their tribes for each generation through stories. These stories told how to please the gods and where the best food was to be found. They told of dangers to be avoided. Eventually, these groups developed storytellers whose role it was to communicate this oral history. In essence, we all grew up listening to stories about our past. Since the beginning of written language, initially on stone and clay tablets, we could keep this information for generations. With the advent of radio and television, the stories became more numerous, more intense, more colorful, and often more violent. Although a good storyteller could activate and excite children and adults, television has brought storytelling to a new level. There is an immediacy about listening to news about murder, rape, riot, flood, fire, earthquake, tornado, and other disasters that are seen in living color and are happening to real people.

What kinds of stories emotionally affect children? The child's task is to learn. A child learns initially from parents, family, and other sources, such as media, school, friends, and so on. The kinds of stories that affect a child differ with the emotional makeup of each child. All children go through a stage of fearing monsters or having other fears; this is a normal part of their development. However, for the child who lacks maturity or is going through an emotional trauma, watching a television program that is full of violence may be unsettling or potentially destructive. Even for adults, some television stories are unsettling. Many of us have been disturbed by watching an important person's funeral on television or by watching an event that has happened or may happen to us. Because stories of child abuse, spousal abuse, rape, murder, and violence are now endemic on our television sets and

upsetting to us, as adults, we must monitor what our children view.

How and when do you censor inappropriate television programs? Parents must define how their television will be used. For example, do you use television as a baby-sitter? Can your children view any program they desire? Do your children watch television when you're not home? Do you have channels on your set that children should never watch? Are your children watching too much television? All of these are personal value questions. That is, your child may watch more or less television than my child. What is important is not these differences, but what is best for your child specifically. Because we are talking about children of different ages, different maturity levels, and with different parents, we can only state some general points of view.

- Children should watch a limited number of hours of television per week. Although television is an excellent educational and entertainment medium, children also need physical activity. More than a few hours of television per day is too much. Some parents do not allow television during the school week. This may be an excellent solution, allowing your child to get physical exercise, socialize with friends and time for homework.
- Certain channels may be inappropriate for your child at any time. Put a block on those channels so your child cannot see them. Read

the instruction manual to your television set or call your local cable station to obtain information about blocking certain channels.

- Depending on your child's maturity, age, and emotional development, certain types of programs should be banned. For example, some children are so upset by monster movies or cartoons that it affects their sleep. Ban them.

- Because television can be an excellent educational medium, use it wisely. For example, "Sesame Street" is an excellent educational program for young children. Many such programs exist for every age level. Teachers sometimes recommend children watch a program if it fits in with what they are teaching at school.

How do you censor inappropriate movies? The movie industry has attempted to rate movies so parents can identify films that are appropriate for their children. Unfortunately, some parents still bring their children to see movies that are clearly inappropriate for them. You must understand your child. If your child is upset by certain behaviors or scared by certain stories, then he or she should not watch those movies. Ultimately, it is your responsibility to decide.

To watch the news or not? Problems of living in the real world. Recently we have seen more children become upset by watching the news—not only news of atrocities in the world abroad,

but news here at home of violence, murder, rape, fire, floods, tornadoes, and earthquakes that are upsetting to us all. The news media sometimes even sensationalizes the small stories. Children live in the real world and must be exposed to this world; thus you as a parent have to determine what they are ready to watch. The answer to the problem is simple. If watching the news is upsetting to your child, he or she should not watch it for a while. You as a parent have to use your maturity and understanding to determine what your child can and should watch.

Recommendations:

1. Review frequently the television programs, movies, videos, and video games that your children watch.

2. Discuss with your spouse which programs are definitely not acceptable, which are questionable, and which are acceptable.

3. Eliminate those that are unacceptable. Allow the acceptable programs, and monitor those that are questionable. If the child's attitude, language, or behavior begins to worsen, eliminate the questionable programs.

How do you know which toys are appropriate for your child?

What use are toys to your child? If we think of toys as merely playthings, we make a major mistake. Toys are a child's means of learning about his or her environment. Appropriate toys at the appropriate age can facilitate a child's understanding about the relationship of things to each other and to the world at large. Unfortunately, these are not always the toys we choose for our children. We have all seen a child prefer a colorful box to a present itself, or witnessed a child's fascination with pots and pans rather than the toys we choose. A toy can have a different meaning to a child than it does to us as parents. Sometimes an unlikely stuffed figure can become a child's most prized possession. Toys help children think and understand.

Games for children. Games for adults. Children begin life attracted to various toys, and as they grow, they become game players. Sometimes these are games children play alone. Sometimes these are games children play together. Socialization often occurs at an early age through playing games. As the child grows, games become more important. Our nation and indeed the world is often preoccu-pied with games. Whether it is a two-person game, such as chess, backgammon, or a team sport, such as baseball or football, we all seem to play games. Work is often thought of as a game. We use the game model in business to develop the idea of a working team. A study of civilizations like the Romans or Mayans has shown evidence of games. One might say that since the beginning of recorded history we have evidence that playing games was important or even vital to understanding a country. The games of Sparta, especially the marathon, are still important today.

What toys are age-appropriate? Older children are clear about what games they want to play, as are adults. But the young child is dependent on parents and family to determine what games or toys are appropriate. If we think of toys as fulfilling a learning need then we can better select the appropriate toy. Toy stores are sometimes helpful in selecting general age-appropriate toys, but parents must know their own child. As young children develop their sensory motor and visual perceptual growth, appropriate toys may include colorful manipulative toys. For example, squeezable toys, blocks, and large, easily held toys that cannot be swallowed are most useful. As children grow, stuffed toys, building toys, and larger screw-together toys are appropriate. The next step requires smaller blocks that can be stuck together. At some point, books with large letters and colorful pictures are useful. As children mature and start reading, many books are available. Toys that are manipulative or require handling small pieces come into play. Eventually, games and electronic games become more popular and interesting to children. During this entire sequence, children sometimes enjoy cars, dolls, and new toys introduced by the toy manufacturers. As parents you must ensure that your toy selection fits your child's needs.

When do you give toys to your children? Like most difficult questions there are several answers. Toys are given on special occasions, as rewards for good behavior, and as learning tools when a child would benefit from them. Remember, if you use toys as learning devices, you must introduce them when the child can benefit from them. Toys don't have to be expensive. Paper, pencils, crayons, and painting supplies can be most helpful. Toys should be fun. Toys should stimulate imagination. Toys should teach the child something new. All these factors should be considered when you buy a toy.

How society decides what toys should be available to your child. It is a fact of our society that advertising and technology affect most aspects of our life. This is especially true with toys. Children want what they see advertised on television and in stores and what they play with at their friends' homes. There is fashion in toys just as in clothes. When something new is offered and demand is high, a toy may become scarce and very desirable to your child. Whether he or she should have it depends on you as a parent.

What about violent toys and video games? There are two frequently asked questions regarding toys:
- Should my child be allowed to play with toy guns?
- Is it unhealthy for my child to play video games?

Violent toys. The use of toy guns, knives, bombs, and other violent toys, are primarily targeted to young boys ages six to twelve years. The majority of girls at this age are not interested in these toys. Before there were guns and technological weapons and before there was television, young boys built spears, sharpened sticks, developed sling shots, and threw rocks as a way of extending their power into the environment around them. The psychological make-up of most young boys is about developing their power to achieve and protect. Powerful weapons, games of battle, competition for strength, speed, or endurance are all designed to help prepare young boys for entrance into the adult world, where the battleground is business, work, money, social standing, material possessions, and so on. A boy's primary instinct is to go out there and "get it" or "make it," and the faster he is able to do that the better he is.

In a healthy environment, a child is able to translate this need for power into real life skills and relationships. As a boy moves through adolescence, he needs to feel his power academically, athletically, artistically, or socially. He needs to see that he will achieve somewhere in the adult world. If a boy sees himself failing at this task or cannot see any opportunities for himself in the adult world, then he may carry immature behaviors of his youth, for example, guns, fighting, and so on, into his adult life. It is extremely important for boys to have successful male role models to emulate, and for boys to have real opportunities to express their talents.

It may be that the toy is less important to a boy than is the ability to feel his power and bring it into the world in an appropriate way. The crucial time for this is between the ages of ten and twenty years.

Video games. Should I let my child play with video games? They seem so violent and aggressive. He or she seems to be addicted to them. Are they good for my child?

You might ask yourself why children find video games so appealing. When you go to the arcades, notice how many boys are there and how many girls are there. You will see that there is usually a preponderance of boys actually playing the video games. The girls, for the most part, are watching the boys or playing games of skill rather than playing the violent games. What does this say about the needs of boys and the needs of girls?

Because video games are relatively new on the scene, no really long-term research has been done to determine their potential dangers or benefits. But parents and professionals have a variety of opinions.

The dangers of video games. Some parents and professionals believe that video games:

- reinforce violent tendencies in children,
- build and reinforce unwanted attitudes about male and female roles,
- develop escapist and addictive patterns in children,
- reinforce violent solutions to problems,
- over-stimulate a child's psychological makeup because the images are created by the adult mind, which can usually handle stronger depictions.

The benefits of video games. Some parents and professionals believe that video games

- provide a release for pent-up hostile and aggressive tendencies in children,
- help the child overcome feelings of insecurity or inferiority,
- develop concentration and attention,
- develop thinking skills,
- develop eye/hand coordination,
- develop the ability to handle competition.

Are video games good or are they bad? We don't know yet. Each family will have to make their own decision. For some, moderation is the key to success.

Recommendations: Watch your child's behavior after he or she has spent time playing video games. Is he or she more relaxed and happy? If he or she is more cooperative and considerate to others, your child may be gaining some benefit from the games. If, on the other hand, your child is more aggressive, more tired, more moody, less cooperative, or less considerate, then he or she probably is not benefiting from video games. Your child's post video behavior should be brought to his or her attention, and the games should be restricted or possibly eliminated.

How do you know how many toys to give a child, and how often?

Children use toys for various purposes. Toys are designed to enhance a child's pleasure, excitement, imagination, skill, or knowledge. Toys are meant to add something of value to a child's life. Toys stimulate play. They are not substitutes for love, happiness, feelings of self-worth, or fulfillment.

Why parents give toys to children. We give our children toys for many reasons. We want our children to be happy. We want to show them how much we appreciate them. We want our children to learn. We want to reward our children for work well done. We want to give our children more than we had as children. We also

give children toys for less noble reasons. Sometimes we want to keep our children quiet and occupied. Sometimes we feel guilty because we have not spent enough time with them. We want them to love us. Whatever the reason or reasons, there are some basic guidelines for giving children toys.

General guidelines for giving toys. First, determine if the toy is a gift, a reward, or a something to build knowledge and skill. Each one can be approached differently.

- **If the toy is simply a gift** to express love or appreciation, it can be given at any time or on special occasions, such as birthdays and holidays. As a gift, the toy should be given without strings attached. That means there is no special requirement for liking the toy or protecting it, only a polite thank-you if the child is of sufficient age (four years and up). If a child can't appreciate the monetary or emotional value of the gift, then give him or her something else. If you require considerable appreciation in return for the gift, then it is not a gift, it is a manipulation.

- **If the toy is a reward** for good behavior or an achieved goal, then it should be given only after the goal is achieved. Motivation is weaker to work hard for something after you have received a reward. There is great satisfaction, and often greater appreciation, for toys when they are earned. It can give a child a sense of confidence and pride when he or she works to achieve something. However, making every toy an "earned" toy creates a different distortion. As parents, we want our children to have the ability to accept gifts and to earn them. This balanced approach gives children a better preparation for later relationships.

- **If the toy is to develop skill and knowledge** it should be given when the child is ready. A child is ready if he or she has some interest in the toy and sufficient skill to achieve some immediate success with the toy. A toy that is too advanced for a child's abilities can leave the child so frustrated that he or she loses interest or feels bad about himself or herself. A toy that is too advanced can sometimes create arguments between a parent who wants the child to develop a skill (like riding a bicycle) and the child who finds the skill too scary or difficult. If you find yourself in this situation, drop back to a simpler task. For instance, in the above example, if the child is not ready for a bicycle, buy the child a toy that has four wheels that he or she can peddle and steer. Have the child walk or sit on things to develop balance and coordination. Make the exercises very fun and enjoyable.

How do you know when children have too much?

- When the toys aren't appreciated, played with, or protected, the child

may have too many toys. Some toys are played with until they break. Some toys are not played with, but protected on a shelf or in a special spot. Both examples are usually appreciated. Toys that are neither played with nor protected are usually not right for the child and probably could be discarded.

- When a child has more toys than his or her attention span can handle, the child may have too many toys. In other words, the child flits from toy to toy without exploring a variety of ways to play with one or two toys. This can leave many children overwhelmed, particularly if the child is young. A toy is interesting if it can capture and hold the child's imagination. Having too many toys can send a subtle message that toys are easily acquired and, therefore, easily replaced. It can suggest to a child that toys are not special or valuable. The child can conclude that there is no need to value the toys.

- When there isn't enough closet space or room for all the toys, there may be too many. If a toy hasn't been played with for several months, you might ask the child if he or she wants to keep it or recycle it. Giving the toy to a charitable organization, letting a friend or relative use the toy for a while, or selling the toy at a garage sale are all ways to recycle an unused toy. If the child protests, you may want to keep it. See if you can determine why the child wants it. For some children, keeping a toy may be a way to hang on to feelings of love, specialness, comfort, or control over the environment. When you set some limits on the child's outside environment, the child will begin to develop a stronger inside environment.

Recommendations:
1. To be meaningful, a reward must be earned.
2. Rewards that come too frequently begin to lose meaning.

How do you know what after-school activities are appropriate for your child?

What purpose do the activities serve?
Too often parents see after-school activities as unimportant or as a holding place for children so the parents can work. In fact, after-school activities can be very important to the child, especially when both parents work. After-school activities may serve a variety of purposes, including physical activity, development of socialization and peer relationship skills, homework, and so on.

What are the needs of the child?
What are the needs of the parent?
Children need physical activities. After sitting in a classroom for six hours, children need to move, to expend energy, to develop their bodies, as well as to develop their social skills in team-related and one-on-one activities. After being in a controlled situation all day, children look forward to the freedom of choosing activities for themselves.

Parents, on the other hand, need to know that their child is in a protected environment. Of course, parents also want to meet the child's needs for exercise and play. Parents may also want their child to finish homework during after-school hours. For working parents, a good after-school program can resolve many of these issues.

What do you want to accomplish during this time? While school provides children with a protected environment, good physical development, and possible homework opportunities, children do not receive time for adequate socialization during school hours. Children do play at recess and at lunch during school, but after-school programs give children a chance to develop social skills in a relaxed atmosphere. If you, as a parent want your child to develop specific social skills, communicate your concerns to whomever is in charge of after-school activities.

Are the activities appropriate and safe for your child? Physical safety and activity appropriateness are paramount for your child. In some situations, such as public or private school after-school programs, you may have some idea of the safety considerations. If you are not sure, ask. In private situations, especially, you may want to observe your child, from a distance if possible, to see if he or she gets appropriate attention. Some children have to be encouraged to socialize or get involved in more strenuous physical activity. If there are any health factors related to your child's activity, you should let the counselor or teacher know in advance. Children with special health needs should be especially protected. It is important that parents actively inform the caretaker.

How do you know if you are achieving your goal? One important parental task is to check often on your child's activities. A program with a great name may, in fact, not live up to that name. If you set a goal to be reached by your child in one month or three months, then you have progress you can measure. If the goal is not met, you may decide to change the goal, or you may decide to change your child's setting.

Recommendations:
1. Make after-school activities useful by first assessing the child's needs.
2. Do what you can, given your time, money, and availability of programs.
3. Evaluate every three months to see whether you are achieving your goals.

How do you know what to say to a child who is getting a new brother or sister?

A change in your child's life. For all of us, parent and child, the transition period of change can be disruptive. Change threatens the child's stability and can be difficult. Often, a new brother or sister is the first major change or trauma in a child's life. The change can sometimes raise new fears in an already fearful child. Remember that some children accept new siblings without much outward concern.

What might the child show? Typically, children need some time to absorb the fact that there will be changes. Going from being the idol of his or her parents' eyes to playing second fiddle is a big transition for a child. Although many parents should and do prepare their child by expressing love and reassurance that they will always love the child the child quickly realizes that an intruder is coming. He or she may show anger or hostility to the idea of a sibling initially. The child may withdraw into his or her own fantasies of feeling hurt, or may openly express the fact that he or she   doesn't want a new brother or sister.

After the sibling is born, a new phase

begins. The child may embrace the new member as someone he or she can care for and love, or the child may show his or her anger in a number of ways. The child may show his or her jealousy of the baby by hitting, pushing, biting, or otherwise trying to hurt the baby. He or she may outwardly do nothing to hurt the baby, but have fantasies of the baby being kidnapped or hurt. Clearly, in many cases, the child needs time to accept the new arrival.

How do you avoid the child's anger and jealousy? There are several ways to help avoid jealousy and anger at the birth of a new sibling. One is to make the child a part of the process right from the beginning. Parents should discuss the impending birth with the child, and make him or her a part of what will happen in the future. This way, the child has a chance to get used to the idea and, hopefully, accept it. If the child does not accept the idea, then he or she at least has a chance to think about what is coming, which may lessen the blow.

Giving the child information as the pregnancy progresses is an excellent way to make your child a participant in the process. Let the child know what is happening. If the baby kicks let the child touch the mother's stomach and feel the kicks. As preparations are made for the baby, let the child help select furniture and toys.

What you can do to make the new baby a more positive experience for the child. As human beings, we tend to be less afraid of things we understand. The more information and involvement your child has, the more likely he or she will accept the new baby.

If your child has a role as protector of the baby, as teacher of the baby, and as helper in the everyday care of the baby, the more positive your child will become. As time passes and your child realizes his or her place as the older child in the family is secure, the better the chance of an easy adjustment.

Recommendations:

1. Include the child in preparing for the new baby and encourage him or her to help after the baby arrives.
2. If necessary, reward the child for being helpful.
3. After the baby comes, spend as much individual time with the older child as is possible and gradually increase the time spent with baby, child, and parent.

How do you know when it is appropriate to leave your child home alone?

Leaving your child home alone depends on several major issues. How far away are you going? How long will you be away? What adult resources—in terms of neighbors, friends, and relatives—are nearby? What is the maturity level of your child?

In most states there are laws that make it a criminal offense to leave an underage minor home alone. You might contact your local police department to find out the laws in your area.

At what age is it OK to leave my child at home alone? It is probably a good idea not to let any child stay home alone before the age of twelve. However, the question is often raised when children are nine, ten, and eleven. There are many working parents who are not home when their children come home from school. These children, sometimes called "latchkey" kids, let themselves in and must care for themselves until a parent arrives. There are also many situations when a parent might make a quick trip to the market or run a quick errand while the child is watching TV or playing alone. Usually these trips or errands take less than an hour.

If the parent wants to leave the child alone for a short time, the parent should consider the following questions:

1. Is there a neighbor nearby who can help the child in an emergency? Is the child comfortable going to the neighbor if he or she is frightened or in need? Is the child able to go to the neighbor's home alone?
2. Is the parent easily reachable by phone? Does the child have the number, and is he or she able to ask the proper questions of whomever answers the phone?
3. Does the child know how to dial 911 and give the proper information? Have you rehearsed this thoroughly (without actually calling 911)?
4. Is the house properly secured?

If the answer to any of these questions is "no," then it is probably not safe to leave the child alone.

Between the ages of twelve and fifteen, many children of normal maturity can be left alone at home for a few hours to manage themselves. It is important to make sure that the four conditions mentioned above are met and that there is some adult support within a five-minute drive. It is also a good idea for children of this age to receive a class or two in first aid. Most local hospitals provide free classes on a regular schedule. First aid classes are sometimes advertised under baby-sitting.

Between the ages of sixteen and nineteen, many children are capable of staying home by themselves not only for hours at a time, but also overnight and, sometimes, over weekends.

Is my child mature enough? Maturity means the child has sufficient self-control to avoid things that are dangerous, for example, matches, knives, alcohol, smoking, firearms, and so on. Maturity means the child has the ability to discriminate minor crises from major crises. Maturity means the child can predict the consequences of his or her actions, and it means his or her value system is oriented to an adult perspective.

You might ask yourself certain questions about your child. How does your child behave when you are home? Does your child show the appropriate actions and reactions to problem situations? Does your child have the right priorities? Does he or she follow instructions well? Will your child obey the limits set by you? If the answer to these questions is "yes," then your child is probably ready to be alone for a short period of time.

Self-care and self-protection are learned. If your child is twelve or older, and he or she wants the experience of being home alone, you can start out with short absences. If the child is not anxious and there are no problems, you can extend your absence to a few hours. If you have a young or middle teenager, you can also start off slowly and build up time away as the child demonstrates his or her capacity to handle himself or herself and the house. It is still not a bad idea to have friends, relatives, or neighbors drop by or call at certain times to give and get reassurance. It is important to remember that children can demonstrate good maturity for periods of time and then, in a moment, regress to younger behavior.

Baby-sitting. Baby-sitting is another situation in which young children are left home alone, this time with younger children to care for. Baby-sitting usually begins at or around the ages of

twelve to fourteen. Usually girls start baby-sitting before boys because girls tend to mature earlier than boys, and girls tend to have a higher interest in baby-sitting.

One of the best preparations for baby-sitting outside of the home is to baby-sit younger siblings. Siblings will be at their worst when Mom or Dad leaves the house. The parents, however, can get a good idea of how their older son or daughter manages the problems that arise. Parents can then guide the child toward more effective ways of managing the younger children.

Another good way to prepare your child for baby-sitting is to have him or her attend a baby-sitting class, sometimes presented by hospitals, libraries, and the Red Cross.

At first, it's not a bad idea to have your child baby-sit siblings, cousins, or friends, where you have access should your son or daughter need your help.

Recommendations: Children under the age of ten should never be left alone while the parent is out.

How do you know what to say to your child about divorce or separation?

What divorce or separation means to a child. There is little that affects a child as much as divorce or separation of parents. Not only is it traumatic for parents, but the child feels both a sense of loss, a feeling that his or her world is disintegrating, and, frequently, a sense that the problem was somehow caused by his or her own bad behavior.

How a child shows he or she is upset about divorce. The child's reaction to divorce may be one of disbelief. How could the parents do this to him or her? The child may blame both parents. The child certainly will be angry at both parents, even though he or she may understand logically why one parent left the other. A second, more difficult, but almost universal, reaction is the child's feeling that if he or she had behaved better, the parents would not have divorced. Children also often try to get the parents back together again. This may fly in the face of reality, but children still harbor the fantasy of bringing the nuclear family together again. When their attempts fail, children feel depressed, angry, and abandoned. This feeling of abandonment is universal, even though the child is loved and cared for by one or both parents.

What can you do to prevent these symptoms? There are a number of ways to help children feel better, although it is inevitable that they will suffer from some sad feelings. Both parents can reassure their children that they are loved and cared for. Parents can reassure children that they will see the noncustodial parent often. Parents can tell the children again and again that they are not the cause of the divorce.

What do you actually say to your child about the divorce? The words you use to tell your children about the divorce are very powerful and should be thought out in advance. This may mean suppressing your anger toward your spouse so that your children are not more traumatized. What you say is another way to prevent the amount of damage that occurs. What words you use are dependent on the age and maturity of the child.

1. Tell the child that his or her parents will be living apart because they are not happy together.
2. Tell the child that you and the other parent love him or her and that he or she will live with one of you and see the other parent often. Tell the child that he or she will spend vacations and holidays alternately with both parents.
3. Tell the child that he or she is not the cause of the divorce.

4. Tell the child that he or she will always have two parents who will love and care for him or her.
5. Do not forget to hold or touch your child. Children need a physical hug to reassure them that they are still loved.

How to minimize the child's reaction. Tell your child about the divorce in advance, and prepare him or her for the impending changes.

Based on the child's age, you can expect some different reactions. Get your child a book about divorce and discuss what will happen. Sometimes the child's major fear is, Who will take care of me?

Recommendations:

1. Reassure the child that both parents love him or her and that both parents are going to have time with him or her.
2. Reassure the child that nothing he or she did had anything to do with the divorce.
3. If the divorce entails a move, it can be helpful to have the child help decorate his or her new room.
4. Select and read one or two books on divorce with your child or children.

How do you know what to say to your child about death?

In our society, certain subjects are difficult to discuss. Death is one subject that is difficult for some parents to talk about. The question is always, At what age should I raise the subject of death?

Because death is part of our lives and an inescapable fact, we must let our children know that they can discuss it with us when they are ready. As parents, we must recognize when our children hold back because of embarrassment or sensitivity, and we must be able to open a discussion with them.

Clearly we must talk to children in a language they understand based on their age and maturity. In this way, we discover what they know, what they don't know, and how much information they can accept. What we say depends on us as parents. How comfortable are we discussing this subject? We quickly get in touch with our own anxieties about how long we have to live and what death means to us. Children's questions about death are often touched off by the death of a parent, relative, or pet. Sometimes just watching a TV program, such as the news, may trigger your child's anxiety about losing you or being left alone.

How a child comprehends death depends on several factors. The first we mentioned is maturity, or the child's stage of development. The second is the kind of education and experience a child has had. This primarily has to do with how the family handles the subject, the religious beliefs of the child and the family, and any ethnic or cultural factors.

While many of us are unclear about what happens after death, we can communicate what we do know. Remember, the task is not just to give your child information, it is to relieve his or her anxiety while controlling your own. Also, some children may want a more simple explanation than we can give, while other children will ask questions we can't answer.

How do you talk to your child about death? The discussion with children about death usually emerges from one of two directions: either the child initiates the discussion, or the parent must inform the child about a pet, a friend, or a relative who has passed away. Each discussion requires a different approach.

Sometimes children ask questions about death on their own. The average age for children to think about death is between the ages of five and nine. Typical questions that children ask are, Where do you go after you die? Why do people die? Are you going to die? Does dying hurt?. These questions about death and afterlife may bring up further questions about God, good and evil, and what happens to good people and bad people after death. It is good preparation for you and your spouse to

have conversations about the particular beliefs and values you want to impart to your children. It is usually best simply to answer the questions that your child asks without giving more information than he or she can handle. Your child's questions will tell you how much he or she can handle. You might tell your child, for example, that he or she will be cared for no matter what happens; your child's fear of death may mean he or she is afraid of being left alone. It is all right to tell children what you know and believe. It is also all right to tell children that there are some things you don't know or understand.

The second occasion in which you may discuss death with a child is when a pet, a friend, or a relative has died. For a child, the emotional involvement would decide the need for an explanation. When a pet or family member dies and the child has not previously been exposed to death, the parent should do the following:

1. Set aside some time when the child is relaxed and attentive and tell the child directly that you have some sad news.

2. Tell the child simply what has happened, for instance, the pet has died, or a relative had an accident and died.

3. Watch your child's reaction and answer any questions he or she has. If your child expresses a strong reaction, he or she may wish to be held and reassured. Don't force it. If there will be a funeral or a memorial service, you may wish to consider

whether you want your child to attend. (See more information about funerals below.)

4. If a pet dies and you want to have a burial ceremony or ritual, have your child help you plan and create it. Rituals often help children let go of something important in their lives. Rituals also help people gain some sense of control over an event that was out of their control.

If you see your child squirming, looking away, or getting distracted while you are trying to discuss death with him or her, you are probably giving too much information. You should wait until the child is more receptive. If the child asks a lot of questions, then you are probably not giving enough information. Use the child's attention and interest level to help you gauge how much information to supply.

What do you say to children at different ages? Children go through a series of stages as they mature. This involves a better understanding of reality and an ability to absorb facts about their world.

- The child from birth to school age deals with reality as he or she understands it. It may be colored by watching television, for example, watching TV characters die and cartoon characters fall off cliffs. Children at this age may see death as reversible, not permanent.
- From kindergarten to about fourth grade, children begin to understand that all living things die. However, death is seen as something that

happens out there, and it is not usually personalized, for example, it will never happen to them or their parents.

- After about fourth grade, children begin to grasp the permanence and irreversibility of death. That his or her parents will die some day is a difficult fact that a child must face. The fact that the child will someday die is clear, but far away.

Like adults, children handle shocking situations in a series of stages. The first of these stages, as in any trauma, is denial, or, Oh no, that couldn't have happened. This distancing allows the child or adult to absorb the truth and deal with it. Some children cry when a loved one dies. Some children appear to be totally insensitive. The parent must understand that inwardly, the child is working through a great deal of feelings. The child may be angry that the person died, feel depressed and guilty that he or she was somehow involved, or show some other unusual behavior. There is an explanation for the child's behavior, although we may not know it immediately.

Should your child attend a funeral? Children under the age of four often do not understand what is happening at a funeral and may not understand why people are sad. Children of this age may be disruptive, confused, and gain little from attending a funeral. Children five years of age and older should be encouraged to attend family funerals, with some exceptions depending on maturity. If a child has not been exposed to death before this age, then some specific detail should be given about what will happen at the funeral and any questions should be answered. If you have an anxious child with a vivid imagination who would tend to worry, consider telling him or her about the funeral on the day before the service. Under the right circumstances, allowing the child to attend a funeral deepens understanding about the life cycle.

A note about grief. Children and adults show their grief in various ways. Some children deny their feelings and show no outward signs of grief. This does not mean they are not sad, but simply that they are uncomfortable with the expression of grief. You, as a parent, may also be uncomfortable, but grief can be used as an opportunity to bring you and your child closer together.

The intensity of the grief may be proportional to the individual's emotional ties to the pet or relative who died. The more intense the grief, the longer the grieving may last. Grief is an emotional state that seems to come and go in waves, so it is perfectly normal for a child to be sad for a time, then to appear happy. Out of the blue, months later, the child may feel sad again. These wave-like states are more intense and frequent at first, then gradually become less intense and less frequent over time.

Recommendations:
1. The best way to avoid complica-

tions when dealing with difficult situations in life is to maintain open communication among family members.
2. There are many books on the market that can be read aloud, to help your child understand and deal with death.
3. If you are not comfortable discussing death with your child, you can get recommendations from your pediatrician, teacher, or other outside professionals.

How do you know if a child needs more time with you?

The obvious way to know when a child needs more time with you is when the child asks you to play with him or her. Many times a child will ask one parent where the other parent is. Questions like, Where is Daddy? Where is Mommy? How come Daddy is so busy, and so on, are indicators that the child misses the other parent. As families become more child-centered, parents listen more to the needs of their children.

A second way to assess the child's need for time with you is to look at his or her behavior. When a child needs more attention, he or she will change his or her behavior in a noticeable way.

The child may become more aggressive, more fearful, more withdrawn, or more pleasing. If a lack of attention becomes chronic, some children will get sick or become more accident prone.

Quality time versus quantity. The truth of the matter is that children need and want both quantity and quality time. *Quality time* usually refers to time spent with the child when he or she is the focus of your attention. This means that the two of you do things that the child wants to do, or the two of you do things you both enjoy. It could be anything from reading, skating, and building models, to playing imaginary games, hiking, and so on. Quality time requires a parental attitude that is receptive to the child's needs and wants. The ideal would be for the parent to create a free and protected space for the child. The space is "free" if the child feels that he or she can say and do what he or she really wants. The space is "protected" if what the child wants to do is safe for himself and others. The space is also protected if the child is free from interruption from siblings. This may sound easier than it is to achieve in most normal households. To create quality time, it may be necessary to take off your "parental hat"; that is, quality time might be a period when you don't teach, direct, correct, instruct, or guide the child unless the child directly asks for your help.

The *quantity* of time is also important. Children who are around their parents a good deal of time get to observe and learn their parents' value systems; they get to learn how parents parent, how families are raised, and how a man or a woman operates in the world. Children pick up all kinds of information. Being around a parent also frequently helps the child feel secure, by knowing somebody is there to answer questions and to give help and comfort when needed. Even when parents are running errands, going shopping, or doing chores, children are learning about life. Sometimes children will take the opportunity to ask you important questions. With some awareness and practice, you can learn to pay attention to both the goal and the process of getting there.

What to do. If you think your child needs more attention, simply add fifteen to thirty minutes of uninterrupted time with your child each day. The younger the child, the more this time should to be oriented toward play, for play is the major language of the child. Simply tell the child that you have x number of minutes to spend together. Ask your child what he or she would like to do during that time. Let the child take the lead. If your schedule is very busy, or one parent spends a great deal of time away from the house, then time with the child must be planned in advance. If you can give a child predictable and regular time together, the child will use that time to get what he or she needs from you.

When to say when. What if my child wants my constant attention? How do I know if my child's needs are way out of line? For the most part, when a child is full, he or she will stop asking for your time and being needy. However, in cases where the child has not developed sufficient independence, he or she can be overly demanding of the parent's attention. In most of these cases, the problem arises because the parent has not set proper boundaries or limits between the parent and the child.

A common scenario might go like this: The parents says no to the child. The child starts to scream, cry, or throw a temper tantrum. The parent gets angry and yells at the child. The child gets more hysterical. The parent gives in and gives the child what he or she wants. Has this ever happened to you?

What does this teach the child? It teaches the child that the parent really isn't in control of the child or the situation. Two feelings result in the child from this. One, the child likes having power over the adult, so he or she wants to do it more. Two, the child becomes fearful because there isn't a strong figure to protect him or her. If this pattern continues, you end up with a bossy and demanding child during waking hours, and a clingy and fearful child at bedtime or when a parent leaves.

Setting limits. Setting limits is very important because it helps the child develop an ability to contain his or her behavior. A child who constantly requires your attention may be a child who is unable to contain his or her feelings. Following through quickly and consistently on any direction given to a child—regardless of the child's attempts to ignore the direction—will develop a sense of trust and containment for the child.

A word about divorce. Recent surveys indicate a side benefit for children of divorce. In many, if not most, cases a child's quality and quantity time with the father improves. Apparently, fathers—either because they have restricted time with the children or because they are required to provide more complete care during the visitations—schedule their time to really be with their children. Many children come into our offices saying that they actually have a better time now with their father than they did before the divorce! Wouldn't it be nice to have this kind of relationship without a divorce?

Recommendations:
1. Create a "free and protected" space for the child.
2. Create predictable times when you can be together without interruption.
3. Set limits on a child who is overly needy for attention.

How do you know if your child is overly scheduled?

What do we mean by overly scheduled? Parents know what the word "stress" means. The stress of work, of taking care of the family, and of including as many activities as possible sometimes seems overwhelming. We must be aware that children feel this same stress when they have too much to do. The world as we know it has more opportunities today than ever before, and those opportunities appear to increase on a daily basis. There is no way any individual or family can participate in all that is offered in one lifetime. As we attempt to be the best parent possible, we have to make decisions and choices among many very good opportunities for our children. The choices aren't easy. If you or your child is like most of us, you tend to overeat at a buffet. As a nation, we tend to overeat, spend more than we make, and cram too much into every day both for ourselves and our children. We have too many irons in the fire.

Symptoms of being overly scheduled. When we or our children overextend our energies, we become tired, grouchy, irritable, mopey, curt, or overactive. If we stay in this overextended state for too long, we can see the effects of our stress. It isn't long before the weakest link in our chain begins to crack. It may be mental, emotional, or physical. We may see it in our child's school performance. We may see it in our child's relationship with others. Then we know the child is overly scheduled.

Children who are overly scheduled may pick fights with their siblings; they may feel that they do not get enough attention from their parents; they may withdraw; they may overeat; they may develop frequent colds; they may do poorly in school; they may crave watching television more; they may become more testy at home; or they may act out in other ways to get parents' attention. Children, just like adults, can get caught up in what others do, and they may feel like they have to keep up with their friends. Because Johnny's best friend does many things, Johnny has to do them too.

What can you do about it? Children between the ages of five and thirteen are probably most at risk for being overly scheduled. With the numerous after-school sports, art and music classes, martial arts, gymnastics and dance classes that are offered for this age group, many children want to do it all. If you add to that homework, doctor visits, and family obligations, you have effectively eliminated play and rest—the two most effective balancing agents for work.

Play can be defined as "enacted imagination." That means the freedom to try your imagination. In most after-school sports, art, or music programs, activities are structured so that children will learn and develop certain skills. It may be interesting, exciting, and fun for the child, but it is not play, and it does not usually recreate or renew the child's spirit. Playing alone or with friends, where the children develop the rules and structures, is often more renewing.

Children need time to play, and they need time to rest. Downtime may be equally as important as playtime. Many children use television to create a mild state of relaxation. If children were encouraged or allowed to take a short nap of twenty or thirty minutes, they might get the same relaxation benefit as watching two or three hours of television.

How to prevent overscheduling your children. Parents should sit down together and determine the top three or four values that they want their children to learn. From this base, parents can make choices that will best serve their children. The values of courage, experience and exploration, must be balanced with the values of control, reserve, and sufficiency.

Recommendations:
1. A child who is overly scheduled will begin to deteriorate mentally, emotionally, or physically. Watch for signs of stress.
2. Prioritize and reduce the number of activities in which the child is involved.
3. Increase the amount of unstructured free time.

How do you know when your child is ready for more responsibility?

What does responsibility mean to a parent and to a child? One difficulty in this area is that responsibility has different meanings for a parent and a child. To a parent, responsibility usually means that the child listens to the parent and then does what is asked by the parent in a prompt and effective manner. The child, however, may interpret the request as a request, not an order, or as a demand to be done sometime in the future, not immediately. With these conflicting expectations, conflict between parent and child is inevitable.

What is the purpose of responsibility? The purpose of responsibility is to ensure the child matures and deals with the realities of life in an age-appropriate manner. Appropriate levels of responsibility are necessary for healthy growth in the child. As the child takes on more responsibility for himself or herself and others, the child begins to feel more grown-up and a part of the family and society. Although this is often unconscious on the child's part, it is important. Hopefully, when the child leaves home, he or she will be responsible for this self-care, as well as for fulfilling his or her duties to society. For example, driving a car demands a great responsibility to not harm the property or persons of others.

How does the responsible and irresponsible child act? Although parents often complain about a child's irresponsibility and the conflict usually comes to a head in adolescence, the issue starts at a very young age. The term "responsible" may mean different things to different parents. Many parents make very few demands on a child and then wonder why the child does not respond in a more responsible manner. Parents must start making age-appropriate demands at a very young age. One rule of thumb is to give your child one responsibility for every year old they are. For instance:

- A one-year-old might be asked to help put a few toys in a box, or help dress himself or herself.
- A two-year-old might be asked to do both.
- A three-year-old might be asked to perform the two tasks above and say the magic words "please" and "thank you."
- A four-year-old might be asked to perform the tasks above and to brush his or her teeth.
- A seven-year-old might be asked to put away toys and clothes, do homework, and help out in the kitchen.
- A ten-year-old might be asked to perform all of the above tasks and help feed the pets and work in the yard.

All of these tasks and more may become the child's responsibility depending on the intelligence, maturation, and ability of the individual child. Some children have more responsibilities, and some have almost none. When you have determined that a child can perform an action, but he or she does not, that child may not be responsible.

What can you, as a parent, do to make your child more responsible? Some parents infantalize their children; that is, they require no responsibilities at all of their young children. When their children reach adolescence, parents are shocked at their children's lack of responsibility. Even if you have household help, it is important for your child to have age-appropriate chores. Among a child's first responsibilities should be self-care, room maintenance, and schoolwork.

As children move into the teenage years, their interests naturally begin to shift from home activities toward social activities. Parents often see a drop in performance of household responsibilities as well as school activities during these years. This usually creates some parental alarm and soon there is conflict. This is a good time to sit down with a child to discuss values and priorities, both yours and your child's. Your child may not be aware that his or her behavior is signaling new values and priorities. There is no use pretending that your child's values and priorities match yours. For most teenagers, it is an overwhelming task to try to meet the needs of parents, school, friends, and self. The discussion should include compromises and priorities that both the child and parent can adopt. Teenagers tend to accomplish much more readily those tasks they consider fair and reasonable. Remember, teenagers may often overestimate their ability to satisfy everybody so they can get what they want. Any agreements made should be on a trial basis with an appointed time to review. It is important for parents to maintain a certain level of patience; remember, this is still a learning process for the child. Being right for the parent may not be enough. Parents must also remember that this is a maturational and growth period for the child. If the child acted the way you would act, he or she would not be a teenager.

Recommendations:

1. If a child can perform an activity with moderate effort, he or she can be asked to be responsible for it.
2. One rule of thumb is to give a child one responsibility for each year of their age.
3. Responsibilities should be for oneself, for the family, and as they get older for others outside the family.

How do you know when your child is ready for sleep overs?

What is a sleep over? A sleep over is when a child invites a friend to spend the night at his or her house, usually in his or her room, or is invited by a friend to do the same. Both situations give rise to different possibilities.

Thoughts to consider when your child wants a sleep over. As a general rule, your child is ready for sleep overs when he or she begins to ask for them. Usually children begin to invite friends for sleep overs between the ages of five and seven. Many children may be used to sleep overs from spending the night at Grandma's or a cousin's house. In the beginning, young children should be familiar and comfortable with the adults who will supervise the sleep over.

Another sleep over readiness measure for your child is whether he or she is able to spend three or four hours playing with another child without fighting or missing the parents. Sometimes when a child is able to get ready for bed and sleep alone he or she has the basic independence and self-management skills needed to sleep at a friend's house. If the child also has the emotional independence to leave the parents and the home overnight, he or she may be ready for sleep overs.

Parents' role in sleep overs. The first time your child sleeps over at a friend's house, it is a good idea for you as parents to stay home and be available in the event of a late night call. Remember, this is an important growth step for the child, involving separation anxiety and responsibility in a new situation. If, for any reason, the child should call, your voice should indicate calm, care, and confidence in the child's ability to handle the sleep over. A little reassurance can go a long way. If the child is very anxious for no apparent reason, it may mean that your child is not yet ready, that something has happened, or that the child is ill. Reassure the child that it is fine for you to pick him or her up and do so promptly. As annoying as this may be, it will increase the child's trust in you and help him or her to try again at a later date. If the child comes home simply because he or she missed you, it would be a good idea to wait at least another three months before allowing the next sleep over. The child may ask again before that time, but making him or her wait will increase the child's determination to make it work, as well as allow some time for maturation. You want the child to have several successful experiences early on.

When is your child not ready for sleep overs? Usually the child is not ready for sleep overs when he or she cannot sleep alone, or if he or she demonstrates very little independence and responsibility. A child who still wets the bed at night can enjoy sleep overs provided he or she is not overly embarrassed. The other parents and child should be made aware of the situation and feel comfortable with it. Usually children over the age of six who still wet the bed at night feel too embarrassed to spend the night at other people's homes.

Some other considerations. It probably goes without saying that parents should be well-acquainted with the other child's parents and confident in their ability to supervise and handle any problems that may arise. It is also important to have their phone number handy. If for some reason you will not be home, make sure the other parents have your pediatrician's phone number as well.

Children who are sick or whose care requires skilled medical training, should stay at home with their parents until they are physically well.

Recommendations:
1. Consider sleep overs when your child begins to ask for them.
2. A child may be ready for sleep overs when he or she can get ready for bed and sleep alone without assistance.

How do you know what kind of music is appropriate for your child?

As we mature, our interest and taste in music changes. Although this is a healthy phenomenon, parents often find it difficult accepting the growing child's musical needs and the child's attempts to be like other children.

What does music do? Music activates thoughts, emotions, and behavior. People are drawn to music that either excites or calms them. Young children tend to like music that is exciting and different. Songs with lyrics always bring into question the issue of values and interests. As children grow and change, their taste in music may change from exciting to romantic to more serene songs. As we grow and mature, we may prefer music that is more complex and meaningful. We must understand the lyrics of our children's songs to see if they represent the values that we want our children to adopt. If they do not, what will we do?

Because proper parenting dictates that we make ourselves aware of our children's musical likes and dislikes, we must try to understand why our children choose particular music. Children may choose songs that represent their maturational level, for example, aggressive songs, romantic songs, calming songs, or even funny songs. Each one says something about who your child thinks he or she is or how he or she would like to be. Your child may think it's cool to listen to the kind of music that his or her friends like.

Symptoms of music problems. Because music and lyrics often tell a story, they offer children an easy way to withdraw into fantasy. Some children listen to music excessively, imagining themselves as the heroic or prime character in a song. Music can be abused as easily as any other form of fantasy, and parents must be alert to what is happening with their child.

What can you do about it? What should you do about it? A good rule of parenting is never to try to control something that is beyond your control. Rather than censor the kinds of music our children listen to, we might first try to understand why they choose this kind of music. Then, we may have the opportunity to introduce our children to other kinds of music. As an example, one parent took his young daughter to see a ballet. At age five, she was bored and really preferred less sophisticated music. At age eight, she fell in love with the ballet, an interest she holds to this day.

Recommendations: Music is an important part of your child's development and one of the joys of being alive. If you are unhappy with your child's taste in music, make sure that it is not just your child's taste that bothers you. If it is, maybe your child has a right to select his or her own music. If it is excessive, or the kind of music you feel is harmful, try introducing your child to other types of music. If you simply cannot tolerate listening to your child's choice of music, buy him or her a set of headphones, and keep peace in the family.

How do you know what curfew is appropriate for your child?

As parents, we are confronted with this question at one time or another. The answer depends on a number of considerations. How old is your child? Where is your child going? Who will accompany your child? Is it a school night or a weekend? How safe is it?

How old is your child? Children under the age of ten should always be supervised when they are away from the house at night. Usually they will be at a friend's house or at a movie or a birthday party where there are adults.

Children between the ages of ten and fourteen are usually a little more independent and capable of staying home alone for a few hours. Children this age are able to stay at a movie theater, skat-

ing rink, arcade, or shopping mall with their friends without parental supervision for a limited time. However, in this age range, there is a wide discrepancy of maturity, and children must be evaluated for safety and responsibility in each situation.

Depending upon the situation, children fifteen to seventeen years old are usually responsible enough to stay out until midnight, give or take an hour.

Children eighteen and older probably can stay out as late as they like. If, however, they still live at home, they should be considerate of family members and household rules.

Where is your child going? It should go without saying that you should know where your child is going. If your child is going to a friend's house, you should know the parents and know where the house is. This is usually not a problem for children under the age of twelve.

The problem usually arises as children move into the teenage years. Children's social groups begin to expand, and there are many new kids moving into and out of groups. Teenagers go to houses of people you've never met and may not ever meet. More transitory relationships are formed. Sometimes it is hard to keep up with a teenager's social life. The problem is compounded when your child or his peer group reaches driving age, because then teenagers can travel greater distances and can greatly expand their boundaries.

For children ages sixteen and up,

there may be regular friends, "hang outs," clubs, parks, and so on, where your child and his or her friends go. Try to find out from your child where these place are. Then take the time some weekend evening to see for yourself what these places are like. You don't have to take your child with you or tell your child of your plans. You don't want your child to be embarrassed or feel like you don't trust him or her. It just might help some parents feel a little more secure to know where their child is when he or she is away from home.

Some parents invest in a beeper or cellular phone so their children can reach them in a crisis.

Who will accompany your child? This is another important factor about staying out. Some children have friends that make parents feel secure, and some children have friends that make parents worry. Before adolescence, parents usually can influence whom the child has as friends. As children move into junior high and high school, peer groups usually expand and there is more exploration of attitudes and values (not to mention haircuts and dress).

Always encourage your child to bring friends home so you can meet them. Make it as informal as possible. Have friends come over to watch movies, have a barbecue, go out for dinner, go on a camping trip, or short vacation—any activity in which they have to interact with you as an adult. In a short time you'll get a good sense of who they are as people. Don't be seduced or repelled by the appearance of your child's friends. Sometimes a very clean-cut preppie friend may be a bad influence, while an earringed, tattooed, long-haired friend may be a good influence for your child. Take the time to talk to your child' friends.

Curfews and bedtimes. Before the age of ten, most children have a bedtime between the hours of 8:00 PM and 9:00 PM Many children have fifteen to thirty minutes of quiet time before bedtime. They get ready for bed (bath, pajamas, and so on), then they read a story or sing a song. Some bedtimes start at 7:30 PM, while others may begin at 9:30 PM.

Between the ages of ten and fifteen, bedtimes usually range between 9:30 PM and 11:30 PM The older the child, the more flexible the bedtime.

For older children and teenagers, whether it is a school night often determines earlier or later bedtimes. The most difficult curfews to set are for children fourteen to seventeen years old. Children this age push for their independence and the freedom to set their own curfews. Yet they are not capable of setting limits for themselves, and oftentimes overextend their energies. After a child reaches eighteen it usually becomes pointless to try to set curfews. Your only leverage at this point is your child's consideration for other family members. If your child is consistently uncooperative, then he or she should be asked to live somewhere else.

Recommendations:
1. Children under ten need supervision.
2. Children eleven to fourteen need supervision, although not necessarily parental supervision.
3. Children fifteen to seventeen can usually be out alone, although they need curfews.
4. Children eighteen and older may not need curfews, but they should consider other family members and household rules.
5. Where your child is going and who is accompanying your child are important factors in determining curfews.

How do you know at what age you should talk to your child about sex?

The question of sex. It is sad that in our culture one of the most important basic instincts—sex—is still a taboo subject between parents and children. Many parents find it too embarrassing to talk to their children about sex. Most of us learn about sex from our friends, and most often we get incorrect information. We learn from TV, from listening to our parents and siblings, and, if we are fortunate, from classes in school. Children's first education about sex is often taught from a negative viewpoint. "Don't touch yourself" or "You will learn when you grow up" are common answers. As parents, we are responsible for our children's values and behavior. Sex education ideally should be taught at home.

How old should children be to discuss sex? You should answer your child's questions about sex whenever he or she asks. Your answers should be constructed to match the child's maturity and level of understanding. You should also talk to your child about sex when you know that he or she is misinformed. Some children fail to gain a full understanding of what sex means to the opposite sex because they are not interested, are too embarrassed to ask, or are insensitive to their partner.

People learn about sex throughout their life. What children know about sex (or where babies come from) at the age of four is different than what they know about sex at the age of nine. Children learn a great deal more about sex during adolescence, when they get information from their peers and some children become sexually active. Sex is different before and after marriage, before and after children, and before and after middle age. What you can tell your child about sex is often a great deal more than what they ask. Many three-, four-, and five-year-olds believe that babies come from Mommy's tummy and that Daddy has a seed that goes into Mommy's tummy. It meets with Mommy's egg and together they make a baby. Three-, four-, and five-year-olds also know that Daddy has a penis and Mommy has a vagina. Children this age also know what sex organs they have. If they do not know, you should tell them.

How children learn about sex away from home. Children ages eight, nine, and ten will receive more scientific information in school about reproduction and the human growth cycle. Children this age will learn about male and female reproductive organs. They will learn about male erections and female menstruation. They may learn about intercourse.

This learning does not take place in isolation. Children will try to supplement what they learn in school by asking siblings and friends questions. There are many excellent books geared to different age groups that explain the whole mystery of sexuality.

Children in the early teen years may start to explore their social/sexual development and how to approach each other as sexual beings. Oftentimes sexual information about birth control, sexually transmitted diseases, and sexual responsibility is taught in school. Information about heterosexuality and homosexuality is given during the ten- to fifteen-year-old range. In middle to late adolescence, many children get to know the opposite sex on a more intimate, individual basis. Issues about love and respect are learned. Moral and family values should be reinforced and discussed repeatedly during this period.

Whose responsibility is it to teach children about sex? The argument about who should teach children about sex—school or parents—is not resolved. The problem, in part, is that many parents do not take this responsibility seriously. Sometimes this is due to parental reticence; sometimes it is due to parental ignorance. Ask any married woman if her husband really understands her sexual needs and, unfortunately, too often you will hear "no."

Where can parents learn about sex? We all know the basics, but that is not enough. There are professional sex therapists who can answer parents' questions, then parents can educate their children. One danger is that parents let this issue go until it is too late. Telling a child about the mysteries of sexuality when he or she is eighteen is usually too late. At that age, a child won't listen or may feel he or she knows more than you. Start young.

Recommendations:
1. You should answer your child's questions about sex whenever he or she asks.
2. People learn about sex throughout their lives. Be prepared to answer questions.
3. Monitor what the child learns through school-related programs, and fill in any information you believe to be important.
4. As the child enters early and middle adolescence, inquire about his or her values regarding sex. Open a discussion if needed.

How do you know at what age you should talk to your daughter about menstruation?

Like sexuality, you should talk to your child about menstruation whenever he or she asks and needs to know the correct information.

Where do children learn about menstruation? Both boys and girls learn about menstruation in several ways. They learn from their sisters, from their girlfriends, from parents, and from school. They also may learn from reading if parents get them some of the excellent books published on the subject.

What do you say to younger children? One six-year-old girl recently asked her mother, "What's that thing you put in your bottom?" A five-year-old boy who walked in on his mother as she was undressing brought his mother a bandage after noticing that her underwear had a little blood on it. It is not unusual for children in the four-, five-, and six-year-old age range to notice unusual items in Mommy's bathroom or to come across a used tampon or minipad. The mother of one five-year-old girl told the story about how her daughter spotted a used tampon wrapped in tissue and loudly announced at their annual family gathering that somebody had a bloody nose. Of course she was holding the tampon up so that the owner would claim it!

Children in the four-, five-, and six-year-old age range commonly ask where babies come from. If they then ask about bleeding or any of the materials that deal with menstruation, a simple explanation will usually do.

Tell the child that babies grow in a special place in Mommy's body (uterus) before they are born. Describe the uterus as a little soft cave that holds the baby until it's big enough to be born. Tell the child that every month Mommy's body puts special food and vitamins in that cave just in case a baby comes. The special food is inside the blood. If the baby doesn't come then the body lets go of the blood food and it comes out of Mommy's vagina. Tell the child that sometimes it takes a few days for all the blood food to come out, so Mommy uses special pads to soak up the blood.

If the child is interested you can let the child examine a tampon or minipad to see how it is made. If the child seems shy or afraid, simply reassure the child that all the items are safe, and that Mommy is perfectly fine. It is important for both boys and girls to see this natural bodily function as healthy and normal.

What should I say to my daughter before she starts menstruating? Before young girls begin to menstruate they show early signs of puberty. Their breast develop, they grow pubic hair, their legs thicken, their hips widen, and their facial features take on adult characteristics. Emotionally and physically, girls may begin to experience premenstrual mood swings, food cravings, irritability, aches and pains, etc. In some young girls, you may observe these signs anywhere from six months to a year before the first actual period. This is a good time to sit down with your daughter and explain what is happening to her physically and emotionally. By this time, most public school children have had some education about the onset of puberty in both boys and girls. However, it is a good idea to have a more personal and thorough conversation with your child. You could talk about premenstrual syndrome (PMS), and how diet, exercise, and rest are important to keep a healthy balance before, during, and after your period. If your daughter experiences any grouchy to weepy mood swings, you might suggest ways to cope. Think of ways that have helped you. The important thing to communicate is that this is a normal and valuable part of being a woman. Any attitudes that suggest the menstrual process is dirty, weak, shameful, or disgusting should be quickly dismissed. It is important that young girls come into this process with clear information, high self-confidence, and a positive and open attitude. Boys should also be taught about menstruation when they show an interest or when you, as parents, feel they should understand what their sister is going through. For boys, menstruation may be a mysterious process, but they also need clear information presented with an open and positive attitude.

What is the father's role? To honor a woman's menstrual cycle is to honor the natural rhythms of the earth. A woman's body rhythm clearly reflects the phases of the moon, the rising and setting of the sun, the seasons of the year, and the cycle of birth, life, and death. As a young girl passes from childhood into womanhood, she begins to participate in the larger mystery of life. Because of this, she should be recognized and honored in some special way not only by her mother, but also by her father. It is the father's role to help validate his daughter's femaleness and sexuality. If the father is frightened by or disapproves of his daughter's maturation, he can send her strong negative messages about men. She may later find it difficult to be herself around men.

Some fathers take their daughters out to dinner (maybe a fancy restaurant), give them a graduation card, take them shopping, write them a letter or poem, buy them a dozen red roses, or do something that openly acknowledges their daughter's coming into womanhood.

What if I'm not sure? The only error parents can make is to avoid or deny this important issue. Parents may not talk about menstruation because they are embarrassed or because they feel unable to explain the subject clearly. If you are unsure, there are plenty of books that are written especially for parents and adolescent children at your local bookstore. Also, most local hospitals have educational programs for the general public.

Recommendations:
1. Answer any questions about menstruation whenever a child asks.
2. Discussions, film strips, and books about menstruation are usually introduced to girls as they reach ages eight or nine, depending on the maturity level of the child.
3. Fathers should participate at some level in honoring a girl's transition into womanhood.

How do you know when your child is ready to drive?

What do we mean by readiness?
Readiness is one of those complex words that takes into account a child's physical, emotional, and maturational skills. A child must possess readiness to handle the responsibilities of a machine that offers freedom, but also the potential to hurt others. Your child is ready to drive when he or she demonstrates the physical skills to drive in a safe manner, the emotional confidence to drive, and the maturity to make good instant decisions. The child must demonstrate the ability to focus, to concentrate, and show good judgment. The child must realize when he or she is too emotionally impulsive or too tired to drive. Maturity means knowing what to do in case of accidents, police pull overs, flat tires, or car breakdowns. These situations should be rehearsed thoroughly in advance.

What you can do about readiness skills. Parents can make sure the adolescent has learned to drive well before turning over the keys. Readiness is also related to general maturity. If the child does not show a sense of responsibility in other areas, the child may not show this sense about handling a car. Because driving gives a child a sense of freedom, you must assess the degree of control your child possesses.

Preventing problems with the car. In general children handle a car better if they have saved for its purchase. Children who are given a car may not understand its value. Those who have worked and saved for at least a part of their car tend to be much more responsible about their vehicle. The child must know that if an accident occurs or the car is misused, access will be restricted or removed until the child matures in attitude or ability. Parents are responsible for the child until the age of eighteen and they have the right to revoke the child's driving license in most states. The car can also be used as part of a contract with the child; for example, "You can drive if you maintain your grades." At age sixteen or eighteen this sometimes is a major factor in the child's good behavior.

Recommendations:
1. Make sure the child is mentally, emotionally, and physically able to handle driving.
2. If the child shows problems, delay driving until the child matures or has a good deal more practice.

How do you know when your child is ready to date?

How socialization develops. Learning how to interact with other children begins at an early age, but dating begins during adolescence. There has been a significant social change in the past few years; children often begin to socialize with the opposite sex in small social groups. Although some of this behavior was always a part of the social spectrum, it is now even more so. As children grow older, they grow more interested in the opposite sex. When this interest heightens depends upon the child's maturity and the mores of the family, school, and social group.

The start of dating. Somewhere between twelve and fifteen years of age, children begin to express an interest in socializing with the opposite sex. Usually, children in this age group date in small groups of four to six. Movies, miniature golf, bowling, birthday parties, and so on, are the setting for these get-togethers. Many children, however, prefer nonstructured activities, such as hanging out at the malls, shopping centers, or parks. Most kids know where the best hang outs are. The difference between structured and nonstructured activities usually is the presence of adult supervision. Hanging out usually is not supervised. Children of this age group begin to move away from adults and into the world of their peers, where sex, drugs, and rock and roll may or may not be part of the scene.

Children in this age group usually are concerned with honing their image, learning about the opposite sex, learning and developing social skills, and looking cool among their friends. Of course, not all children follow this pattern. You may have a perfectly normal and healthy child who shows little interest in the opposite sex until a much later time.

Children in this age group may be ready to join social groups and date when they demonstrate the following behaviors:
- They express an interest in doing so.
- They can spend several hours with their friends in an enjoyable way.
- They can spend time together

unsupervised without getting into trouble.

- They are responsible about being where they say they will be.
- They are ready to go when it is time to go.

If children can follow these five functions in a consistent way, they are usually ready for the privileges of group socialization or group dating. If children begin to fail in any one of these areas, it is appropriate for parents to restrict them temporarily until they learn how to develop more self-control.

The development of dating. As children mature between the ages of sixteen and nineteen, dating starts to become formal. Sex, love, and intimacy become the issues involved. Children learn about responsibility in a relationship and different levels of communication. Feelings can soar and crash. Deep relationships can be formed, and hearts can be broken. It is through this reality testing that adolescents become young adults.

Children in this age group are ready to date when they exhibit the following behaviors:

- They express an interest in dating one on one.
- They have discussed with you their values on the use or avoidance of drugs and alcohol.
- They have discussed with you their knowledge of and values regarding sex, and the responsibilities toward and prevention of possible disease.
- They have demonstrated their capacity to be where they say they

will be, and to return when they say they will return.

If the child has not mastered the abilities listed for the twelve to fifteen age group, it is very likely he or she will have trouble mastering the abilities in the sixteen to nineteen age group.

Parental concern about dating arises when there is a large age difference in the children involved, for instance, a child in the twelve to fifteen age group wants to date a child in the sixteen to nineteen age group. It is usually not a good idea for these age groups to mix, because the older child and the younger child do not share similar interests, or if they do, they don't remain similar for very long. As a rule of thumb, any dating combination in the teen years where there is more than a three-year age difference should be examined carefully.

What you can do as a parent. Parents have both a firm and a delicate role to play. Parents should be firm in instilling their children with the parents' values and mores. Parents should be delicate, however, in discussing these values and mores with their children, because the children may be embarrassed. Children are often confused by dating, by their own growing sexuality, and by the demands of both their parents and society. If parents come down hard on a child, the child may rebel and refuse to discuss the issue with parents. Ideally, a child should be able to come to parents for advice and counsel.

Recommendations:
1. Try to begin a conversation with your child in as nonthreatening a way as possible. You may find his or her suggestions agreeable.
2. Tell your child what the limits are: where they can go and what time they have to return home.
3. Make it clear that you must be called in plenty of time if there is any deviation from the agreed-upon schedule.

How do you know when your child is ready for a part-time job?

What work means to a parent and to a child. The work ethic is very important in American society. We are taught that work is good. Work is necessary. Work of one kind or another is a part of a grown-up's responsibility. In contrast, children usually follow the pleasure principal. Children, adolescents, and some adults seem to want to play if they can, whenever they can, and however they can to avoid work. For some, work has a negative connotation. If you say, "That's work," in a negative tone of voice, it means it is something you do not really want to do. For most of us, as we mature, work and responsibility become a part of our everyday life that we accept. For children it differs.

Children sometimes have difficulty dealing with work in the form of chores and schoolwork. Children must be taught the value of work, the benefits of work, and the interest and enjoyment of work. Those of us who have jobs that we enjoy are the fortunate ones in this society.

How do we prepare children for work?
Parents can teach children to be responsible when they are adolescents by gradually giving them more responsibility. Children should be given part-time jobs, depending on the child, at about the age of three. The child may be asked to put toys back in a box, or make some contribution toward the home environment. Some children earn an allowance for completing chores around the house. Other families have values that frown on paying children for chores that are part of being a family. Learning to give without receiving a monetary reward helps develop the skills and attitudes necessary to become a productive member of society.

Part-time jobs usually start in adolescence, although there are many industrious and ambitious children who start earlier. A child is ready for a part-time job when he or she has other aspects of life in order. If the child handles academics, social life, family life, and physical well being with responsibility, then you may add a part-time job to teach your child about the value of work and money. Usually it is a good idea to discuss priorities with the child who wants to take on a part-time job. A child must know, for example, that he or she may not have as much time with friends, and parents must understand that the child may not have as much time with the family. Sometimes, if a child is overextended, his or her grades may start to slip or the child may get sick too frequently.

A child's readiness. A child is ready for a part time job when he or she demonstrates the following:

- The child has a clear set of priorities.
- The child has reliable and consistent behavior.

A child who cannot get out of bed and to school on time regularly may not be a good candidate for a part-time job.

It is important to remember that for children of this age everything is about learning and preparing for an adult life. During the first few weeks of a child's part-time job, parents should sit down with the child weekly to find out what the child is learning. Sometimes children have to slow down and pace themselves. At other times, they have to work a little harder. Try to help your child find a suitable balance.

Remember, adolescents or older children must learn that working is a skill. Learning a skill means inevitable success and failure. Your child may not do well in his or her first job. That is one reason your child has a job: to learn. Your child will grow up and mature. Don't despair.

Recommendations:

1. Working helps the adolescent reach maturity sooner by teaching responsibility and money-handling skills. At the right age allow your child to work.
2. Allow your child to work as long as he or she desires after other essential duties are completed.
3. Work out some arrangements for saving, as well as spending, money.

How do you know what to say to your child about money?

What does money mean to us as people and parents? In our society, money is sometimes the most private of issues. We might discuss sex with someone, but we rarely discuss how much money we earn. What does money mean to you? Is it the source of all good? Is it the source of all evil? Or, is it neither good nor bad in and of itself, but rather, a means by which people accomplish both good and evil. It is a fact of life for most of us that money is something we engage in getting, spending, losing, saving, or building up. Perhaps the best guidance we can give our children about money is to be neither seduced nor intimidated by its power.

What do we want our children to know about money? Because we as parents have widely divergent values about money, we must decide what we want to teach our children about money. Sometimes parents' philosophies differ about the making and spending of money. This can produce many arguments in the family. Remember, children learn most values from parents. What messages about money do you send to your children?

How children learn about money. Around the age of four, five, or six, children learn the concept that money buys things. They learn that to have and to spend money is to have power. This learning continues and grows throughout childhood and adolescence. Children learn from listening and watching. They learn from parents, friends, and others what the mysterious power of money is.

Basically children have to learn two things:
• What it takes to get or earn money.
• What it takes to manage money.
Managing money involves spending, saving, and building. Earning money usually involves effort. Sometimes we expend a lot of effort to make a little money. Sometimes we expend a little effort to make a lot of money. Earning money often requires the output of energy, imagination, and enthusiasm. Managing money usually requires discipline, self-control, structure, and good judgment.

Allowances. Many families introduce their children to earning, saving, and spending money through an allowance for chores done around the house. Some children earn stickers, and the stickers earn special treats or prizes. Stickers may work for children ages five to nine, but money usually is closer to their interest level.

Some parents believe that a child should not receive money for doing chores because family members should work and contribute to the family. This is a marvelous idea theoretically, and it has merit. However, for most children, earning money teaches valuable lessons about work and enhances self-esteem as well.

If you choose to let your child have an allowance, the amount of money you give can vary widely. Children in the five- to ten-year-old age may receive from $2 to $10 a week, depending on the money available in the family and on the parents' value system. Children in the ten- to fifteen-year-old age range might receive anywhere from $5 to $25 per week, depending on the child's maturity and the chores performed. For children sixteen and up, money needs are usually greater, especially if the child drives. Food, gas, car insurance, and other costs should be factored into the allowance.

Chores. A good rule of thumb for younger children is to have them complete one chore for each year old they are. For example, a five-year-old might have to (1) get dressed in the morning, (2) eat breakfast, (3) brush his or her teeth, (4) take an evening bath, (5) and go to bed on time. If the child learns to do this daily, he or she may receive an allowance at the end of the day or week, depending on the child's ability to associate the reward to the effort.

Working outside the home. Children may start working outside the home at various ages. Children may mow the grass, do odd jobs, deliver newspapers, and so on. The older a child gets, the more likely he or she is to have some job outside the home. Whether the child baby-sits or has another job, parents should help the child plan what he or she will do with the earned money. This is a golden opportunity for children to learn good money management techniques.

Recommendations:
1. The only way a child learns to manage money is to earn it, save it, and spend it. Let your child learn to equate money with time spent working.
2. Allow the child to save money for something he or she wants. Delayed gratification is a lesson the child will learn by waiting to buy what he or she wants.

How do you know what to expect from your children when they leave home?

What do parent and child feel when a child leaves home? Many children, but not all, leave home at age seventeen or eighteen. Some stay much longer because they cannot bear to leave home, or they simply are not ready to leave. Although parents often plan and save for this moment, it is sometimes very painful for one or both parents to have a child leave. Separation anxiety cuts both ways. Parents miss their children, and children miss their parents, their room, and their safe, comfortable life. Children who long to get away from the pressure of their parents and who look forward to going to college suddenly find that they have what they want. They also find that they suddenly have many decisions to make. Both parent and child feel a sense of loss. Parents have to adjust to an "empty nest," or at least to one less child. Children realize all the good things they had at home that are no longer available. Children may have difficulty structuring their lives to include all the chores that a parent performed in the past. While loving their freedom, children finally come to appreciate the good deal they had at home. Although these feelings vary from child to child and parent to parent, there usually is great similarity in these feelings.

Even if children are prepared to leave home, they may be fearful that they won't succeed. Sometimes children are not prepared or mature enough. Other times, children leave and do extremely well, which can cause a sense of abandonment for the parents.

Problems that may arise. Children leave home for many reasons, only one of which is to go to college. When they leave, children often turn to parents with problems they feel they cannot solve. Some possible problems include getting into debt and needing financial assistance. Children may encounter an unplanned pregnancy and the need for child care. A child may fail at school without plans for a job or career. Sometimes, as children become young adults, they divorce and are unable to support themselves, or they get fired from a job, and so on. In any event it is always good for parents to have contingency plans in mind should any of these events occur.

Sometimes parents do not have as much contact with their children as they would like. The child may not call or write, or the child may choose to exclude the parents from his or her new life. This can create pain and hurt feelings. Then, when the child calls, it is because he or she needs or wants something. Parents can sometimes feel used or taken for granted. In most cases when children first leave the parental home, they do not think of

gratitude for parenting well done. This is something that may come many years down the road, usually after children have had their own children and they begin to realize the effort and sacrifice needed to do the job responsibly.

Some thoughts to keep in mind. Parenting is never done. When you are older, your child will still see you as a resource in times of difficulty. Your child may want financial help; your child may want you to baby-sit your grandchildren; your child may simply want the comfort of knowing you are around. Parents must care for themselves, and plan ahead for any eventuality.

Recommendations:

1. It is healthy for children to leave home and go to college. Control your own feelings of loss so that your child does not feel guilty.

2. Keep your feelings of anxiety under control. You probably have taught your child the important lessons he or she will need to survive in college.

3. For better or worse, most children seem to come home for extended periods of time. That and the ease of phone calls will allow for an easier adjustment.

How do you know how to get your child to attend religious services?

Several important factors are involved with this question. What are the parents' beliefs? What is the parents' behavior? What is the child's age?

Parental beliefs are important. When young, children tend to believe what their parents believe; only later do they begin to challenge all parental beliefs in an effort to become independent and autonomous. Young children cannot be expected to have the maturity to understand spiritual values. They learn from you. As children reach adolescence, they begin to understand, hopefully, the meaning and value of a spiritual orientation. It may not be until they become adults that children realize how much spiritual values can contribute to their happiness and fulfillment.

How do I get my child to attend services? Whatever parents' spiritual and religious values, the most effective way to gain children's compliance is when parents regularly and continuously attend religious services. If, in your home, every Sunday without fail, or every Friday night, you attend religious services, your children will learn the habit. If, on the other hand, you attend services sporadically, then your children will learn that religious services are not too important, and they may not want to attend regularly or at all.

Remember, you cannot force belief. You can make your children attend services, but if you want them to believe what you do, you must prepare them early. We all want to do what is enjoyable and avoid those activities that are painful, unpleasant, or boring. If children see religious services as an enjoyable part of their week, they will be eager to attend.

What makes services enjoyable to a child? Until a child becomes mature enough to appreciate the meaning and benefits of spiritual beliefs he or she will only want to attend religious services that have meaning for him or her. For a young child of five or six, these benefits may come through various routes: the religious stories that are given; the social relationships that develop; the hands-on activities the child is involved in, and, finally, the meaning the child gets from these activities. Many religious organizations today have a variety of services designed specifically for children and adolescents.

As children reach adolescence, the situation changes. Social factors also change. If your child's friends all attend services then your child will find it agreeable to attend. If your child feels he or she is allowed to formulate his or her own beliefs rather than being forced to accept your beliefs, your child will be more likely to attend services.

Remember, adolescents have to go through a period of challenging all parental values. Initially, this may mean rejecting whatever parents believe, and later slowly realizing the value of those ideas. Some children, again, are different. They can accept matters of faith at an early age and never challenge them. These children are more likely to accept attending services as an essential or normal part of everyday life. How a parent relates to a child can play a key difference in how the child accepts parental authority.

Aim for long-term versus short-term goals. The most important thing a parent can do is maintain a consistent attitude toward his or her spiritual practice. As children grow, marry, and have their own children, they often reclaim the values that they left behind as adolescents. Be patient; it is never too late to begin a spiritual or religious practice.

Recommendations:
1. If you want your child to attend services regularly, you must attend them regularly.
2. Explore child programs within your religious institution. Make sure they are child centered.

How do you know how to get your child to discuss daily activities and experiences?

How was your day today? Fine. How was school today? Fine. What did you learn today? Nothing. Tell me about your day. There's nothing to tell. It's just normal. How do you feel? Fine. Is every thing OK? Yes. Can I go now? Does any of this sound familiar?

Why is it that children seem reluctant to share the details of their experiences with their parents? Think back to your own childhood. Why didn't you share information with your parents? Some of us shared a little, and some of us shared a lot. However, very few of us shared anything if we believed that the parent would get angry, be critical, blame us, punish us, give us a lecture, tell us what to do, be more concerned about his or her own feelings and needs, not understand, or simply not care.

Sometimes our parents were more concerned with our behavior than our thoughts or feelings. Many parents today try to reverse that emphasis. They want their children to share something of their inner life with them.

Develop good relationships first.
Communication is a skill that primarily develops through the relationship with the parents. Communication develops along with several other attributes such as trust, acceptance, understanding, and interest. It is, in part, a habit that is reinforced and encouraged by the parents.

Trust occurs when children feel safe that they won't be hurt, that they won't be punished, or that what they say won't be used against them at a later time. Sometimes children don't share because they don't believe the information will be held in confidence. These children have seen parents share "cute" stories with other family members or friends, sometimes bringing them embarrassment. Such storytelling may be insignificant to an adult but it can break down a child's trust in communication.

Trust also occurs when a child believes he or she has a choice about parental involvement. Sometimes children are reluctant to include parents in their world, because parents have all kinds of ideas about what should be done and they begin to direct the child's action. Parents often want to take charge. By taking charge, the parent communicates that the child isn't doing a good enough job and really isn't competent. In some cases, it is necessary to step in, but in the majority of social and school situations, the child usually wants to solve his or her problems alone. A parent can avoid this trap by simply asking a child if he or she wants any help from you. In this way, you give the child the choice to work independently or use your help. This communicates that you trust the child, and that you are there for him or her. This encourages the child to include you more often. Remember, trust is something built over time, not overnight.

Acceptance is the ability to listen to information without judging it. Parents are usually very quick to place some value judgment on a child's thoughts or activities. By stating or implying that something is good or bad, right or wrong, safe or dangerous, the parent begins to shape and define what has been shared by the child. Most people, including children, believe that there is no room for their thoughts or values with a judgmental person. Your child may think to himself or herself, I'll be much more cautious about what I share with this person next time. If I have to share, then I'll give very safe answers like, "fine," Judgment is probably the single biggest obstacle to good communication.

Should you tell your child what is good or bad, right or wrong, safe or dangerous? Yes, of course. However, in effective communication, you have to wait until the child feels fully heard and understood. When this happens, the child is much more likely to take in what you have to say, especially if it is contrary to what he or she thinks. Good communication is like good breathing. You have to wait until the air is out before you try to take new air in. If a child only gets out one or two sentences before the parent makes some judgment, the child will not be able to fully take in any new information. The child will usually stop communicating with that parent.

Understanding literally means to stand under some one. Anytime a person really feels understood, they feel supported; they feel stronger, validated, and cared for. You don't necessarily have to agree with someone for them to feel fully understood. However, you do have to let them know that you heard what they said (you may have to repeat it to them), you can appreciate how they came to that thought or activity, and you can relate to the feelings that they may have. If you can get this far, you have achieved a major piece of communication. You probably will get your counseling license soon!

If you have ever been on the receiving end of having someone really understand you, then you know how satisfying the experience is. Chances are, the next time you want to share something, this is the person you will go to first.

Interest is important to convey to a child, while respecting the child's privacy or independence. Parents who seem overly interested or not interested usually get shut out or excluded. If a gentle inquiry into the child's daily activities yields no results, tell the child you would like to ask him or her a few questions about friends, school, and so on, and ask when would be a good time for the two of you to talk. When and where you talk can be very useful. If you keep it short, specific, and painless, you will get a bigger response next time.

Pay attention to the time and place. Choosing the right time and place to share information about your day is also important. Find a time and place that is quiet with few distractions; when the child is somewhat rested is often an optimum time. When a child first gets home from school, he or she may be tired or eager to play, neither of which suggests a good time to talk. Some children complain in counseling that parents bombard them with a thousand questions as soon as they get home from school. If a child feels this way, it's not the right time for a heartfelt discussion.

If a child wants to talk with you, try to stop what you are doing and give the child your full attention. The younger the child, the more immediate is his or her need to get your attention. If you are able to do this, you tell the child that you are interested in him or her and you are available for him or her. This creates security in the child. If you are unable to stop what you are doing, or unable to give the child your full attention, see if you can defer the conversation for a little while. Try to be available as soon as possible. However, don't delay conversations too often, or you will begin to communicate to the child that he or she is not a priority in your life. Over time, this can create angry, hurt, and insecure feelings in a child. He or she will begin to exclude you from conversations, or the child will become more demanding of your time and attention. Some children who feel ignored will strive to get your attention all the time. This can sometimes create a vicious cycle in which we push the child away and he or she strives harder to be with us. When parents are clearly not available, it is best to indicate that to a child and say something like, "I know you have something important to talk about, but I have to finish this task, and then I can take the time to talk with you." A child may or may not accept this, but it at least recognizes that the child has something important to say.

Children give signals to parents.
Children give parents signals when they have to talk about something important. If the child doesn't approach you directly, then he or she may get your attention by withdrawing, getting angry more frequently, or appearing more insecure. A child may also signal the need to talk by how he or she comes to you. The child may hold his or her head or body differently. The child may approach you and not say anything. If you take the time to observe your child, you usually can learn how your child signals that he or she wants to talk to you.

There are sex differences and individual differences. Clearly, children differ in their ability to express themselves. Some children communicate easily, while others do not. Some children lack the vocabulary to say what they mean and become easily frustrated. If you have the sense that your child wants to talk to you, simply ask the child if he or she would like to talk to you. If you do not get an immediate

no, then the answer is yes. Make a time and a place to have that conversation.

There is no question, girls, with their early maturity and better verbal skills, can often communicate with words more easily than boys. It is no surprise that it is girls who are most often on the phone. Many girls find talking about things relieving and satisfying, especially if they are under stress.

Many boys, on the other hand, especially as they get older, don't like "rehashing" the day's events. To some, it is simply reliving the day's stresses that they are trying to forget. Talking about the stress simply adds more stress. For this type of child, tell the child, in advance, that you would like to talk with him and ask when would be a good time. When you do talk with him, have some specific questions in mind like, What are you studying in math? or What do you like most about your best friend, Joey? What's one thing you like (or don't like) about playing on the baseball team? If you get an I don't know answer, you might change your question to, Just tell me one thing about the subject. Accept whatever the child has to say, and thank him for answering your question. If you get a few rejections, just thank the child and wait for a better time.

Should you give or not give advice?
Offer advice when it is requested, and don't offer advice when it is not requested. This is good communication. However, there are times when it is good to break these rules.

Giving advice when it is not requested is risky at best. However, as a parent your job is to guide and protect your child. It is important to give unsolicited advice when you believe the child is going in the wrong direction, especially if there are serious consequences. In fact if the situation is very serious, advice is not needed—restrictive actions are. Give advice sparingly when it is not requested. Given too frequently and in too many nonserious situations, unsolicited advice from a parent will break down communication between parent and child.

Withholding advice, even when it is requested, is appropriate when you want the child to make his or her own decision on a certain matter. You may feel that the child is too dependent on your judgment. As long as you can live with the child's choice and the child is very able to handle the consequences, then the choice should be the child's. Parents who expect too much from their child, or who overestimate their child's abilities, can make the child feel unsupported. Eventually, the child won't ask for advice, even in important matters.

Here are some practical tips.
1. **Create a time and space conducive to talking**, for instance, just before bed; riding in the car alone with the child; early in the morning before getting up; at dinner, when you are sitting down and not watching television; any quiet and somewhat private moment during the day.
2. **Be specific.** Asking, How was your day? What did you do today? may

be too broad and general. It may be better to ask, Tell me one thing that you liked that happened today, or Who did you spend most of your time with at recess today? or What kind of mood was your teacher in today?
3. **Be brief** if the child isn't volunteering a lot of information. Three or four questions like the above examples will usually be enough to give you some idea of what your child's day was like. If you have more questions, save them for a later time.
4. **Be pleasant.** Have a friendly tone of voice. Don't walk away angry, hurt, or disappointed.
5. **Don't criticize, ridicule, or judge,** if possible, what the child says.
6. **Be grateful.** Thank the child for sharing with you. If the child is open to it, give him or her a hug. Tell the child you love him or her.

Recommendations:
1. The more you listen to your child, the more the child will talk.
2. Be very careful not to be critical or offer advice if you want your child to talk freely.
3. Your child will only communicate when he or she is ready, which may not be the time when you are ready to listen. Find the time to listen.

How do you know how to handle constant fighting among your children?

Why do children fight? Fighting is a behavior that comes from a need to protect something or to achieve something. A child may feel the need to protect his or her room, toys, friends, or relationship with the parents from an invading sibling. On the other hand, a child may feel the need to achieve more freedom to do what he or she wants, to gain more control over who does what or has what, or to elicit more attention from the people in his or her environment.

As infants, all of us are born vulnerable and dependent. This is scary and unpleasant at best. For that reason, most of us learn to please, fight, or withdraw to gain some control and, thereby, reduce our anxiety. Children are too young to protect themselves completely, and they are too young to achieve everything they want. Consequently, they look to adults for that protection and achievement. It is left to the parents to decide how much protection and how much power each child needs. The needs for power and protection vary greatly among children. If you have two or more children, you will clearly see this variation.

The younger the child, the more power and protection is needed from the parents. As the child grows older, he or she gradually learns how to take, how to negotiate, how to wait, how to compromise, how to share, and how to do without. As a child learns these skills he or she gradually learns how to achieve and how to protect.

When parents are not present mentally, emotionally, or physically, fighting among children increases.

Because children are dependent, they are highly responsive to the moods, energies, and behaviors of parents. Children can easily sense a shift in the parents' attention. How many parents have had the experience of being most needed as soon as they get on the phone!

Parents have very busy lives. There are so many things to do, and so many responsibilities to tend to that it is very easy for parents to become absorbed in their own activities. Children, and especially sensitive children, will feel the absence of attention. In time, the parent's absence creates anxiety or anger in the child, who eventually shows it behaviorally. Some children will become more withdrawn, some more fearful, and some more defiant. Usually, if the parent's attention is absent for too long, children begin to fight among themselves as a way to draw in the parents.

What do I do first?
1.   When children fight, the first thing a parent should do is to get centered. Take a deep breath (two or three,

if needed), calm yourself, and gather your confidence.

2. Stop the fighting by physically separating the children so they cannot touch or reach each other. You may have to put the children in different rooms, temporarily, until they can calm down enough to talk to each other.

3. Assess what each child is trying to accomplish by fighting. Is the child trying to get something, or is the child trying to protect something? Simply ask each child, What do you want?

a. Fights that are related to *achieving* occur when two children want one thing at the same time. The children want the same toy; they want to control the television or video game; they want to control the direction of play; they want to sit in the front seat of the car; they want to sit next to a certain person; they want one parent's attention; they want what the other one has; and so on.

Explain to each child that two people cannot do or have the same thing at exactly the same time, but back up that statement by explaining the need to share, negotiate, compromise, take turns, or do without. Some parents opt to buy two (or more) of everything, so that each child has his or her own. This can provide short-term resolution of the conflict, but eventually children must learn to share. And in this case, sooner is better than later.

Use these techniques to teach your child to share:

• Take away the toy or privilege until the children can agree on a solution; this often gets the children's attention.

• Set time limits and have the children take turns.

• Trade one toy or privilege for another, for example, You can play with my video game, if I can play with your football.

One mother of four children between the ages of five and twelve posted a sign on the back of each child's door, "Share, Negotiate, Compromise, Take Turns, or DO WITHOUT!" The children lost toys, television, clothes, treats, and quite a bit in the first few weeks, because nobody liked to share, negotiate, compromise, or take turns. It wasn't much fun, and it required sacrifice. The children only really learned to share when they were *absolutely convinced* that doing without was much worse than having something at least part of the time. After the first few weeks, the noise and fighting was reduced by at least ninety percent.

Setting rules that determine who gets to do what, when, and where can be done singly by parents, done in combination with the children, or done by the children themselves. It is best to have the agreement reached before the toy or privilege is used and to have a consequence set up for anyone who does not abide by the agreement. Sometimes these rules are written up and posted where everyone can see them. The rules may have to be changed, periodically as children grow and situations change.

Sharing, waiting, and taking turns are behaviors that parents must introduce to their children beginning between ages two and five. Parents should require their children to practice these skills between the ages of four and twelve. If children do not have some of these skills by the age of twelve, they will probably experience significant social, behavioral, and relationship problems. These children may need some professional outside help. Teenagers usually can be reasoned with in terms of sharing and cooperation, especially if phone, car, money, and social privileges are attached to the discussion.

b. Fights that are related to *protection* occur when one child provokes the other by name-calling, hitting, invading the other's space, taking the other's toy without permission, destroying something that the other child is building, interrupting a conversation that the other child is having with a parent or friend, and so on.

These fights represent the other side of the coin. Social skills require that you share, and they also require that you respect boundaries, yours and others. Children have a right to their bodies, possessions, space, thoughts, feelings, and so on. These rights usually increase as children get older and more independent.

It sometimes seems that children are born with personalities that are shy, protective, and/or possessive. Other children seem to be born with personalities that have no sense about what belongs to whom, and they share everything: toys, food, clothing, and so on. Whatever style of personality a child comes in to the world with, he or she will have to learn the other. And it usually requires some pain or sacrifice. However, if a child can learn the other side early, it will save him or her great pain later on.

When you ask the child, What do you want? and the child answers something like, I want him to leave me alone. I want him to stop bugging me. I want him to get out of my room. I want him to stop hitting me. I want him to stop calling me names. I want him to leave my stuff alone, you can pretty well assume the child does not feel protected.

It is fairly common for this complaint to come from an older child who is being "invaded" by a younger sibling. Younger siblings usually want to play with older siblings because they are more stimulating or interesting. Younger siblings may want to copy or compete with older siblings to feel bigger, stronger, or more mature. Younger siblings may want to play with older siblings to gain approval and attention. Sometimes older siblings have more privileges or competence, which can be interpreted as power by a younger sibling.

If you get answers from one of

your children that suggest he or she feels the need for more protection, do some of the following:

• Acknowledge that the child has some right to privacy, possessions, space, or whatever is in question, if you also agree. In other words a child may feel he or she has the right to say who can or cannot come into his or her room. You may or may not agree. You may have to define for the child where he or she does and does not have rights.

• Define for both or all the children what some temporary or limited rights might be, for example, they have the right not to be hit, not to be called names, not to have their creations destroyed, not to have their personal toys taken without permission, and so on.

• Set rules with consequences, for example, You are not allowed to borrow your sister's clothes without asking first. If you do, you will not be allowed to borrow any of her clothes for a month (or six months!). You are not allowed in your brother's room when he's not here, unless I give you permission. If you do, you'll lose television privileges for two days (or a week!).

• Explain to the children that rules are necessary structures for people who have not learned how to properly share or respect boundaries. When they can do this on their own, they may not need the rules, but they have to learn how to do both.

• You might consider teaching your children the importance of manners. Manners are nothing more than small rules that show extra respect for boundaries. Saying, please, thank you, excuse me, not interrupting when someone is talking, and knocking before entering a room occupied by someone, are all courtesies that respect boundaries.

• Before you finish helping the children, ask yourself if you have been too busy lately. Maybe you have been sick or stressed and your energies have been down. Maybe things have been wonderful, and you have been absorbed in new things in your life, with the end result being that the children have not had your full attention lately.

• Set aside time either to be with the children as a group or to be with each child individually, to reestablish your connection to them. It may take several weeks, or maybe even a few months, of consistent attention before the children regain their security. One or two outings may not be enough, depending on how long you have been absent.

Should I let the children work it out themselves, or should I try to solve the problem for them? This is always a hard question to answer, because we start off solving all of our infant's problems, but gradually we want our children to learn how to solve their own problems without our assistance. Here are a few suggestions:

1. Ask yourself, Does the child have the basic skills to solve the prob-

lem? Does the child know how to clean up his or her room? Does the child have any skills related to sharing, taking turns, waiting, and so on? Have you observed the child exhibiting these behaviors naturally, without coaching? When a child can perform a behavior with minimum effort, he or she will use it independently. If the skill requires a good deal of effort, a child will be less likely to use it without assistance. We want to build problem-solving skills until they can be used with minimum effort whenever possible.

2. If the children have the basic skills to solve the problem, and there is sufficient time for them to work it out (sometimes there isn't enough time or they don't have the proper surroundings to do it themselves), then it is usually better to let the children work it out themselves.

3. In the beginning, have the children stand or sit in front of you and ask them to work it out right there. Tell them they cannot go back to play or do whatever they were doing until they have solved the problem. Don't let the children leave until you are sure each child is satisfied. As an outside observer you might offer some suggestions for trades and compromises, but let the children make the decisions. Don't offer too many. Don't let the children leave if one child is still angry or upset, even if the children have agreed on a solution. Ask the upset child if he or she thinks the deal is fair. If the

child says yes, simply comfort him or her until he or she feels better. If the child says no (which is usually the case with a child who is still upset), then tell the children the problem is not yet solved. If a child leaves upset, it will only be a short time before the next altercation erupts—and it's usually a bigger eruption.

Solving a problem in this way usually requires more patience than most children have. So, one, two, or three times is usually all it takes before the children want to solve a problem outside your presence. Simply saying something like, If you're fighting, everybody come here so we can solve it, usually gives children enough incentive to resolve it themselves.

4. Listen to what each child needs or wants, and make decisions about what each child has to do. Take this approach when children don't have the skills or special knowledge required to solve problems alone; when there are very young children involved; when time is short or you are in a place where the children cannot discuss the problem (for instance, a church or restaurant); or when there is a wide age discrepancy in the children.

If you make the decision, expect some arguing—especially from older children. You can allow an appropriate objection, but if it is carried on past a few seconds, or if it is filled with rudeness, bad language, criticism, or blame, you can tack on a possible consequence, such as a time out, grounding, loss of a privilege, and so on.

Recommendations:
1. Be careful not to be pulled into the argument.
2. When you have made a decision, tell your children what to do. Tell them; do not ask them.
3. Be sure that the children cannot work out the problem themselves before you intervene.

How do you know how to handle sibling rivalry?

What is sibling rivalry? The word "rivalry" means a competition for the achievement of some goal. The goal might be a parent's attention and/or affection, or control over the family's environment or status in the family, such as who gets to sit in the front seat. The instincts for achievement and control are natural and necessary for survival. Consequently, some competition in the family is healthy and should be accepted, as long as it is balanced with cooperation and teamwork. Both values are needed to succeed in the world.

Know your own values. Some parents believe that children should work it out

among themselves; they consider fighting to be a natural part of the process. These parents might argue that fighting helps develop thinking skills, negotiating tactics, toughness, and strength of character. Other parents believe that children should work to get along peacefully, developing cooperation and teamwork. These parents believe fighting promotes bad feelings, which destroy teamwork, and serves no constructive purpose. For some strange reason, these two very different types of people often find each other in the world and decide to marry. Then they decide to be parents.

If you have found yourself in this position, consider your children lucky. You may have a difficult time with your spouse, but, hopefully, the children will take some values from each parent and be better prepared for the future than they would if they were raised only by one parent. If you are a single parent please don't be offended. Whatever your main value system, your children will be exposed to the opposite from outside sources. What is important is that you also recognize some value in the opposite position.

What causes sibling rivalry? Besides the natural instinct to control, there are a few other factors that influence sibling rivalry.

Personality Styles can greatly enhance or diminish sibling rivalry. In a recent workshop of more than two hundred parents, the question was asked, How many parents of two or more children have children with almost opposite personalities? More than ninety percent raised their hands. Only a very few parents said that their children had very similar personalities. Whoever designs families seems to like wholeness, because whatever comes out the second time is, in most cases, vastly different than what came out the first time. If the first two are alike, then the third child will offset the other two.

If you have two or more children, invariably one of them will be more aggressive, stubborn, strong-willed, and independent than the others. On the surface, this child may appear to be more interested in power and control. Usually this child will have to be given some limits to respect the space and possessions of other children in the family. On the other side of the coin a more passive or gentle child should be encouraged to stand up for himself or herself or his or her possessions.

Personality Compatibility between a parent and a child can also influence sibling rivalry. Some parents just naturally get along better with one child than another. You might feel more relaxed around one child; you might smile or laugh more; you might be more affectionate; you might have easier communication; you might talk more; you might generally have more common interests; and so on. Even though you may love your children equally, but differently, for their own qualities, your children will notice a disparity. It is even possible to love one child more, yet get along better with

another child. From your children's point of view, whomever you get along with best or spend the most time with is the one you love the best. As parents, we simply have to be aware of this possibility.

If you think this applies to you, spend special time (maybe alone) with the more difficult child in an activity that he or she enjoys. This is an important way to diminish the childhood perception that you love one child best. As children get older, you can discuss how your relationship may be different with each child but how that doesn't discount the love that you feel for each of them.

Family and Cultural Traits also greatly influence sibling rivalry. Whatever qualities the family or culture holds as valuable enhances the status of the child who possesses those qualities. The more traits the child has, the more valuable the child might be. If the oldest son looks just like Dad, or the oldest daughter looks just like Mom (assuming this is desirable), it can make that child seem more special and can get him or her more attention from friends or relatives. If the child is a successful student, athlete, artist, or beauty queen, the child may draw more positive attention from both inside and outside the family. A child who has fewer desirable qualities may receive less positive attention and feel less than special.

A strong and ambitious child who does not receive positive attention may rebel and seek negative attention. He or she might become the "black sheep" of the family. Many families have one. These black sheep usually represent attitudes and values that have not been integrated into the family system. Given some love and understanding, these children usually can help other family members develop compassion, strength, and maturity.

Birth Order can also play a role in sibling rivalry. Often the firstborn child had some time to enjoy Mom and Dad all to himself or herself. Along comes child number two, and the firstborn's attention might be cut down to half or, maybe, all the way to zero. Sometimes the newborn is very cute and charming, and sometimes the newborn is cranky and restless. But almost all the time, the newborn gets more attention than the older sibling. It's not uncommon for the older child to bear some resentment.

Even if there is a good bond between the newborn and the older child, conflict usually arises as the newborn reaches the toddler age. A toddler can bite, pinch, scratch, throw, and invade the older child's "territory." Most parents are more patient and understanding of the toddler, realizing it's just a stage; but the older sibling has a different viewpoint. When the older sibling is "attacked" by the younger sibling, the older child is often told not to hit back because he or she is bigger. Oftentimes, the older sibling is encouraged to share and give more to the younger sibling. Sometimes the older sibling has more responsibilities and requirements than the younger child. These facts, which may accumulate over some time, can create a picture of great unfairness in the mind of an older sibling, which can last, in some cases, throughout the siblings' lives.

One way to help diminish these feelings is to show the older child that you understand his or her plight by helping the child to protect his or her space and his or her possessions. This is not easy with a toddler who seems to be everywhere at once. But over time, as limits are set on the younger child, the older sibling can feel a sense of fairness. If the older child is over the age of six or seven you might ask the child if he or she thinks he or she is being treated fairly with regard to siblings. If the child says no, it doesn't necessarily mean you have to change anything. You'll just have to evaluate what the child says.

Age Range is another factor in sibling rivalry. In families where there is more than a five-year difference between the eldest child and the youngest child, there is usually a difference in parenting behaviors. By the fourth or fifth child, parents do things quite differently than they did with the first child. Parents are usually more casual and relaxed about parenting. Younger siblings usually don't have as many photographs in the family album, and they don't usually get as many baby toys or clothes as the firstborn. Younger siblings may not get as much attention as the firstborn. The mother may work to help support the family by the third or fourth child, although lack of parental attention may be balanced by an increased attention from older siblings.

An older child may perceive that he or she was raised with more restrictions than a younger sibling who seems to have more freedoms at an earlier age. It is important for parents to recognize that they mature as people during the parenting years, so that the last child may have been raised by a more mature adult than the first child. This is a natural part of life. If a child, in the heat of an argument, wants to point out all that he or she didn't get, it is usually best to respond calmly and to acknowledge, without self-blame, what the child didn't get, balanced by what the child did get.

Some experts say that middle children have the most difficulty, because they may not get the attention that the first or last child gets. Middle children are sometimes referred to as the "lost children." Sometimes a middle child gets bossed around by the older child and invaded by the younger child. In any case, there seems to be a great deal of pressure for middle children, and they can often get overlooked. Be sure to take time to check in with your middle child.

What are the do's and don'ts?

1. Do spend time with each child individually in an activity that he or she enjoys. If you enter your child's world, he or she will be more likely to enter yours. Even if this seems impossible, reorient your priorities and make it happen. These are the

times that mean the most to us. These are the times that parental influence can be the greatest. *Nothing gives a child greater validation and feelings of self-worth than having a parent spend individual and enjoyable time with him or her.*

2. Don't make comparisons between siblings. Don't say, for instance, Why don't you act more like your brother or sister! Even if you feel that way, the words can damage your child's feelings of self-worth and dramatically increase sibling rivalry.

Recommendations:

1. Remember, rivalry between siblings is normal. If you are not upset by the rivalry you can be of better help.
2. If your child seems to be too needy of your time, you need to understand why. If you cannot figure it out, seek professional help.

How do you know how to handle a nagging, clinging, or whiny child?

Why are they like this? We assume that the child is not overly tired or coming down with an illness, both of which can produce clinging and whiny behavior. Rather, we are talking about a pattern of behavior that has been present for more than three months and seems to be part of the child's overall personality.

Consistent clinging or whining is a symptom of the child's dependency. The child either feels unable to do things for himself or herself or the child has learned that it's just easier to get someone else to do it. Usually these children like to be around the parents or, perhaps an older sibling. These children might follow parents or siblings around, or they may need constant attention. These children may want to be held or picked up frequently. They may experience a great deal of anxiety when separated from their mother.

As the child gets older, he or she may be more of a homebody. The child may cling to one special friendship at a time, rather than develop several friendships. The child may have some difficulty going to school and may seek constant help for homework, especially with bigger projects for science or social studies. As teenagers, these children may be slower to mature. They may not be eager to learn to drive or to date, although some of these children are very interested in dating so that they can be close to someone. These children can sometimes be controlling and easily jealous in their relationships.

There are at least three factors that can produce some of these dependent behaviors:

- Slow development is one biological factor. Some children grow at a slower rate. They demonstrate delayed development at all the growth markers; walking, talking, perception, coordination, social development, tooth development, puberty, and so on. If the parents have an expectation or a desire for the child to grow up faster, the parents can end up pushing the child, which oftentimes achieves the opposite result.

- Rejection of a child can produce more dependent behavior in a child. For whatever reasons (and there are many), the bonding between the mother and child may be nonpositive or weak. The child may be unappealing as an infant to the mother. The child may have had colic, an illness, or some disfigurement that pushed the mother away. The mother may have been depressed or exhausted during the pregnancy or after the delivery. The child may have been an unplanned pregnancy, and the mother may have felt forced to have and raise the child. Mothers are, as you may recall, human beings, and they have their limitations.

  If the child senses this weaker bond, he or she will not feel secure, so he or she will usually seek to get those close, warm feelings. As the child develops, he or she may be a pleaser, trying to be the "good" child, but never really developing the courage to be himself or herself, or the child may directly seek to have one or both parents involved in every aspect of his or her life. The early sense of rejection and the feelings of low self-worth, if not resolved, lead to most of the addictive patterns that we have today. Drugs, alcohol, food, work, exercise, and the like can all be substitutes for the feelings of comfort and power we were unable to get and hold onto.

Sometimes a child can start off well, but something happens along the way that produces more dependent behavior. A mother goes back to work to make ends meet. The father is transferred, and the family moves away from all that is familiar. A parent dies. There is a divorce. The list is endless. However, if the early bonding experience was positive, it is usually easier to recoup a child's courage and independence.

• A second psychological factor occurs if there is an overly close bond between the mother (it can also be the father) and the child. An anxious parent intent upon being the perfect parent can hover over a child, anticipating every wish before it is even expressed. The child is never allowed to struggle, be alone, or do without. Consequently the child doesn't develop the internal resources to manage himself or herself physically, emotionally, or mentally. The child doesn't develop the internal capacities for security and comfort.

Besides the anxious parent, there is also the needy parent who feels either alone or unloved, or who has been unable to achieve intimacy with other adults. Sometimes when these people become parents, they foster a close relationship with the child to satisfy their own needs. Oftentimes, these parents are overly protective, overly controlling, and overly involved with their children.

What can I do about it?

1. If the child is a late bloomer you simply have to reduce your expectations and get the child assistance with education, if needed. Remember, late bloomers can be just as successful and happy as early bloomers; they just do it later.

2. If you have a needy, whiny child who turns you off, don't try to get away from him or her. It will only make the child pursue you more. Remember, the child doesn't understand why he or she feels this way. You have to move toward the child, but in a way that makes you feel comfortable and confident. With a young child pick an activity or a series of activities that you might enjoy together. The activities could last anywhere from five minutes to thirty minutes in length. Focus on being with your child in a positive way. Make it fun and pleasant. The goal of the activity is second to the relationship during that time.

3. Structure the time with the child. Younger children, ages two to five, usually do better with many short, but frequent, times with a parent. You can use a kitchen timer with a bell to signal when it's time to play with Mommy. Set the timer with ten-minute intervals to start. A

young or needy child may resist at first, but if the parent is consistent, the child will accept the structure.

Usually within a couple of days, the child gets bored with the parent having so much control, and the child begins to develop more stimulating independent play. Most often, within a few days, the parents can increase the time between playtimes by five minutes or so, and it is no longer a problem for the child. What is important is that the parent begins to feel a little more control in the relationship.

When you give time to a child, don't give to the point of exhaustion, because you will have to withdraw in an equal or greater proportion to recover your energy and you will soon begin to resent the child. Give only to the point where you begin to tire, then stop. You will still have some reserve to do other things, and you will recover more quickly. If you stop a little early, give the child your attention another time. If you keep your promise, the child will begin to trust you, and this trust will give the child the ability to wait.

When you have young children, it is often impossible to get dishes done, the house cleaned, and laundry washed while the children are home and awake. Some men or women, however, feel that they are not good enough unless they can do it all. If you have young children, lower your personal expectations for what you can achieve.

Older children, ages six to twelve, can often wait several days to a week or more to have special time with a parent. Set up a special time that includes activities the child enjoys. If you don't enjoy the activities the child chooses, and you cannot find activities of common interest, then cut down either on the amount of time you spend doing the activities or on the frequency with which you do them, but not both. Pick one or the other. Above all else, you must strive for consistency, that is, what builds trust in the child. Trust is the foundation for independence.

4. Encourage time apart. Starting from toddler age and up, encourage and require personal time, alone time, or independent time. These concepts are introduced by many parents at a very early age. Sleepovers, visits with relatives, summer camps, outings with friends in which the parents don't attend, occasional weekends away for the parents, all help to encourage independence in children.

Recommendations:

1. The more you encourage your child to have activities away from home, the less dependent he or she may become.
2. If your child cannot find activities away from home you can help by phoning such groups as Boy Scouts, Girl Scouts, school clubs, athletic activities, karate, or other activities that the child should be encouraged to join, at least on a trial basis.

How do you know what to do when your child wants things that you can't afford?

Wanting it is not usually the problem. Nagging is annoying and the guilt of not being a "good enough provider" creates the problem. If the child communicates, directly or indirectly, that you've let him or her down, you can't help but feel that twinge of guilt. This is especially true when a child's best friend or "all of his or her friends" have something that the child doesn't have. It could be clothes or toys or opportunities, but somebody always has something your child desires.

What the child runs up against is the concept of limits. If a parent understands and appreciates the value of limits, it is easier to set limits with the child. Families that stay within their financial limits create a stability that enables them not only to grow, but also to handle emergencies that arise. Families that constantly spend more than they make, increase their debt and stress while they decrease their stability. Invariably, these families get caught short, and they have to make drastic changes to rebalance. The drastic changes create undo stress. If the child wants something that the parents feel is appropriate, but they cannot afford

it, then some kind of plan can be made that may include the child's efforts to acquire the object or opportunity. In most cases, the desired object is also more greatly appreciated and cared for when it is achieved.

A second value may have to be learned about possessions. Children don't readily understand the concept that money and possessions can't bring them happiness, because it is hard for children to distinguish between pleasure and real happiness. Money can certainly bring pleasures and certain levels of security, but pleasures tend to be fleeting. Satisfaction and fulfillment of goals achieved, self-acceptance, and self-appreciation tend to lead to deeper levels of true happiness. Children want to have what others have so they don't feel lacking, or left out, or that they don't belong. Children usually want to feel like part of a group and that they have some status or power in that group. Ask your child to discuss with you other ways in which he or she can feel good in a group. Maybe some older siblings or friends could offer some ideas. When children hear what other kids really think they don't feel so alone. Children may also be very surprised to hear what other kids think.

Recommendations:
1. Children who do not immediately get the toy they want will often forget and want something else the following week.
2. Help your child plan and save for something he or she wants. Learning to wait is a valuable lesson.

How do you know how to handle parental guilt?

What is parental guilt? Parenting = Guilt. You get parental guilt the moment your children are conceived, and it can last a lifetime. You can be sixty-five-years-old, and if your forty-year-old son or daughter still messes up, you will, at some level, blame yourself.

Why are we prone to guilt? The problem is that we are grossly underprepared for parenting. How many parenting classes did you take either in high school or college? How many classes did you take about raising two-year-olds; dealing with colicky babies; handling sibling rivalry; handling various child personalities; setting limits and discipline; communicating at a child's level; raising teenagers, and all that goes with that? How much practice did you have caring for children before you had them? Did you ever try to get children to do things that they didn't want to do before you had children? Did you take any classes in how to keep a relationship together when you have children? Did you know how hard it would be before you started?

The problem is that almost none of us had sufficient information or skill to raise children when we started our families. You got more information about and practice at driving a car than being a parent. You probably got more information and training for your job or career than you got for parenting.

When you have lots of information and lots of practice, you still make mistakes. But when you have little information and little practice, you make lots of mistakes. Most of us really love our children, and we really want to help them grow up healthy, happy, and well-prepared for life. So, when we see our children get hurt, fail, or grow up a little crooked, we feel guilty. The guilt is compounded by the fact that often-times, we are the ones who hurt our children the most. Especially for young children, parents are the most powerful people in the child's life. The power we have can be used for healing or for hurting. None of us is perfect, so our power will be used to both heal and hurt, in most cases. We feel guilty when we hurt somebody we love. We feel like we've failed when we hurt somebody we were supposed to help. Welcome to parenting.

A second part of the problem is that we grow and change along with our children. Every five to ten years, we have a different awareness, different perceptions, different feelings, different skills, different needs, thus we parent differently. At a parenting seminar, one father of six said that children ought to be like pancakes, you should be able to throw out the first one or two. He was just kidding, but his point was well understood by the other parents. The fact is, we learn as we go along, and both we and our children pay for our parenting mistakes. Most of us learn fairly quickly that it is not humanly possible to be a perfect parent.

Is guilt good or bad? Good guilt lets us know when we have let ourselves down. We have betrayed our own ideals or we have hurt someone we love. If we listen to good guilt, we might stop drinking or smoking because it "models weakness" to our children, or lessens our capacity to relate to each other. When people have children, they often let go of self-indulgent activities either because they have less time and money for those activities, or because they want to model healthier behavior for the children. Good guilt helps change behavior for the better.

Bad guilt disables us. Bad guilt comes from unrealistic expectations and excessive self-criticism. If we are overwhelmed and obsessive about our parental inadequacies, we do not have the strength to withstand the many mistakes we make in learning to parent. We will either be overly strict and demanding of our children, or we will constantly be overwhelmed, disorganized, and depressed. When we take either extreme, it adds to our guilt and produces resentment toward our children. Guilt is inevitable. A little bit may be good, too much can be deadly. How we handle guilt is important.

Children can use guilt to manipulate parents. All of us have difficulty with some type of child behavior. It might be the aggressive child, the fearful child, the depressed child, the dependent child, the lazy child, the whiny child, the selfish child, or the pleasing child. One of these behaviors pushes our button the most, and the child probably knows it. Children are able to sense their parents' vulnerability. Also, the child has nothing better to do for the first five years of life than to learn how to control his or her environment. Because you are part of that environment, the child has to learn how to control you. If you feel inadequate or bad that you have not given your child some opportunity or that you became angry at the child unfairly (because you've had a bad day), then you are a ripe target for some guilt-inducing comment from your child.

In addition, working parents often feel guilt because they fear they do not spend enough time with their children. A father may feel guilty because he does not participate in his child's sports program. A working mother might feel guilty when her child does poorly in school because she's too tired to help the child with homework when she comes home in the evening. Many parents feel guilty when their child is at day care. Some parents feel they do not give enough toys, clothes, or other material item to their child, or do not provide something the child wants. Children pick this up and use it to express their anger, or they use it to get what they want.

What do you do when you feel guilty? There are several things you can do when you feel guilty:

1. Stop. Take a deep breath. Think for a few minutes about *your priorities*. Are they love? Are they material success? Are they good feelings among family members? Write them down if you have to. Because it is not possible to do everything, it is essential to determine what is most important in the long run. If we are talking about priorities, such items as basic food, clothing, shelter, and education probably come before the latest fashion or toy, although your child won't think so. If we are talking about feelings, such as emotions as basic love, respect, appreciation, and gratitude for personal belongings come before desire for whatever the child wants to get. If we are talking about behavior, children have to learn independence and self-assertiveness, as well as patience and cooperation. You can teach these values regardless of your financial situation.

2. Determine where the majority of your time and energy goes. Energy flows where attention goes. Wherever you place most of your energy is where your priority lies. Think about it. Does most of your energy go to the children, a relationship, yourself, work? All of these areas (and a few more) demand our attention. We feel guilty if any one of these is ignored. As a parent, you are the major source of giving to the children, especially if they are younger. It is not only important, but crucial, for you to maintain your sanity and stability. If this means taking time for yourself, or a particular relationship, then you must do it, even though your children might protest. If you have nothing, then you have nothing to give. If you give beyond your means, then you begin to develop a good deal of resentment toward yourself, your spouse, or your children.

3. Distinguish between wants and needs. Everybody may be able to meet the needs for food, clothing, shelter, education, and some loving attention. However, not everyone may get as much as they want. Get used to the idea of setting limits. Setting limits with a child activates the child's internal resources to meet his or her needs.

4. If your guilt is excessive or debilitating, you may be reacting to memories of your own childhood, which may or may not have anything to do with what your children need now. Or you may have some very unrealistic expectations about parenting. In either case, some short-term parent counseling would be advisable.

Recommendations:
1. As a parent, you need to be aware of your own feelings; if you are not, you may be easily manipulated.
2. Be aware of how your child tries to manipulate you.
3. If you are not able to control your child's manipulations you may need to seek professional help.

How do you know how to accept imperfections in your parenting?

As mentioned in the previous chapter, guilt is one result of being a parent who tries too hard. There are other feelings and thoughts that come to parents who try to be the best parents they can be.

Parents feel imperfect when there's not enough money. Parents often want the best for their children, even if they can't possibly afford it. What children need is affection, security, and a stable home life, as well as the essentials of life, such as nourishment and warmth. Good medical care and good education are also high on the list for parents. It is very easy for most parents—especially in America—to get swept up into material success. It is easy for parents to cross over children's wants into children's needs. Then parents feel responsible to provide their children with these items. Basic commercial marketing tells us that we have to buy a certain product or we will lack something. Not many of us want to lack something, and we certainly don't want our children to lack anything. Simply let your child know that there are many more things to buy than you can afford. If you can accept this reality comfortably, you will teach your child an important lesson about money.

Parents feel imperfect when they don't have enough time or energy. Perhaps unlike any other time in history, good opportunities abound for our children. If you look at all the after-school programs alone that are available in art, music, dance, athletics, travel, and so on, you will be amazed. There are community-based programs and private programs. There are state and federal programs, as well as programs that provide additional education and foster special interests. There simply is not enough time or energy to participate in them all. Choices have to be made, and good opportunities have to be left behind. Overloading your child's schedule, even with good things, will eventually weaken him or her.

Parents feel imperfect when they have bad habits. It is true that you raise *your* children. This means your children learn your behaviors. They learn your values. They learn to solve problems the way you do. If you lose your temper, yell and scream, chances are one or two of your children will do the same. In other words, you are the model for what your children become. If you say one thing and do another, your children learn that. Even if you are perfect, chances are you had to go through a learning process, and chances are your spouse isn't perfect. If you can change some of your bad behaviors, whatever they are, your child learns that it can be done. If you cannot, then at least identify those behaviors as undesirable.

Parents feel imperfect when their children pick up their bad habits.
What about those aspects of your behavior that you cannot change? Children are adaptable, but at a price. This is both fortunate and unfortunate. If you are a parent who is very angry and punitive, your child will learn to live with it, but at a price. The price may be a very unhappy and depressed child. Or, the price may be a child who becomes disturbed in other ways. Sometimes children learn to distance themselves from a difficult parent. Because children have no choice, they learn to deal with the unhappy situation. Clearly, if parents can change their behavior they should do so. Most likely, your child will survive you as a parent. The child's desire to have a relationship with you as an adult depends on what you do as a parent now. Some children don't call home for a good reason.

What can you do now?
1. It is important to remember that there are no perfect parents and no perfect children. There are simply parents and children who have strong and weak points. If you are willing to compliment yourself on your strong points and work on your weak points, you will model very constructive behavior for your children. Accepting yourself in this more loving way will allow you to

be more accepting toward your children.
2. Separate your sense of self-worth from your children's performance. It is their performance, not yours. You may have to find other areas of your life that make you feel good about yourself.
3. Parents should ask spouses or close friends for an evaluation of their parenting skills. If these people are not available, parents should talk to a professional or take a parenting class.

Recommendations:
1. Recognize your strong points and your weak points.
2. Compliment yourself on your strong points and work on your weak points.
3. Accept yourself in a more loving way; this will allow you to be more accepting of your children.

How do you know how to deal with your children when you are going through a crisis?

What we as parents sometimes forget is that, no matter how we feel, the lives of our children go on with the inevitable ups and downs. Also, our children seem to have an uncanny ability to sense when we are vulnerable, and when they can take advantage of us. The younger or more dependent the child is the more insecure the child becomes when we are vulnerable. To the child, our vulnerability appears as weakness. Because both of these statements are true, we, as parents, have to develop a way to get the support we need, while providing support and security for our children. If we can do this, we may also be able to turn these negative situations into positive ones for our children.

What do you say to your children when you are in crisis?

1. STOP. What we mean by "stop" is that you must get your children's attention. Children must learn to listen to what you say. Saying "stop," or holding your hand up, is a good way to get children to stop the usual flow of whatever is happening.
2. The next step is to tell the child how you feel. As you discuss how you feel, you have to tell the child what changes are to be made. That is, what you want your child to do or not to do. This may involve many possibilities, some of which are listed below:
a. I may be crying in the future. It's not something you have done. It is about _____.
b. I am angry about something at my job. If I am irritable and angry at home, it is not because of you. But at this time, it is best to leave me alone.
c. I am overwhelmed doing _____ at present. This is making me irritable and angry. It would be very helpful if you would (for example, clean your room, make your own lunch, and so on.).
d. During this period, I need to be alone to think. I may not talk or play with you much, but it doesn't mean I don't love you. I'll get over it soon.

Trusting your child with your feelings and asking for your child's help contributes to the child's feelings of growth and maturity. If your child continually resists cooperating, you may have to give the child a time out, or you may have to ask other adults for help.

Crisis has some benefits. Death of someone we love, taxes, quarrels, illness, divorce, work problems, disasters, and the like, can all cause us to feel vulnerable and in crisis. Not only are we upset, but our children, who sense this fact, can also become anxious and upset. Sometimes this happens overtly and sometimes children themselves don't realize what motivates their feelings and behaviors.

One benefit of crisis is that it gives us the opportunity to teach our children to be sensitive to other people's needs. Often, children grow up thinking they are the center of the world. In fact, they are self-centered; only as children mature and learn do they become more sensitive and caring. Children learn these lessons as parents teach them time and time again about patience, independence, sharing, and giving.

Recommendations:
1. Use the situation to help make the family bond closer.
2. Think of the crisis as a teaching opportunity; this will allow you not to feel guilty.

How do you know what to do when you have a child with whom you cannot relate?

Children, like adults, have a full range of personalities. Just as there are adults we don't particularly care for, sometimes we have children whom we love, but don't really like. Parents can't easily relate to these children. This may be for several reasons.

- Sometimes the child represents something from the parents' past that is difficult to face. All of us, as adults, have some part of our own personality or past that we don't particularly like. We may have overcome or denied these feelings or behaviors successfully. When we see our undesirable personality or disagreeable behavior in our child, we may want to run away from it or deny it. This may mean dissociating from our child. Sometimes a child is too active and loud; sometimes too aggressive or selfish; or sometimes too passive, lazy, or quiet. The unattractive trait can be any one of these qualities and more. It is important to determine what behavior in your child is difficult to accept.

- The child's very existence may interfere with the parents marital relationship. As much as our children give to us, they take away some things as well. Sometimes what we lose is simply the freedom we had before there were young children or dependents to care for. This is not a problem that is easily solved. As we go through the various stages of life—from child to adolescent to young adult—we make gains and sacrifices, as well as effect changes in our lifestyle. The responsibility of a child is one of those permanent changes that is difficult for some to assume.

- The child's presence interferes with a parent's career. This can be especially true for a woman who is torn between the traditional role of primary caregiver and her role at work. The problem is to balance being a parent at home and an achiever at work.

- The parent has never learned to deal with young children. Those of us who are only children, or the youngest child in a family, or who did not grow up around children, may not have learned the skills needed to be a parent. Those of us who were raised by rejecting parents may have no skills other than to reject our own children.

- Being a parent is not something you planned for and it is not something you really want. This leaves us feeling unready to be parents. Because parenting is one of the major jobs we perform, and we are totally untrained for the position, we sometimes feel at odds with fulfilling the role, especially if we have little experience with children.

What must parents do? The first thing to do is to admit that you are having difficulty. This will open the door for help and for you to learn. Second, take some time to determine what your child likes, somewhat likes and dislikes. Your child may have limited likes, none of which you can understand. Find something that you can both enjoy. You may have to experiment with some new activities until you find something. Third, plan for short times when you and your child are together, until you both have the confidence to be together in an enjoyable way. Fourth, focus on having fun, rather than teaching, controlling, or directing.

You may find answers in childrearing books, childrearing courses, or from professionals. Sometimes just observing other parents may be helpful. Doing what other parents do with their children may help you relate to your child. Asking your child what he or she likes to do is another way to begin relating. Children are great teachers.

Look and learn. Whatever the reason for the difficulty, parents must resolve the underlying problem. Parents may be able to do this alone, or they may require help from a professional psychologist or family counselor.

How can you relate to your child?
One way to relate to a child is simply to spend time with the child. Children will talk to fill a void. That is, if you put two adults, or two children, or a child and an adult alone together in a room, eventually there will be communication. If you play with a child—difficult as it may be for you—eventually problems, such as fear and lack of trust, are overcome.

Recommendations: If the situation raises questions about your feelings that you do not understand, talk to a professional such as a psychologist or other mental health specialist.

How do you know how to relate to your spouse's children when you are the stepparent?

Some experts in the field suggest there are three stages to stepparenting:

First, there is the period in which the stepparent is very giving toward the children. The stepparents buy them things, stay out of their business, do lots of things for them, take them places, and essentially try to please the children. If these actions fail (as they often do) to get the children to trust, respect, and appreciate the stepparent, then the relationship goes into stage two.

In the second stage, the stepparent gets irritated and frustrated because the stepchildren apparently are not bonding positively with the stepparent. The stepparent's authority isn't being accepted, and the stepparent does not feel included in a meaningful way into the family. The stepparent may become more authoritative, or he or she may become more critical of the other parent, trying to get the biological parent to make the children do what the stepparent wants them to do. This usually results in numerous arguments between the children and the stepparent and sometimes between the spouses. Sometimes, when the stepparent asserts some authority, the ex-spouse is drawn into an argument with the new stepparent. It can get quite nasty.

Stage three occurs when the arguments have reached a point where the adults have to sit down and work out an agreement regarding the stepparent's role of authority. This, in turn, is brought to the children, and, with luck, is supported by all the adults involved. It doesn't always work out this way, and some situations never resolve themselves.

Here are some important factors. One important factor is the age of the children. This is important for two reasons. The first is that it may be more difficult for an older child to accept a new parent. Any child between the age of five and sixteen probably is still in a strongly bonded relationship with the natural parent. Before this age frame and after this age frame, the stepparent may have an easier time. The child may blame the stepparent for the divorce, or see the stepparent as a threat to the child's fantasy of the parents getting back together.

Age is also important is because the longer the child lived with the now-absent parent, the greater the bond. The greater the bond the more protective the child will feel about that parent. If the child feels protective of both parents, it can become quite difficult for the stepparent to bond with the stepchild. If you remember that it took at least five years, when the child was most dependent and vulnerable, for the child to learn to trust the natural parents and accept their authority, it can help you to be a patient stepparent in the bonding process. The child has to trust you and feel your support long before he or she will accept your authority. If you try to press that authority before the trust is built, you will either overwhelm the child and turn him or her off, or the child will rebel.

There is a second important factor to keep in mind: it takes two to make a relationship. Sometimes a stepparent gets lucky and hits it off immediately with a child. There is an instant chemistry. If this happens, you have a big head start. Foster it for a good six months to a year, if you can, before you ask the child to do things that he or she may not want to do. On the other hand, if there is no immediate connection, or if there is a good connection but the child is cautious because he or she doesn't want to feel like he or she is betraying the other parent, then you may have to go more slowly.

What are the do's and don'ts?

1. Be yourself. Children have an instinctive sense to spot any false behavior on your part. They may not instantly love you. They may instantly hate you without you having done anything, but this can be overcome.

2. Understand the limits of the relationship with your spouse. Will you become an equal player in this relationship to the children? Or, will you just be your spouse's other half, so that the children relate to you as a friend, not an authority figure? Remember, the children may take their cues from the biological parent.

3. Understand your spouse's mixed loyalties. Before you came on board your spouse's primary loyalties were to the children. Now that you are in the picture, there will be a change, but it might take time. You cannot be a protector one moment and give up that role entirely the next. Many second marriages become rocky over this issue. In some marriages, this problem is never solved because

it is not addressed directly, and the marriage suffers. Work on the problem, but give it time. There is the loyalty of your spouse to the children and the loyalty of the children to the absent parent to consider. With very young children, the problem may be resolved easier. With older children, there may be more difficulty.

4. Give it time. Do not enter the situation thinking that everything will now be different. You may have to deal with resistance for a while. As you show the new family who you are and what you are willing to do and not do, they will, in most cases, come to appreciate you.

5. Spend time with the children and your new spouse. Getting married doesn't mean giving up your work, if both parents work. One way to let the children know you is to go places together. Another is to talk about what is important to them. Every child has continuous mini-crises that are soon over. If children see you as accepting, honest, and supportive they will come to accept you.

6. Do not bad-mouth the absent parent. Remember, the children will have divided loyalties, maybe on a permanent basis. You can tell them what you expect, as well as what you will give.

Recommendations:

1. Try to understand what specific part of being a stepparent bothers you. Is it the children or your spouse?

2. Your role must be very clear to you and your spouse to work out the problems.

How do you know how to help your child adjust to a new stepparent?

You have just married, and now you either have to introduce a relatively new parent to your children, or you have to help your children accept that someone you lived with will now take on an official parental role. You can best help your children adjust to this situation by clarifying your relationship with your spouse and answering some questions for yourself.

What role do you want your spouse to play? As a protector of your children, are you willing to share that role with someone else, fully and without reservations? Or, do you want your spouse to have a limited role? What role does your spouse want to play? It is very important to come to some agreement before you to get married.

Consider some of these issues.
- **Talk.** Depending on the age of your children, you should have a conference with them to tell them what they can expect in the future. We

are all anxious about changes small and large. This certainly is a large or major change in your children's lives. They need to know the limits of this new relationship. They may need help in handling divided loyalties to the absent parent. They need to know that the stepparent is your equivalent, or second or third, when it comes to being in charge.

- **Love.** Children have to know that you still love them, even though you have somebody else in your life. Although this may be obvious to you, it may not be clear to your children, unless you spell it out.
- **Anger.** Children may be angry at you for bringing somebody new into the family. Or they may be angry at your spouse, no matter what happens. You have to accept your child's anger, let it pass, and move on. As the child learns more about the new spouse and finds that the changes are not so drastic, the anxiety and the anger will disappear. Only in rare instances, when the anger does not disappear, will parents have to seek professional help.
- **Information.** Help your new spouse with information about each child. What does the child like and dislike. What are the child's strengths and weaknesses? When should you be careful with the child? Suggest ways for your spouse to improve the situation.
- **Involvement.** As your new spouse gets involved in the child's life in such areas as school, sports, after-

school activities, purchases, and so on, the child will learn to both accept this person and relate more closely. It takes time.

- **Finality.** As children learn that the situation is permanent, no matter how they feel or what they do, they will begin to accept the situation. This acceptance may come before the children begin to trust or to love the new parent. The more the children are with someone, the more the tendency is to accept that person.

Recommendations:

1. Expect some initial resistance; this is normal. Usually, the more time spent together between your child and spouse, the more improvement you will see.
2. Only when the resistance seems intractable should you seek professional help.

As a single parent, how do you know how to introduce your dating to your children?

At some point after your divorce or separation you may begin dating. This is healthy for you, but the question is how to tell your children and/or have them involved.

What is the problem? Generally there are two major problems in this area.

First, children usually don't have a concept for dating. They don't usually understand that it is somewhat exploratory and transitory in nature. Children quickly jump to the possibility of marriage and having a new mother or father. This, in turn, gets children geared up to either bond with or rebel against the potential new family member. In either case, the reaction is premature and gets the child emotionally involved unnecessarily. This can create great hardships for a child.

Second, children can feel threatened by the changes that occur when a parent starts dating. There is almost immediately a sense of loss with the parent, who is now dividing his or her attention between the children and the new friend. Children are very sensitive to the loss of attention. Even if parents give the same amount of time physically, children can tell when the parent's mind is somewhere else. Clearly, children tend to love their parents and often find it difficult to accept any changes in this relationship. Children may be afraid of change. They may be afraid they will lose their parent's love. They may be afraid that the new person will take away their parent. Because they have not yet bonded to this person, children also do not know what to expect. They do not understand the parent's need for companionship or sex. They do not have the maturity to understand the need to share your life with someone.

What is the solution? Generally it is not a good idea to introduce your children to a date in the early stages of your relationship. You can tell your children that you are going out to dinner with friends or to meet someone. If the relationship lasts beyond three or four dates and it looks like the two of you will continue to date, you can refer to your date as a new friend. At this time, you can have the person pick you up at the house, or you can introduce him or her to your children. Usually it is not a good idea to have the new friend spend time with your children until there is a commitment toward your relationship. Otherwise, the children will begin to bond with him or her. It may be a little inconvenient for you to keep your date and your children separated, but it will save your children a lot of stress later if you decide to end the relationship.

If you meet someone and it appears that you will be going out evenings or on weekends, it might be important to tell your children that you are dating. In most cases, if you have younger children, they really won't have a clear picture of what that means. You may need to answer their spoken and unspoken questions. Does this mean you don't love them? Does this mean you will leave them? If the child is old enough, he or she may ask you if you will have sex with this person. Some questions you should answer directly and honestly. Some questions, however, are personal, and you should tell your children that you will not answer them. For some questions, you simply may not know the answer. It is better to tell your children what you can, and tell them where the limits are, rather than lie to them. In all cases, children need reassurance that you will take care of them.

Should you bring this person home? Although introducing a constant stream of people to your child is not good, there is no reason not to introduce your child to someone you like and with whom you have a continuing relationship. The children may have to learn some new social skills: for instance, how to talk to this person, and when to leave him or her alone. Remember, the children will assess this person as a possible parent, just as the person will assess the children, as possible stepchildren. Family outings or extended time together should be reserved until there is some commitment to the relationship. It is the commitment to the relationship that provides protection for the children. Children don't carry the mature perspective about relationships that adults do, and usually they are ill-prepared for the relationship to end. They can get very hurt.

Should your friend sleep over? Again, generally, the answer is no, not unless there is a spoken commitment to the relationship. This question raises a number of other issues. It depends primarily on your morality and your view of the relationship. In our society, many dating couples do spend the night together. If this happens you should explain this new stage in your relationship to your children. That you really care for this person or that you have moved to a more serious relationship may be good enough reasons to make the change. Remember, you are a model for your children. Would you like your child to have the same value system? This is an especially difficult question if you have a child between the ages of nine and sixteen, because children this age are highly aware of the sexual aspect of sleeping together. These children may feel strongly that your actions are wrong. It is important that your words and your actions match, otherwise you will lose credibility with this child. This is a very important time for moral development.

Recommendations:

1. Try to be aware of your children's feelings about having to share you, as well as getting used to a new person.

2. It is important for children, depending on the their ages, to learn that you have a life of your own apart from them, and that this does not mean you do not love them.

How do you know what is the best custody arrangement for your child?

What is the problem? In the heat of divorce, parents sometimes make major errors in custody arrangements for their children. Custody has to fit in with the needs of both working schedules to make sure the children are well cared for. Custody should be fair in regard to vacations and holidays for both parents. No one questions the necessity of meeting the needs of both parents. The problem lies in the fact that, up to this point, there is usually little consideration for what is really best for the child. Somehow, in the heat of the arguments, children's needs are forgotten or neglected. The court does not usually ask children under the age of twelve what they want and why they want it. Sometimes, this is a grave error.

Different arrangements can work.

- The most usual custody arrangement is for children to live with their mother and see their father every other weekend and once during the week. Considering that almost all fathers and many mothers work, this is usually a pretty good arrangement. It runs into difficulty when the child has his or her own plans for some event on a weekend, and the parents get angry. Or, the child has plans on father's night to see the child, and the father gets upset because the mother won't allow him to see the child another night.

- Another custody arrangement is for the child to spend three and a half days of the week with each parent. For some children, this is not a good arrangement because it is too disruptive. Both parents should work out the arrangement so that the child's school and social activities are constant.

- Some children are awarded to one parent for six months and the other for six months. This is often a poor arrangement. Children need stability just as the parents do. Children have to have a home, a school, and a set of friends. Having two of each can create more stress on a child than he or she can handle.

What is the best arrangement? The best custody arrangement is one that first takes into consideration the needs and desires of each individual child, and second is flexible enough to allow for changes without court order as the child grows.

Children have different needs. Some need to see a particular parent more often than another. Sometimes a child is more dependent on one parent than another, and this can differ among children in a family. What works well for one child may not work well for

another. It is important to listen to and understand each child's needs and desires. It doesn't mean that the children will get everything they want immediately, but it is important for the parents to know what each child desires. Perhaps, in time, schedules can be arranged to better suit a child's needs.

When custody arrangements are made, it is very common for courts and outside family specialists to group all the children together, so that whatever rules are established apply equally to all the children. Because it is more complicated to take into account each child's needs, some children suffer more than others. It sometimes is wonderful for a child with several siblings to have individual time with a parent. Also, sometimes allowing just two children who get along to stay together makes it easier both on the children and the parents. When children have these types of options, they benefit from the custody situation.

As children grow, their needs and desires to be with one parent over the other change, and there has to be sufficient flexibility in the custody arrangement for a child to spend more time with the parent. This very often occurs in the ten- to fourteen-year-old age range. Often, tension increases between the mother and the early adolescent child. Either the mother will have difficulty controlling a child growing in size and defiance, or the child will ask (or threaten) to live with the father. It is beneficial to have some flexibility in place, without having to go to court to make changes. If the parent who primarily has the child is dependent upon the child-support money, the emotional intimacy, or the child's attachment on an ego level, there can be real problems.

Some parents settle on a fifty percent legal and fifty percent physical custody arrangement, with a separate agreement that allows the child to live with one parent more of the time. This may or may not include different child support money. However, whoever has the child for the greater amount of time should construct the household budget to account for changes in the child-support money. Otherwise, it can be very difficult to allow a child to switch households at a certain point, if it becomes necessary.

When two parents become financially and emotionally independent of the children, they can best provide for those children.

What can be done when there are child-parent problems? Sometimes a divorce is precipitated by the way a child is treated by one parent. As an example, if a father neglects a child or is physically abusive to the extent the child does not want to see him, that information should be shared with the court. Often the courts will hear various claims by both sides in a custody battle, and without extensive proof of such claims, the court will usually apportion fifty percent custody to both parents. Both parents have a right to see the child by law. The child does not have the opportunity to state whether he or she wants to see a particular par-

ent, although this situation seems to be changing. Children should be given the opportunity to say what they think and feel about seeing a parent. This information then can be evaluated by the court and a decision made. When allegations of neglect or abuse can be verified, special custody arrangements should be made. If the abuse or neglect is severe, it is worth the time, energy, and expense to get a child expert or social worker to help document the inappropriate parenting before filing for more-restricted custody. In many cases, as the child gets older he or she will want to discontinue visitations. If and when this occurs on a regular basis, it is a good idea to get some outside professional help to evaluate and support the child's needs.

Recommendations:

1. Try to make custody arrangements flexible enough to meet the demands from both parents as well as your child's needs.
2. Remember, as children grow, they demand their own needs be considered. These needs may not fit in with yours.

How do you know how far away from your ex-spouse you should live for the sake of the children?

Although this is not a critical issue in a divorce situation, a correct decision can make life easier and more pleasant for fathers, mothers, and especially children. In a society where both parents often work full-time, children can benefit when parents live within walking distance. This kind of arrangement presupposes that there are parents who can cooperate and who can appreciate the benefits for the child.

Here are some reasons to live close to your child.
- The child experiences less sense of loss for the more-absent parent.
- The child can go to the other parent's home if one parent is out somewhere.
- There are not two groups of neighborhood friends, but one group common to both households.
- If a child has a problem to discuss with either parent, it can easily be accomplished.
- Parents can communicate easily with each other regarding any current problem.
- If a child has problems with homework, both parents are close at hand.

Here are some reasons to live in a different neighborhood.
- Some children will try to run to the other parent's house when they have an argument with the custodial parent, thereby manipulating the situation.
- A parent who feels that his or her privacy or security is in jeopardy will not be comfortable living too close to an ex-spouse. This tension will add stress to the parenting and will not be good for the children.

Recommendations: It can be beneficial for the child if parents live close to each other and in the same school district. However, parents need to balance closeness with a feeling of privacy.

How do you know when your child should have a say in the custody arrangement?

Allow your children to express their needs and feelings. In the vast majority of cases, separating from parents is very difficult for children. Usually children have very little control over the situation, and this adds to their stress. It is important for children of all ages to have the freedom and opportunity to express their feelings of anger, blame, fear, sadness, and any guilt they may have. This can initially reduce some of the stress. They have to have an opportunity to describe what they like and what they don't like about the custody arrangement, at least as a way of letting the parents know how they feel.

When should children have real choice? As children move into early adolescence, somewhere between age ten and fifteen, they push for greater independence and control. This is a time when children can make choices and test out the consequences. Their understanding of the world and relationships is still quite immature, although they may think they know it all. It is a good idea to make these children's choices time-limited at first, so that children can develop a more realistic perception of what it means to live in the other household. Durations of three, six, nine, or twelve months are not uncommon, with opportunity to review at each point. We assume, of course, that the other household is capable of handling the responsibility of raising the child. In most cases, it is very important for the child to feel like he or she has access to both parents.

Parents need to be careful of these areas.

- **Some children will try to escape a strict parent.** There are often many power struggles during this time, and the custody arrangement can be used to pit one parent against the other. A child may perceive one parent to be more strict than the other, and for that reason alone the child may want to live with the other parent. Children fight for privileges, yet they are reluctant or unable to accept the responsibilities that go along with those privileges. If the child moves from a more-restrictive to a less-restrictive environment, the restrictions and responsibilities should be spelled out clearly in the new environment. The expectations for school, home, and friends should also be stated clearly, and the consequences identified should the child begin to drop below set standards.

- **Often children will attempt to reunite the parents.** Some children want desperately to live with the noncustodial parent, but as soon as they are there, they want to go back to the custodial parent. When children go to the noncustodial parent's house, they call the custodial parent all the time or constantly talk about the custodial parent. It seems like these children just can't make up their minds. In many cases, this may be a younger child who simply is not ready for an extended stay away from a primary parent. The primary parent might be the one to whom the child is more strongly bonded and the parent who does most of the caretaking. Being bonded to someone does not necessarily mean you like them best; it means that you are most secure with them.

In other cases, a child may be subconsciously or consciously trying to recapture the feeling of the nuclear family again. The child may be fighting the reality of the divorce. If the child is over six years of age, you can usually set up some limited times during which the child can call the other parent. This outside structure helps the child develop an internal structure that helps him or her cope.

- **A parent may use the child to gain more financial support.**
Oftentimes, and unfortunately, children aren't given more choice in custody settlements because the child-support money is at issue. Sometimes custodial parents become dependent on child support for their own livelihood, and the withdrawal of that money would create hardships, like having to move or lowering their standard of living. Sometimes a supporter who feels stressed to make enough money welcomes a brief respite from the monthly child support payment. In both cases, the child's need is not the first priority. It is shameful and, unfortunately, all too frequent.
- **A parent may use the child to combat loneliness.** It also happens frequently that a parent grows emotionally close to a child and is reluctant to allow the child to live with

the other parent because he or she fears the assumed loneliness. By the same token, an emotionally needy parent may encourage a child to live with him or her to fill an emotional void. In both cases, the parents have to find other adult-level relationships to meet their needs, and refrain from using the child in this way.

- **A parent may use the child for validation.** Some parents think that whomever the child wishes to be with is the best parent or person. It proves that the parent of choice was "right" or "better" somehow than the parent who is being left. It can cause some parents to think, I somehow didn't do a good enough job. Therefore, I must have been a bad or incompetent parent. It can be not only personally rejecting, but also socially embarrassing. They may wonder what their friends will think, especially if their children have asked to be with the other parent. Again, we are not focused on the child's needs.

Why should the child have a choice, especially as he or she approaches adolescence? The child should have a choice about the custody arrangement for four primary reasons:
- **Get a more realistic picture of the other parent.** If a child grew up with predominantly one parent and had infrequent time with the other parent, then what the child knows about the other parent is largely a fantasy. It may be overly positive or

negative, but it is not realistic. If the fantasies are not tested and brought into a realistic view, they will interfere with later relationships. A girl who never got to be with her father might look unrealistically for that "great, good father" quality in her relationships. Or, if she was kept from her father because he was too mean, she might grow up afraid of men. This is not to suggest that a child be placed in a dangerous situation just to experience the other parent. What we are saying is that if a child in late childhood or adolescence expresses a desire to be with the other parent, he or she should, in many cases, be given that choice. Eliminating the fantasies during these early years helps develop more mature and realistic relationships later.

- **To get a more complete picture of the world.** Oftentimes, parents divorce because they have different viewpoints, attitudes, values, or needs. These differences cannot be resolved, and the stresses become too great to sustain a married relationship. The child is a product of both parents and will probably carry some attitudes from both parents. If you eliminate or greatly diminish time spent with the other parent, you can weaken the child's preparation for the world. In many divorces, each parent thinks the other parent teaches the child inappropriate values. One parent is too coddling, too indulgent, too overprotective, or too helpful, while the other parent is too absent, too cold, too harsh, or too demanding. After all, if the parents agreed on many of these points, they might still be together.

If the child expresses a desire to be with the other parent, it may be because he or she wants to develop a greater ability to handle the qualities in the other household. If Mom didn't make it work with Dad, maybe I can, is how some children think. They want to give it a try. If this is the child's attitude, then it might be very helpful for the child to try to develop a more complete relationship with the other parent. If a child is successful in doing this, he or she is much better prepared for adult life. To be able to form a good relationship with both parents is the best preparation for adult life.

- **To give a child a choice is sometimes necessary to accommodate the child's growing social life.** As some children move into adolescence, their friends become extremely important. In fact, friends may act as the bridge between separating from parents and moving into the adult world. So as some children get older, they may want to live with the parent who most supports their social activities. One household may live closer to friends or be set up so the child has more privacy or freedom. This has to be weighed against the child's level of responsibility, but all things considered, if the child can handle it, then it may be in the child's best interest.

- **To allow children a little more room to grow as they move into adolescence.** For some children, a shift occurs when they move into adolescence. They become very "cool" and grown-up. They put down others as babyish or annoying. They often are very intolerant of younger siblings and want to retreat from the noise, activities, interruptions, and demands of younger children. While it is important for young adolescents to learn to develop tolerance and patience, it may also be appropriate for them to have their own space. If they express a desire to live with the other parent, it should be considered and discussed.

Recommendations:

1. Do not tell your child that he or she has a say in custody arrangements unless you are willing to listen to and possibly accept his or her recommendations. Provide an opportunity, however, for your child to express his or her feelings about the arrangement.
2. Try not to be upset by your child's changing wishes. Be prepared in advance as to how you are going to handle them.

How do you know how to handle a child who doesn't want to go on visitations to your ex-spouse?

Working with the problem. In the dissolution of a marriage, the court gives you custody of the child, but gives your spouse the child on weekends, holidays, or some combination of these. This may sound initially workable and satisfactory to many parents until the child refuses to go to the other spouse, and the ex-spouse accuses you of disobeying the court mandate.

Some reasons the child doesn't want to go on the visits.
- The child doesn't like his or her activities to be interrupted.
- The child doesn't have as much fun at the other household.
- The child doesn't have as many belongings at the other household.
- The child doesn't have friends near the other house.
- The child doesn't get along easily with the other parent.
- The child doesn't get along with the stepparent or stepchildren at the other house.

- The child is afraid to leave the custodial parent.
- The child has a closer bond with one parent.
- The child is afraid of the other parent.
- The child is caught in a fight between the parents, and the child feels guilty when he or she leaves either parent.

What can you do to help the situation?

1. If the law requires it, you must comply. If you are not happy about the visitation schedule, try to make changes legally. There are a variety of public and private professionals who will help you if you are convinced that the arrangement is not in the best interest of the child. You may have to look around for those who can work within your financial constraints. Be open-minded. If three or more professionals tell you that your worries are unfounded, you may have to reexamine your motivations.

2. Sit down with your child and ask him or her what in particular he or she doesn't like about going to the other parent's house. Ask the child if there is something about the physical space that he or she doesn't like. Ask if there is something about the other parent or household members that he or she doesn't like. Ask if there is something about leaving your house or yourself that makes going to the other house difficult. Usually one of these questions will be close to the real reason. You may also ask the child how he or she feels when he or she goes to the other house. Ask the child if he or she tends to feel more mad, sad, or afraid at the other house. If the child picks one of these over the other, you will gain additional clues. Whatever the child says, ask him or her to give you an example of how he or she felt at the other house. This can help you sort out what is difficult from what is inappropriate.

3. It is important to remember that it is very common for two divorced parents to have different value systems. Parents may have very different ideas about how to raise children. When parents separate, each parent has more control in their separate households. So a child may have a strict parent in one household and a very lenient parent in the other household. In most cases, the child will want to spend more time with the lenient parent. It is possible for two parents to have very different households and have both still be appropriate. If you are not sure, you can seek an outside neutral third party for feedback. If you get mixed opinions from the outside party, then you probably will have difficulty making changes.

4. If you or your child is in an uncomfortable situation, and you cannot change the visitation arrangement, then you must wait until the child gets older and the courts give him or her more say in the custody or visitation schedule. You and your

child may need some counseling to help you tolerate the situation in the meantime.

5. Once you have some information from the child make sure the child will tell the other parent what he or she told you. If the child is unwilling, you may have to wait until the child gets more confidence and is able to make his or her opinion known to both parents. Sometimes, children caught in divorce will say one thing to one parent and another thing to the other parent. Children will sometimes say whatever they think the parent wants to hear. When the child is ready to tell both parents how he or she feels, it is a good time to have a meeting.

Recommendations:

1. If you can, discuss this situation with your former spouse, or with your child and your former spouse.
2. Try not to let your own needs interfere with your child's needs.

How do you know when to give your child choices about visitations?

Visitations may create a problem. In late childhood (ages nine to twelve)

and early adolescence, many children are ready to test their decision-making skills. They make choices that begin to affect their lives. At this age, children can be more outspoken about their likes and dislikes. Developmentally, children this age may separate from one parent and bond differently with the other parent. A child's need to be with friends may take precedence over his or her need to be with parents. Sometimes children express a desire to change the visitation schedule. The problem is that there is usually a rigid legal agreement with financial repercussions in place.

Is this good for the child? Generally, changing the visitation schedule is a good idea, assuming that both parents can and will go along with the change (this is not frequently the case). It is also a good opportunity for the child to experiment. This also assumes that the child will be held to his or her responsibilities in both households. Making a change because a twelve-year-old child wants to spend more time at the parent's house where he or she will not be held accountable for homework, regular bedtimes, appropriate friends, and so on, is not an appropriate choice.

How to resolve the problem of visitation. It may be quite difficult to work our a new visitation schedule because of how rigid divorce laws have become. In the eyes of the court, children are possessions with limited freedom. As children move into adolescence, they may be able to push for their own desires, but there is no guarantee that they will be met legally. Parents have to establish some flexibility in the custody arrangement during the initial divorce settlement, and both parties have to be able to support themselves in the event that the custody arrangement changes (see pages 76-78).

The first approach is for the parents to discuss the issue without the child present. Once the child has made his or her wishes known to both parents, the parents should discuss the child's needs separate from the visitation schedule's financial and physical necessities. Each topic should be discussed separately, otherwise the conversations can become overwhelming and heated. Consult an outside third party to help keep the conversations on track, if needed. Usually the court can supply you with names of such people. It is also important to explain to a child who wishes to make a change that you will help, but that there are legal, financial, and physical problems to be overcome first.

If there is some possibility that the physical, legal, and financial issues can be resolved, then both parents should sit down with the child to discuss rules, responsibilities and expectations for the child.

What happens if you have to go to court? This is usually the last resort and often the most difficult and expensive option. For example, let's say there is a twelve-year-old boy who wants to live with his father and visit his mother on weekends, but the mother refuses to allow it. If all areas of discussion, negotiation, and counseling have been exhausted, and both the father and the child still want to make the change, then they can petition the court to make a change. Often a professional child advocate can be enlisted to help prepare a case on the child's behalf, which is then presented to the court by an attorney. In some cases, the judge may ask to meet the child and the attorneys in chambers, out of the presence of the parents. In other cases, the judge may read a statement from the child. It may depend on how strong and clear the child feels about his or her choice.

Is it worth fighting for your child's needs? Usually the answer is yes, especially if the child's physical and emotional safety is at stake and outside observers agree with the change.

Recommendations: If your child is old enough, see whether your former spouse will allow your child to make decisions as to visitations.

How do you know if you are helping your child too much?

Risks of helping too much. Although we love our children and want to make their lives as easy as possible, we can damage them in several ways by helping too much. We may create the kind of child that we did not intend to make. We may produce a dependent child with no drive, no sense of independence, and no mastery. Children have to develop a sense of themselves to be able to function in the world. We may deprive them of this sense if we help too much.

Children need to learn to be independent. Just as we stop feeding a baby when he or she can feed himself or herself, or stop dressing a child when he or she can dress himself or herself, we have to allow a child to develop self-confidence and mastery of the world. As the child grows from a newborn to adolescent, there is an increasing drive toward independence; it is important for parents to enhance this independence not hamper it.

Children need to learn self-confidence. Out of this mastery of small tasks comes a feeling of self-confidence. The child senses not only the approval of those around him or her, but a healthy feeling that he or she can do things on his or her own. As adults, we tend to enjoy those things we do well. If we are good cooks, then we are rewarded by the comments of those for whom we cook. It is natural for us to want to repeat those things we have mastered and do well. Parents have to foster feelings of self-confidence in their children.

Parents need to allow their children to grow up. Those parents who do for their children what the children can do for themselves run the danger of infantilizing their children. Parents come to us and say their children are immature and do not show a sense of responsibility. They are often right. However, when asked if these parents give their children responsible tasks to perform they often answer no. To teach independence, we must allow children to do what they can do. To develop responsibility, we must trust children to take as much responsibility as they can handle.

How much help should the parent give? The difficulty here is to know what your child can and cannot do. For example, before demanding that your child tie his or her own shoelaces, you have to be sure the child is capable of doing so. You must know your child's limits before you can correctly help him or her. This means you use trial sessions to allow your child to complete a task for the first time. Sometimes there will be failure, and sometimes success.

You can help your child learn the rewards of success. Much of the time, children will let you know when they are ready to try something new. There is a natural, healthy development in children in their drive toward independence. The parent who allows and fosters this independence will have a child who is demonstrably mature and independent. The child will ask for less help and will usually try a task before asking for help. Of course, it is just as important to help a child who is unable to complete a task without assistance. It is one of life's pleasures to assist our children when they need it. It is another sometimes difficult task for parents to differentiate when to help and when to allow the child to work alone.

Recommendations: Just as there is a danger of helping your child too much, there is a danger of helping your child too little. Check with your spouse or someone who knows your child well to get another opinion.

How do you know what to do if you find out your child is sexually involved or abused?

Should you do anything? Of the many anxiety-producing situations parents face, this is near the top of the list. The answer to the question is usually a definite YES. What to do is dependent on your personal mores, your religious beliefs, and your awareness of the problems associated with sexual activity.

How do you handle sex play among younger children? Sexual exploration,

sexual curiosity, and masturbation can start in infancy and last a lifetime. It is very normal for infants to discover their pleasure centers and masturbate. They may use their hands and fingers or simply rub up against an object. If a child seems to be masturbating constantly it may indicate that he or she is bored or in need of comforting. In some cases a child is tired and may need a nap. By the age of three you can identify for a child what is private behavior and what is a public behavior.

Children ages three to five commonly are curious about other children's bodies, too, especially those of the opposite sex. Usually by the age of three they have discovered that boys have a penis and girls have a vagina. They can name and identify the major body parts of both sexes.

At times a parent may find or hear about their child in some stage of undress playing with another child. In most cases this experience creates some mild to moderate alarm in the parent. When this activity is discovered in a day care center or school, the parents of both children are notified of the incident; the children are usually instructed about private parts being kept private. Most often there is nothing to be concerned about as long as the children are roughly the same age.

In some cases a five- or six-year-old child may refer to having sex with another child. They may even refer to having oral sex or anal sex. If this is the case, find out just what the child understands by these terms and where he or she heard about them. This information is all too often available in magazines, videos, and television; the children may also hear about it from other children in nursery school, kindergarten, or day care centers.

Sex play between children where the age difference is two to four years may be a problem. A child who is older or significantly more mature has an advantage over a younger or less mature child and can control or manipulate the younger child against his or her will. This kind of situation needs to be corrected early.

How to deal with consensual sex among older adolescents. There is no question that consensual sex among adolescents has increased over the last few years, and that the age of involvement has gotten younger and younger. By this time, you should have conveyed to your child your beliefs about sexuality. The question here is what to do if your adolescent child is involved sexually and you believe that it is wrong. This is a painful situation for both children and parents. You may be able to break up the relationship if you feel that it is wrong for your child, but remember, if you are heavy handed, you may lose your child's communication and trust. Another possibility is to use the opportunity for communication between you and your child. Your child's sexual activity gives you a chance to talk about the real problems that may be encountered. It gives you the opportunity to talk about morality, about possible pregnancy, and about the responsibilities involved. Finally, it

gives you an opportunity to talk about sexually transmitted diseases, and the consequences associated with them. Your child's sexuality can lead to a permanent break between parent and child, or offer a chance to really be of help now and in the future.

It is important to deal with sexual abuse immediately. Sexual involvement of a child and an adult is clearly child abuse and must be reported to the authorities immediately. In addition, the child's contact with that person must be stopped immediately. This is particularly difficult if the abuser is a member of the family, but the child's need for protection is paramount, and the parent must take action. Both the initial, as well as later, consequences— which sometimes last a lifetime— require that parents take action to both stop the abuse and have their child see an expert in child abuse, such as a psychologist, psychiatrist, or other mental health worker, to help deal with the trauma.

How parents can help. Aside from seeking therapeutic assistance, parents have to help their children at this time by creating an atmosphere of noncritical acceptance. For a child to share these difficult feelings, parents have to control their feelings and allow the child to talk about his or her feelings. This has to be done when the child is able to talk without force from parents. The child may already have feelings of shame or guilt, or blame himself or herself for the sexual activity.

Hopefully, parents can listen so that the child feels free to talk.

Recommendations:
1. Realize that sex play among peers in early childhood is normal.
2. Help children distinguish between private behavior and public behavior.
3. Seek professional help if sexual abuse has occurred.
4. Realize that views about sexuality have changed since you were a child. Examine your own feelings carefully before you decide what to do.

How do you know what to do if you find out your daughter is pregnant?

The parent-child relationship is of great importance. Much of what a parent can do in this situation depends on the parent-child relationship. If there is a history of openness between parent and child, then parents can be helpful in decision-making. The pitfalls between the parent and child are many. Parents' morality may be different than the daughter's. Parents may feel that they should decide what should be done. Adolescents, on the other hand, are involved in separation and individ-

uation at this stage in their lives, and they usually feel that they can make their own decisions. Often, parents and children agree on the final decision, but how the decision is derived is very important and depends, in part, on the parent-child relationship.

Parents need to help their daughter make a decision. Problems arise when parent and child have a difference of opinion about the final decision. Parents may have a different view about abortion than their daughter. Because the child is still a minor, parents may believe that the decision is theirs. Indeed, the financial obligations of having a child may be a burden that some parents are unwilling to face for their daughter. Clearly, the age of the child, the maturity of the child, the involvement of the baby's father, and the father's maturity are of vital importance. Emotions can easily get out of control in this situation, since decisions are colored by so many factors.

Your daughter will be facing many pressures. Your daughter, aside from dealing with the reality of her pregnancy, may have difficulty dealing with pressures from you, from her boyfriend, and from his parents. Again, the greater your daughter's ability to communicate with you without pressure, the better she will be able to make a reasonable decision. Again, although you and your daughter may agree on the final decision, how the decision is reached is very important. Consider that this is a real-life decision your daughter will remember all her life and that she has to feel she made the right decision.

Parents play an important role in decision making. Although parents may, in fact, be very upset, an unplanned pregnancy is an opportunity to help a daughter make a mature decision. If, instead of telling or ordering her to make a certain decision, parents allow the emergence of a thoughtful decision from their daughter, parents help can increase their daughter's sense of responsibility and decrease chance of later recriminations.

The baby's father and the father's family also need to contribute to the decision. It is sometimes possible to contact the baby's father and the father's family when making decisions. This may help your daughter make the correct decision. This is something that can be discussed with your daughter, because the responsibility is at least half his.

Recommendations:
1. Simply forcing your daughter to do what you want may not work. Try to get her cooperation in whatever solution is worked out.
2. After a decision is made, make sure your attitude is not punitive. Your daughter has to feel she has made the right choice.

How do you know what to do if you find out your son has impregnated a girl?

Parents should use a positive strategy. Whether it's a daughter or a son involved in a pregnancy, the impact of the whole situation can be overwhelming. Denial, and anger do not solve the problem. On the other hand, as a parent you can use helpful ways to resolve a very unhappy situation. As parents discuss what to do, their son is also deciding what to do. Parents and child may not agree in part or in total.

Parents need to communicate with their son. This situation presents an opportunity for parents to discuss their son's feelings and any steps that should be taken. This is truly a situation where a young man is faced with a difficult decision. Does your son accept responsibility for his actions? Can you help him take proper responsibility? These are some of the questions that have to be answered very quickly. Rather than parents telling a boy what he must do, it is much better if the son comes to a decision he can live with now and in the future. Parents have to see that their son accepts that responsibility.

Parents and children together should make the final decision. Whether to end the pregnancy is a decision that both the girl and the boy involved have to make. Clearly, both parents' advice comes into play here, but it is the children who will have to live with their decision, and their feelings should be considered.

Your son will play an important part in making a decision. This may be the first major decision your son has to make as an adolescent or young adult. It is beneficial for your son to make his own decision, and live with the consequences of it. Although you may help your son make the decision, you want him to feel he made it. This sets the stage for your son's future decision making. Dealing with the situation in this way may help bring the family closer together, rather than fragment it into angry factions.

Parents need to be careful in playing their role. How a young man sees himself at this age can be critical for his future. If a boy feels he has made a caring, mature decision, taking into consideration the needs of others as well as himself, it will help him mature. Parents who are angry and rejecting accomplish nothing, and they don't help their son make the next positive steps in his development.

Have your son contact the mother of the child. It is good if they can come to a mutual decision that is backed up by both sets of parents. While both sets

of parents may want to assign blame to the other side, this achieves nothing and makes both children feel worse. A mutual decision does not condone the children's behavior or assign blame.

Recommendations:
1. Use the situation to help your son learn to take responsibility and become more mature.
2. Do not expect an adolescent to behave other than like an adolescent. Help him to see the consequences of various outcomes.

How do you know when to offer your child birth control?

Religious factors are important. Some parents are opposed to birth control for religious reasons. However, children should still receive information about the dangers of sexually transmitted diseases and the problems of pregnancy.

When do you offer information about birth control? Parents should always answer children's questions, at a level they can understand, whenever questions are asked. As children grow, they often get information and misinformation from friends. Rather than wait until an accident occurs, parents should teach their children the basics of birth control and protection from disease. Again, teaching is not condoning promiscuous sexual activity, but rather protecting children from future problems.

Who should give the information? Although some school districts teach children about pregnancy and sexually transmitted diseases, parents can never be sure their children comprehend what is taught. It is a fact that most children in our society learn about sex and birth control from someone other than their parents. Yet, parents may be in the most trusted place to help their children.

What information should be given?
- The facts of pregnancy.
- When a woman can and cannot become pregnant.
- Various methods of contraception and birth control.
- Sexually transmitted diseases and their signs and symptoms.
- The dangers of AIDS.

What if parents cannot give this information? Sometimes parents feel unable to discuss birth control with their child, or they are afraid they do not have enough information. Parents may ask a nurse, physician, sex educator, or others to help them educate their child.

Knowing when to give your child birth control information. Birth control is given to adolescents usually for one of two reasons: either the child is sexually active or there is the probability that the child will become sexually active, or, in the case of some teenage girls, there is a need to regulate the menstrual cycle.

In many cases, parents can sense that their son or daughter is involved with a special boyfriend or girlfriend. Parents may observe the children kissing, hugging, or holding hands in a romantic way that suggests they are getting closer. This is usually a good time to ask your child how he or she feels about the boyfriend or girlfriend. If the child answers, We're just friends, it probably means that the children are not ready to enter a sexual relationship. You can always ask the child to discuss his or her values about sex. Ask the child when he or she feels sex is appropriate. You might also ask your child when and with whom he or she thinks sex is appropriate. You will get a better sense of how close your child and the boyfriend or girlfriend are. You can also ask your child if they have already had sex. If you start by asking your child for his or her thoughts, feelings, and values, instead of telling your child what yours are, you are more likely to get the child to open up.

If the answers you get from these questions indicate that your child is turned off by the idea of having sex, or that the children are not even close, then there is probably no need to offer birth control. On the other hand, if the answers to your questions suggest that the children are coming close to having sex or have already started having sex, then it is a good idea to have birth control handy.

For boys the issue of birth control may be a little easier. You can buy a box of condoms for your son to keep on his person, so he will be prepared if and when he has sex.

For girls, birth control is sometimes a more complicated choice. Buying a box of condoms is a good idea; however, your daughter has to be able to make a young man use them when they have sex. Not every teenage girl has this kind of personal strength when it comes to intimate relationships. Some parents don't trust their child's ability to make good decisions in the heat of passion, and prefer to have their daughter put on birth control pills or a patch. Because a girl can get pregnant the very first time she has sex, some parents believe it is better to risk condoning sex, than to risk a possible pregnancy.

What if my son or daughter is only fourteen or fifteen years old?
Unfortunately, it seems that children begin to have sex at younger and younger ages. This is an extremely difficult question, especially if the children, or one of the children, is in the early teens. Usually the girl is younger than the boy, such as when the girl is fourteen, and the boy is sixteen or seventeen. Oftentimes, parents have to step in and discuss with the children involved the inappropriateness of a relationship that is too physically intimate. The child lacks the emotional stability and maturity needed to handle the emotional and physical consequences of sex. Sometimes the children

will have to be separated, or if a young child is in an unhealthy peer group, he or she may have to be removed from the group.

Recommendations:
1. Give information whenever your children ask.
2. Give information about birth control before, during, and after children become sexually active. Assist your child in making decisions about using birth control.

How do you know how to handle how your child dresses?

As a parent, you make all your child's choices in the beginning. As the child grows up, he or she will begin to assert his or her own desires about clothes. Striking a balance between what the child wants to wear and what you believe is appropriate is a time-honored tradition in parenting!

Parents need to know about current children's fashions. Fashion plays a bigger role in our lives than many of us like to admit. It influences us as adults, and it influences our children. We usually have complete choice about what our children wear before they reach the age of six. Once our children get into school, they either want to fit in or stick out, depending on their personality. Clothes can then become a way of making these statements.

Most often between the ages of six and thirteen, children want to wear what other children wear. They want to fit in. They are highly influenced by what they see on television, both in terms of advertisements and TV characters. Movies also capitalize in marketing T-shirts, hats, jackets, shoes, and so on. Some children follow the trends, and other children copy them. Parents usually want their children to wear clothes that are protective, warm, durable, and preferably inexpensive, as children tend to go through clothes pretty quickly.

Parents' knowledge of children's needs is important. Beginning around the age of twelve to thirteen, children may again want to change their dress. They either want to identify with a special group (skaters, surfers, gangs, jocks, preppies, nerds, or whatever is current), or they want to make their own individualistic statement. Sometimes the choices are so outrageous that parents are uncomfortable. This is, after all, the point—going past the parents' boundary. This is a common way that a child begins to feel independent from the parent and/or the adult society at large. As part of the fashion, hair may be colored or cut in a strange manner. There may be strange jewelry, make-up, or body colorings. Be patient!

How do you feel about clothes and appearance? Some parents have little trouble with their child's unusual dress or appearance. They went through it themselves, so they understand the process. But for other parents, it is quite difficult. These parents may want to have neat and tidy-looking children. Wait. If one goes to a college campus, the dress is casual, simple, and minimal. For example, jeans and a shirt are the most common apparel today. Five years from now, these same students will be working in offices, often wearing shirts and ties. Boys tend to be less concerned than girls about clothes, until they begin to date. In either case, parents can be almost certain that dress codes will change as children mature.

Here are some avenues to explore.

1. In most cases, schools have dress codes to promote three basic values. First, there is *safety*. This code may have to do with large loop earrings, sharp jewelry, hats or sunglasses that block vision, shoes that are unsafe, gang apparel that could instigate fights, etc. The second value is to *reduce distraction*. Clothes that are too tight, too short, or too revealing distract from the academic focus. Third, some schools have a dress code to set a *"tone,"* which may be serious, formal, casual, warm, or personal, and that supports the school's academic purpose. These same dressing principles can be explained and used when your children go on outings.

2. Make a contract with your child

that states he or she can wear what he or she wants when out with friends, but that your child may have to dress a bit more formally when attending formal functions. It is important to remember to pick your battles carefully when dealing with adolescents. There are a lot of things with which you can disagree. Pick only those fights you feel most strongly about.

3. For early teenage girls who wear make-up and sexy clothes, you can use the same values as described earlier. Is it safe? Is it a distraction; that is, is the girl dressing to get a certain kind of attention? Is the child aware of the attention she is trying to get? Does she need a certain kind of validation? Finally, what tone is she setting with her dress? Especially with a young teenager, you may still have some control as to where, when, and with whom she can go out.

Recommendations:
1. If the way your child dresses offends no one but yourself, maybe you should ignore it.
2. Children's dress codes change as they mature and inevitably reflect their age group.

How do you know how to raise boys and girls, and should you treat them differently?

Know the difference between sex and gender. Sex is a term used to describe a child's biological attributes as a male or female. *Gender* and *gender identity* refer to our sense of masculinity or femininity. Various authors have described the biological and psychological interactions that result in gender identity. As we develop, we take on certain characteristics that determine our roles as boys and girls, and eventually men and women.

In recent years, a growing body of research has shown that males and females may process common experiences in different ways. Male and female methods of communicating and relating may also be different. The question arises, Should we, as parents, talk to our male and female children differently and treat them differently?

Watching boys and girls at play. One piece of research done a few years back looked at a group of boys at play and a group of girls at play. Among other observations, what the research showed was that when the boys got together, they made a set of rules for a particular game. Any boy who did not want to play by those rules was excluded from the game. He had to sit out a turn, or he was free to go off and start his own game. On the other hand, when girls got together, they too made a set of rules for a particular game. When a girl did not want to play by those rules, the game stopped, the girls renegotiated the rules, and the game resumed. For boys, the rules and the game momentum were more important than contact among the players. For girls, contact among the players was more important than the rules.

If you substitute "work" for "game," you might conclude that for men, being good at work (game) and following the rules of work (game) may come before having close relationships. For women, having good relationships and securing contacts may come before any particular work (game).

The difference between male and female and masculine and feminine is important. If we substitute masculine and feminine for male and female we have a better chance to be accurate. If we assume that all of us have both masculine and feminine behavior attributes we can avoid any rigid stereotype of behavior. There are females who show a good deal of traditional masculine behavior and for whom being competent at the game comes before keeping contact, while there are plenty of males for whom keeping good contact comes before being good at the game.

How young children develop. We find that gender differences are not as important the first few years, although many parents dress their newborn babies in pink or blue to help observers identify them as boys or girls. We used to think that only girls should play with dolls. Now all children play with doll-like toys. Girls may play with trucks and cars as well. Some girls never enjoy playing with dolls. As children grow up, their gender usually becomes clear. There is a greater tendency for boys to play with trucks, guns, and toys that allow them to be more physical. As girls grow, they often play with toys that allow them to imitate their mother's actions; that is, girls use their mothers as role models. It is important to allow children to develop individualistic mannerisms rather than set any limits. To attempt to force children into molds is harmful and rarely works. This can be a major disappointment to many parents because they may have a preconceived notion of what they want their children to be.

Another research project, in the area of communication, demonstrated another difference between young boys and girls. The researchers took a group of children who were able to crawl and stand, but who could not yet walk. The researches put the children one at a time in a room and had their mothers walk out one door and come in another, to stand behind a clear Plexiglas barrier. The mothers had neutral looks on their faces. When the boy children saw their mothers, the majority of the boys immediately began to crawl toward their mother, and tried to climb over or push down the barrier. The majority of the girls, on the other hand, made faces, cried, and called out to their mothers. A few of the boys exhibited the girls' behavior, and a few of the girls exhibited the boys' behavior. What does this suggest?

This might suggest that young children with more masculine traits communicate and relate physically, while those with more feminine traits communicate and relate verbally. This information is important if you are trying to teach something to a child or if you are trying to understand a child's needs.

Allow older children to develop in their own way. As children grow, parents often put enormous pressure on them to be very masculine or feminine; parents sometimes worry about gay and lesbian tendencies or that their children do not fit their preconceived image. The important issue here is not to bully the child or force him or her to become what you want, but to allow the child the freedom to grow in his or her own way. The question is not to treat your child as male or female, but to treat your child as an individual.

As children get older, hopefully, they will be able to integrate those qualities that are not part of their natural tendencies. In this way, children may be better able to relate to those around them.

Here are some final thoughts. In the end, it is probably more important to find a way to relate to each child. Each

child is unique, with his or her own special language. It takes time and effort to get to know and understand each child.

Recommendations:
1. The rules of what is masculine and feminine are changing. Trying to mold your children in one direction usually does not work.
2. Do not sacrifice your relationship with your child to masculine or feminine stereotypes.

How do you know what to do if your child gets arrested?

Be aware of your initial reaction. One of the most traumatic events in the life of a parent is to receive a phone call telling you your child has been arrested. It immediately brings up the image of your child and the horrors of being in a jail for any amount of time. Sometimes these feelings are justified, and children are arrested for doing something wrong or for being in the wrong place at the wrong time. However, parents should pause and ask themselves several questions before taking action.

What to do when your child gets arrested.

1. Ask the police why your child was arrested and when he or she will be released if you come down. This will help you decide whether you should come to the jail with an attorney.
2. Will there be bail involved? If the police indicate that the child will be released on bail, then you should come with cash. Usually jails do not accept checks or credit cards.
3. Most important, is it wise for you to go to the jail to bail out your child? Consider the boy who has had repeated offenses and doesn't listen to your pleadings to change his ways. Will staying in jail overnight impress upon him that he should change his actions? Or will waiting several hours before you go to pick him up do the same thing? Before you rescue him, consider what lesson you want him to learn. If the child believes you will rescue him no matter what he does, he may have no incentive to change his behavior. Certainly there should be a difference in your behavior for first-time offenders and those who may not be guilty of anything other than bad judgment.
4. There may be situations in which you decide to allow your child to accept the consequences of his or her behavior. Parents should not feel guilty about this. For the child who refuses to learn through the usual means, sometimes enduring consequences will do the trick. Bad things may happen in jail—things over which you have no control. But troublesome behavior may be curtailed by the punishment of being in jail in a miserable situation.

How to get help for your child. If your child is arrested, most likely he or she will see a probation officer sometime before going in front of a judge. Depending on the offense, your child may receive a fine, a community service obligation, or a sentence to a juvenile facility. Under any circumstance, your child should receive some type of counseling to help him or her clearly understand why he or she made such a poor choice. Sometimes when children are lost, lonely, afraid, or angry, they make bad decisions to feel better. Sometimes children travel with the wrong crowd and are too influenced by troublesome kids. It is important to discover some of the underlying problems to help build an internal and external structure to prevent your child from being arrested again. There are all kinds of publicly and privately funded programs that the child's probation officer may be able to recommend. Sometimes these programs are called diversion programs.

Recommendations:
1. Be sure to consider the long-term meaning of the arrest. What can your child learn from the situation?
2. The arrest may have different meanings to your child and to you. Try to see the situation from both sides, so that you can use the information constructively.

How do you know what to do if your child over-identifies with a rock star or other celebrity?

How a child's identity develops.
Throughout our lives, we all define and redefine who we are. As very young children, we discover we are a boy or girl who belongs to a certain family. As we grow into adolescence, we redefine ourselves not so much as a family member, but more as an individual among our school peers. As we leave school, perhaps after college, we define ourselves in the workplace. Moving through adulthood, we again redefine ourselves as married or as parents. The years pass, and we must redefine who we are as we go through midlife, and finally, old age. Each stage brings its own challenges and benefits.

Probably the two most critical stages, however, are the very young child, whose identity is largely influenced by the parents, and the adolescent child, who is greatly influenced by peers. Sometimes young adolescents are at greater risk because they are trying to establish an identity apart from their parents, who are usually more conservative, practical, and realistic. Adolescents are often attracted to young role models, such as rock stars and movie stars, who appear as either powerful or popular. At this age, children don't have the experience to know that all that glitters is not gold.

What to do when you do not like the changes in your child. Fortunately for most parents, there is nothing to do but to simply ride it out. Whether this means putting up with long hair, or short hair, or colored hair, remember this is simply a stage that children go through. As children grow and mature, these identifications disappear. The need to be different from parents is very strong in some children. It is how they show their developing independence. It may take a few years, but almost everyone makes it.

Only in a few cases do children identify with an image that is dangerous or unhealthy, or overidentify with an image until it begins to interfere with school, isolates them from friends, and disconnects them completely from the family. Nearly a dozen girls in one high school decided to commit suicide after their favorite rock star committed suicide from an apparent drug overdose. One of the girls was successful, and four others came close, before the parents and the school became aware of the situation.

If a child's attention gets too far away from academics, a healthy peer group, and family requirements, parents usually get more involved. Parents may restrict the time that a child spends with certain individuals and require greater effort toward schoolwork or family involvement. This can result in a variety of unpleasant confrontations, but they may be necessary and helpful to keep the child on track.

What do you do when your child joins a cult? Cults are simply tightly knit groups that usually require a firm commitment and involvement from its members. Cults usually command a great deal of control over individuals in the group. If you think your child is in a cult, you should consult an outside professional.

Recommendations:
1. If your child's attachment to a celebrity is not hurting schoolwork or social life, maybe you do not need to worry.
2. Be careful of trying to set limits that you cannot control.

How do you know how to handle negative or hostile feelings toward your child?

What can parents do about their own feelings? Most parents have a full range of feelings toward their children. These feelings range from love to anger, from joy to disappointment, from fear to excitement, and sometimes even to hate. In our culture, however, only positive feelings are clearly accepted. Yet, many of us have negative feelings toward our children, sometimes we experience these feelings when our children are young, and sometimes we experience them when our children go through adolescence. We are not talking about the angry feelings we have when our children disobey or get in trouble, but the really negative feelings that border on hatred.

What is the source of these feelings? Most of us are programmed to want children, and, indeed, most of us have children who are lovable. Rarely do people talk about what you have to sacrifice to have those children. Most of us are not really prepared for the sacrifices required. Women may have to give up or delay a career. Men may not be able to chance a new career because they have to provide for a child. The parents' sexual life often changes dramatically when children are born. In addition, every child lowers the socioeconomic level of the parents by ten to twenty percent. Although parents may love their children, many will verbalize that, in one sense, they made a big mistake having children. The price was too great for the relatively small rewards.

Any parent may have a difficult child. While all children are sometimes difficult, there are some children who seem difficult always. These children may constantly challenge, may constantly need help, or may be constantly negative or unhappy. After a while, you feel drained when you are around them. If you have a child like this, he or she can create very negative feelings in you.

If you have a child who doesn't meet your expectations, or who is perhaps handicapped in some way, you may feel extreme disappointment or failure. Also, some parents complain that their child is so different from them that they cannot find anything to relate to with that child. These are sad but true feelings.

What parents can do about working with a difficult child.

1. Perhaps the first thing you can do is to find someone who can accept and understand your feelings. It might be a spouse, a friend, a relative, or a professional counselor. Just expressing the feelings can help immediately relieve some of the pressure.

2. Take some time apart from the child, and let him or her stay with others who might relate to him or her better. This doesn't mean you abandon the child, but taking a break can help you better tolerate your situation.

3. Sometimes if you look for just one thing you like about the child, and focus on that it can help turn things around. If you can find one activity that the two of you enjoy, you can slowly build a better attitude toward the child. Even if the child is five-, ten-, or fifteen-years-old, you can

start over if you will take it one step at a time.

4. Get some professional help, either for you or the child. Sometimes this can be an effective way to find a bridge between the two of you.

5. If the situation has reached an intolerable level, and all of the above suggestions have failed, consider sending the child to live with a relative or friend who can relate better to him or her. As the child gets older, boarding school might offer some options. The child may be away during the week and home only for the weekends. While shorter in quantity, the quality of time together might improve.

Parents' feelings may range from negative feelings to hostile fantasies. If your negative feelings progress to hostile fantasies of doing harm to your child, then you are too stressed. If you have daydreams or night dreams of killing or seriously hurting your child, you have to take a break and talk to someone about your feelings. These are powerful feelings, and you must deal with them.

When negative feelings get to this level, we usually blame the child unfairly for things that are not his or her fault. We usually react to deep levels of self-rejection and unfairly put that on the child.

It is important to get some professional help if these thoughts are persistent.

Recommendations:
1. Try to work through your anger in some positive way, such as exercise.
2. If the hostile feelings are persistent, seek professional help.

SCHOOL AND
LEARNING PROBLEMS

How do you know if your child is in a good child care center?

What is a good child care center? A good child care center provides for your child's needs emotionally, physically, and educationally. Although the primary purpose of a child care center is to care for your child when you are working, it can do much more than just baby-sit.

Steps in selecting a child care center.
1. A child care center should be licensed by local authorities. You can check with local city or county agencies to verify whether the center is accredited.
2. The director and/or teachers should have an educational background with young children.
3. Talk to parents who have their children enrolled at the center and get their opinion of the school.

Physical environment. Physical safety is paramount in selecting a place for your child.
- Does the center adequately protect your child, for example, can the child run outside to the street?
- Are the toys child-proofed against injury? Are the climbing toys outside and inside safe from breaking or falling on a child?
- Are the bathrooms adequate? Does the center have children wash their hands, and is there a healthy cleanliness policy?
- Are nutrition times adequate? Are the children given foods that are limited in sugar, fat, salt, and additives?
- Is the school too clean or too dirty? If the school seems very clean, are the children allowed to play in a

sandbox, or with paint and clay, or with toys children this age enjoy?

- Is the furniture adequate and appropriately sized for the children?

Emotional environment. Young children need a great deal of acceptance and warmth in a context that sets reasonable limits for them.

- Is discipline too lax or too severe? Children need limits appropriate to their age. If you can, observe the school in action to check teachers' behavior.
- Are teachers there consistently? Young children bond with loving teachers and may have difficulty if the teachers continually change.
- Does the school have a plan to help both parents and children separate from each other? Are parents allowed to observe their children? Sometimes separation anxiety is a major problem that is solved easily if handled correctly.
- Do the teachers come to your home initially to allow your child to get to know them? This often avoids the problem of separation anxiety.
- Is the atmosphere tense or relaxed? The feeling tone of both children and teachers is an important indicator of how your child may do.
- After attending for a short time, is your child eager to go to the center? Often parents do not listen to young children. Children will often indicate by words or behavior whether the center is good for them.

Educational environment. A good day care center can provide a positive learning experience for your child both socially and academically.

- Does your child have a chance to develop socialization skills? This involves playing with and interacting with other children without being bullied by a stronger, more-aggressive child.
- Does the center have a plan to introduce children to or play with age-appropriate games and toys, such as clay, crayons, gross and fine motor coordination activities, paper and pencil tasks, blocks, puzzles, and other items that help children learn about their environment and about each other? Interactive toys especially help children learn about each other.

Recommendations: When you finally pick the right place for your child, learn how to interact with your child's teacher and the center's director. It may only take a few words when you pick up or deliver your child to check that all is going well. The happier and more confident you are with the center, the more you will communicate this feeling to your child. You can learn many things about your child by just talking with the teachers, things you might not have observed yourself.

1. Be sure to check with other parents whose children attend the child care center.
2. Ask your pediatrician about the child care center. He or she may be able to make recommendations.

3. Be particularly aware of any negative behavior or changes that your child is exhibiting.

How do you know when your child is ready to separate from parents and attend nursery school?

When are the parents ready? Mothers and/or fathers sometimes have major difficulty separating from their two-, three-, or four-year-old children when they attend preschool for the first time. If you are not used to being apart from your child for several hours a day, and preschool will be your first separation experience, then you are at high risk for being a problematic parent for your preschooler's teachers. Fathers generally have less difficulty separating because they are usually at work for eight or more hours a day. Also, fathers may not have had as much daily contact with the child during the child's first few years. Working mothers also have less difficulty with separation.

Mothers and fathers want their children to grow up, but it seems to come all too soon. There are questions like, Am I doing the right thing?, Is he or she old enough?, Will my child make it?, Am I going to mess him or her up? If you are the kind of parent who is anxious about separating, then you should prepare yourself and your child by practicing. You can begin by finding a trustworthy baby-sitter, family member, or even a day-care center that will allow you to drop off your child for fifteen to thirty minutes every day. If this separation is easy, extend your time away to an hour at least three times a week, and gradually increase it to a full three hours, two or three times a week. While you are away from your child do something that takes your mind off the child; go shopping, run errands, read a book, watch a television show, exercise, do chores, call a friend, and don't talk about your child.

If you separate from your child consistently, you will be surprised how quickly (three to four weeks) you will be able to overcome your anxiety. The financial cost for such a venture will be small in comparison to the therapy bills you might otherwise pay later. If the financial cost is a burden, try to find a friend or a relative to baby-sit. A little sacrifice on their part now will make their time with you more pleasant when your child is in school.

Parents sometimes have difficulty separating from their children because, in the early years, parenting can bring a sense of meaning and importance to a parent's life. When the child is gone and able to function well without the parent, some parents feel unimportant and useless. To avoid this, parents should have outside interests that bring purpose, pleasure, and validation to their sense of self.

When is the child ready? Children are usually ready to separate from parents and attend preschool or nursery school when they can play independently and/or when they can be left with other adults for several hours at a time. A child who is very clingy or who cries and whines constantly while the parent is absent is simply not ready for preschool. Many preschools require that the child be potty-trained, another developmental milestone which indicates your child's readiness. If your child is behind in language development and potty training and he or she is clingy, the child is not yet ready for nursery school. You may have to wait at least six months to a year before you try sending him or her.

Another way to tell if your child is ready is to observe him or her with other children the same age. Enrolling your child in a Mommy and Me class, organizing play groups, or observing your child with siblings and cousins may give you an idea of your child's relative maturity in comparison to other children of the same age. It is important to be open and nonjudgmental in your observations. Remember there is a wide range of maturity that is normal for this age group. If you have the opportunity, put your child with a group of older children and see how he or she does. Then put your child in a group of younger children and see how he or she does. This way you can get a picture of your child's readiness. If your child appears more comfortable with the younger children, then it is best to wait and bring your child into a preschool situation as an older child.

Before the age of three, a child's sense of security is largely tied to the parent. By three years of age, many children begin to have an independent sense of self. Children this age have a greater capacity to entertain themselves, interact with others, put trust in adults other than the parents, and generally transfer the safe experience of home to new situations. Because of this, many children are ready for preschool or day care at or about the age of three. Some timid children can be pushed to try the new experience. Perhaps they can go with a friend to preschool or nursery school. Perhaps Mommy can stay until the child feels comfortable in the new situation. Perhaps the child can bring a stuffed animal or favorite toy from home to help lower anxiety by serving as a security object. If after a week or two these methods do not produce good results, it is probably best to wait at least six months to a year until the child is more ready.

Another note: Children pick up on parents' spoken and unspoken feelings. The more relaxed and unrushed you are initially, the easier it is for the child to feel comfortable. Your child's school also may have extensive experience with separation anxiety and the teachers may be able to guide you.

Recommendations:
1. Teach your child to separate from

you by having a baby-sitter do several hours of supervision.

2. The more independently the child plays, the easier the transition to nursery school.

3. Follow the teacher's advice when leaving your child at nursery school.

How do you know if your child is in the right school?

What does the "right school" mean?
When parents ask about the "right school" for their child, it can mean many things. What are the parents' values? Do they want a religious education for their child? Is the child headed toward college? Are the parents looking for enriched programs, regular programs, or programs geared toward the slower student? Would parents prefer an old-fashioned, rigid, and structured school, or an easy-going, creative school that allows children more freedom? Parents must answer these and the following questions, and think about their values and goals for their child. In large communities where there are many public and private schools, the selection can be confusing.

More questions to answer about schools.

1. What do we expect and plan for our child? Is this what our child plans and wants, or are we imposing our hopes on our child?

2. What aspect of our child's education is most important? Religious education? Academic excellence? Sports, or some other factor?

3. Does the school have to be near our home? Will my child drive or take a bus? How long will my child be on the bus and with whom will he or she travel to school?

4. What is our socioeconomic level? Is that important?

5. Do we believe in public or private education; does it make a difference?

6. What is the quality of the neighborhood public school?

7. Will we be happy with the friends my child makes at a particular school?

8. Can our family really afford the cost of an expensive private school for the next few years, or should we save the money for college?

Parents must also consider the emotional, behavioral, and maturational level of their child and ask themselves the following questions:

1. How bright is my child? How do we know? Has our child had an independent evaluation?

2. Is our child happy in his or her present school? Should we change schools?

3. How easily does my child make friends? If we change schools will he or she be able to make new friends easily?

4. Does my child have any academic

weaknesses? Would he or she fit into a school that is geared to advanced, regular, or slower students?

5. Does my child need a school that has special classes for children who are behind in one or more areas?

When in doubt. If a school choice is still not clear to you, consult your child's teacher first and then another professional, such as a child psychologist and/or educator. They may help resolve your confusion and help you make the correct choice.

Recommendations:

1. An excellent way to check out schools it to talk to parents whose children are enrolled in the school you are interested in. Ask them about the prospective teacher.

2. Some publications in your area rate schools. Check with your local librarian.

3. Researching schools takes time. If you have the choice, start a year ahead of time to look for the appropriate school.

How do you know if your child is behind in school?

What does "being behind" mean? *My child's failure is my failure.* Many parents believe this to be true and, therefore, cannot tolerate any deviation from perfect grades, or good grades, whatever that may mean. Therefore, there are various interpretations to the phrase "being behind." Does it mean being behind everybody in the class, being behind some standard set by parents, or being behind what you are aware your child is capable of achieving? Those of us who have gone through the school system and graduated with a high-level degree can recall usually one or more classes in which we did not perform particularly well. Parents who watch their children's school behavior with a very critical eye must keep in mind that a child's functioning is variable. In that variable behavior some children consistently do better in class because they are gifted intellectually, have better work habits, or particularly love some teacher or subject. Most adults choose careers based on what they like. Children do not always have the opportunity to choose classes they enjoy in school.

Some independent measures of a child's functioning in school.

1. Ask your child's teacher about your child's performance. Both school grades and a teacher's comments give you a pretty good indication of how your child is functioning. The assumption is that a child of average intelligence should achieve average grades. As long as a child is functioning at average in class a teacher will not say he or she is behind.

2. Have your child evaluated by a

child psychologist. This independent evaluation will tell you how bright your child is. If your child is above average intellectually, he or she should be performing above average in school. An evaluation will also help you plan for your child's future in terms of performance expectations.

3. Bright parents usually have bright children. If you and your spouse are college graduates, then you can expect your child to be bright and perform well in school.

4. If your child is not doing well in school, you should ask yourself why. You also should take some action, such as having your child evaluated, or changing his or her homework or study habits at home. Could the problem be a learning disability? Could it be due to drugs, truancy, or some emotional problem? As a parent you have to know your child. You have to know your child's intellectual ability. Some children are better than others at using words and ideas. Some are better at creating things and using their hands.

5. Parents need information to help formulate plans and make reasonable demands and expectations of their child. Not all children should go to college, because some do not have the cognitive skills. However, in this day and age, when blue collar workers often make more money than their white collar counterparts, there is less value judgment on those who do not get a college degree.

Listen to your child. One source of information about your child is your child. Parents do not often listen to what their child says. Sometimes the information is there waiting for parents to listen to and act upon. Many children, given the opportunity, will tell their parents about their problems. The informed parent can then make a better decision that will really work, rather than a unilateral decision in which the child plays no part.

Recommendations:

1. Remember that school grading is subjective and may differ with different teachers.

2. Schools differ in how children are graded. If you are not aware of how your child's school is grading compared to other schools, try to find out from the principal of your school.

3. When in doubt, seek independent evaluators such as an educational or child psychologist.

How do you know if your child is dyslexic?

What is dyslexia? Both professionals and parents are often confused by the term "dyslexia." It has become a general term for a variety of specific learning problems. Dyslexia literally means having difficulty with the written word. It is a neurologically based reading disability. This means that the reading disability is not due to poor education, poor parental training, or poor motivation. It is not due to emotional problems. These disabilities can cause reading problems, but they are not dyslexia.

Approximately fifteen percent of all children have learning problems, but only four percent are dyslexic.

What causes dyslexia? Neurologists and brain researchers are still investigating the exact reasons and locations in the brain for this disability. Usually it is inherited, so that if one parent is dyslexic, the child may also be dyslexic. American educators see that there is an underlying inability to process language in dyslexic children. English and European educators see that there is an underlying visual perceptual and sequencing weakness. Both viewpoints are good indicators that dyslexia may be present. The confusion for the specialist is differentiating between dyslexia, attention deficit hyperactivity disorder, learning disabilities, and secondary reading problems.

Dyslexia in some children may be more apparent through their spelling and language. When the dyslexic child hears the spoken word, he or she may omit, substitute, or reverse the sounds and hear a completely different word than what was said. Other children may look at the printed word or letter and read it as something very different; they may read "b" as "d," or "p" as "g", or the word "saw" as "was." Some dyslexic children have difficulty in one

area or the other. Some have difficulty in both.

Dyslexia may occur at four or more critical points in a child's development.

1. A history of reading problems, learning problems, developmental delay, or dyslexia in the family. Since dyslexia is genetic and usually inherited, this is a strong indicator that the child has dyslexia.

2. Damage done to the neurological system from the point of conception until birth. The use of drugs, alcohol, nicotine, medications, etc., can seriously influence the developing fetus. Direct injuries to the mother, or illness during pregnancy, can also directly influence the child's neurological health.

3. Any traumas during the birthing process, such as anoxia or lack of oxygen, incorrect use of forceps, or any medications given to the mother to aid the delivery, may later affect the child.

4. Any injuries to the child, or illnesses such as high fevers or poisoning, can create a neurological impairment.

What are some signs of dyslexia? The following signs occur at different ages, but they can help parents and teachers identify dyslexia. One symptom alone doesn't necessarily make a child dyslexic, but the accumulation of symptoms gives a strong indication.

- Slow to learn the names of letters.
- Slow to learn the names of colors.

- Mixing up words. Saying "aminals" for "animals," or "donimoes" for "dominoes."
- Reversing letters and numbers.
- Difficulty remembering directions.
- Difficulty locating objects that are plainly in sight.
- Skipping lines and losing one's place while reading.
- Spelling errors.
- Constantly mixing up left and right directions.
- Mild speech delay.
- Problems with coordination, such as tying shoes, buttoning a shirt.

These symptoms may be noticed in children under the age of five. If these symptoms persist as the child grows older, they become significant indicators of dyslexia. A nine-year-old who has many of these symptoms has a high probability of dyslexia.

What can you do about it?

1. If your child has many of these symptoms, they will be picked up most likely by your child's teacher. Talk to your child's teacher first.
2. If you see these symptoms in your child, and your child's teacher has not noticed them, bring them to the teacher's attention.
3. If the problems persist or the child performs poorly in school, consult your child's principal. Ask the principal to have the school psychologist do a psychological-educational evaluation on your child.
4. If the school psychologist is not available, consult a private child psychologist.

5. Dyslexia is a problem that requires more professional training than most parents have. If you need help with a dyslexic child, you should seek out a competent professional for assistance. Teachers specifically trained in learning problems, educational therapists, and educational psychologists are equipped to help your child.
6. It is important for parents of a dyslexic child to inform themselves of special programs and special schools that might help the child.

Prevention: Awareness of a dyslexia problem and early intervention, along with warm support for the child, are often the best things parents can do for a dyslexic child.

Recommendations:

1. The term dyslexia is often not understood by teachers or others. You may want to have your child evaluated by a psychologist.
2. Many dyslexics respond to training by an educational therapist. The problem may not continue to be a problem if you get help for your child now.

How do you know if your child has a learning problem?

Edward is a well-behaved child. Teachers love him. Although he only gets C's, his parents and his teachers are satisfied with what he does. Does he have a learning disability?

George is off the wall. He truly is an overactive boy who can't sit still, and he has difficulty listening to his teachers' instructions. He gets C's. Teachers feel he could do better, but they don't have time to give him additional attention. Does he have a learning disability?

Marsha is often in her own dream world. Directions have to be repeated to her. Once she reads something, she never forgets it. She is getting by in school unevenly. In some classes she gets A's, and in others she gets D's. Does she have a learning disability?

What is a learning problem? A learning problem assumes that the child has academic ability that he or she is not maximizing. Learning problems can be physical, emotional, or motivational in nature. They can be the result of poor study habits. Sometimes a child's uneven performance, such as getting A's in some classes and D's in others, show the possibility of a specific learning problem. Sometimes a child who is perceived as bright, but who functions below grade level, may also exhibit a learning disability. A child who has difficulty listening in class, or who is disruptive, may also have underlying learning problems.

Learning problems can manifest themselves individually or in combination with academic performance, language development, visual and auditory perception, and social and emotional areas.

The term "learning disability," sometimes called a "learning problem," means something very specific. It means that your child is either functioning below grade-level expectations, or that your child is functioning below expectations for his or her intelligence and ability.

To know if your child falls into one of these two categories, you need an estimation of your child's intellectual ability. The assumption in public schools is that the average child will do average work in all classes, that is, achieve grades of C or better. Since we know that all children and adults are stronger in some areas, such as language or visual spatial tasks, reading or arithmetic, and so on, we have to understand that these strengths and weaknesses are not learning disabilities, but an inclination of interest or skill in one direction or another.

What to do about it. To find out if your child has problems with learning, consider the following:

If you suspect that the learning problem is academic, ask yourself why.
1. Is your child's academic perfor-

mance uneven? Does your child do poorly in reading but well in math? Is the child a good reader, but a poor speller?

2. Do you find that your child has a strong resistance to some subject areas? For example, does your child hate to write? Does your child hate to read? Does your child hate to do math problems? If so, ask yourself why. Is it a simple matter of interest, or is it a matter of difficulty? Most children avoid subject areas that challenge their abilities. If a child experiences failure in an area, he or she is very likely to resist that area. If a child perceives that he or she is slower in some areas than his or her friends, the child is less likely to work in that area. In a testing situation, a child who has low interest, but good ability, will do well. If the child has low interest and poor ability, you can assume that the low interest is due to the poor ability.

3. Choose a subject with which you suspect your child is having problems. Ask the child to read aloud from a school textbook as an example. See if the child has difficulty reading the material and answering questions about it. Make sure it is material your child has already covered in class. If the child has difficulty, it means that the lack of ability may be creating low interest, and there may be an underlying learning problem.

Sometimes a learning disability manifests itself in the way the child processes visual and auditory language.

Language processes are viewed in three ways: receptive language, associative language, and expressive language. Some children don't immediately understand what is said to them or what they see. You constantly hear the response, Huh? or What? Also, the child gives responses that have nothing to do with the questions you ask. This would be an example of a possible receptive language disorder. Children who understand what you say, but have difficulty transferring the concepts into new situations, may have an associative language disorder. For example, the child who is told to eat fruit, not candy, may constantly ask for a variety of sweets such as cookies, gum, etc., because the child doesn't understand that eating sweets is unhealthy. Parents often feel they are repeating lots of information, and the child is not getting the idea or concept. A third group of children probably can understand what is presented to them. They can generalize it to a variety of situations, but they may have great difficulty organizing and expressing their thoughts and feelings in either oral or written language. These children often say, I don't know, or are very resistant to expressive writing exercises. They may give short, one-word answers to questions. For example, Where did you go? Out. What did you do? Nothing.

Your child may have auditory or visual perception problems. Some children have difficulty locating sound in their environment, for example, locating who is talking in the room. Children who have particular difficulty concentrating when there is noise in the room may have a problem hearing words against a noisy background. They may be easily overwhelmed when there is noise in the background.

Children who have difficulty locating objects in their room or words in a sentence, children who skip lines when they read, or unintentionally skip problems in a math exercise, may be exhibiting a visual perceptual problem. One of the most common of these difficulties is reversing letters or numbers.

Your child may have trouble with coordination. Fine motor coordination involves the small muscle control needed to button a shirt or jacket, or tie a shoelace. Often these children have difficulty with handwriting. Gross motor coordination involves the large muscle control needed to bend, run, throw a ball, kick, catch, and so on. A child who constantly runs into things, trips, and falls, may have an underlying problem with sensory motor development.

A learning disability can manifest itself socially when a child does not perceive situations in the way that most of his or her peers do. The child says or does things that seem inappropriate, as attempts to get attention. These things may appear to be bullying or immature. A child who tries to be funny, but who acts clearly inappropriately, can become rejected or isolated over time. Emotionally, the child often will feel "stupid," "dumb," or "bad." The child may frequently express this verbally.

See if your child fits in one or more of these categories. The more cate-

gories your child fits into, the greater the likelihood that your child has an underlying learning disability.

Recommendations:

1. Learning disabilities need not be permanent. You need to take action as soon as possible to first evaluate your child and then get help in solving the problem.
2. If you do not know of anyone who can help, check with your school district for people with knowledge about special education.
3. Make sure your child has his or her hearing and vision checked to rule out any possibility that there are problems in these areas.

How do you know if your child has a reading problem?

Reading as a school subject. Reading is probably the most controversial area in education. Educational experts fiercely debate *when* a child should read, and *how* a child should be taught. Should a child be instructed to read, or should we wait for the child to initiate interest? If we teach the child, should we begin at age two or three? Should we start at six or seven, when most children in public education begin? Should we wait until eight or nine,

when perceptual and language development is more mature? There seem to
be advantages and disadvantages to
each argument. You have to make the
choice based on your value system.
Good luck!

Let's suppose you've made your
choice, and for some reason you're
beginning to wonder if your child has a
learning problem. Maybe you over-
heard your friend talk about a learning
problem that his or her child has. How
can you find out whether your child
has a problem without signing up for
an expensive psychological evaluation?
Here are some simple and practical
things you can do.

One of the easiest ways to find out if
your child has a reading problem is
simply to ask your child to read aloud
for you. If the child is resistant to reading out loud it usually is because the
child doesn't like to hear himself or
herself make mistakes. Encourage your
child to read for you in any positive
way you can. Complimenting, charming, and rewarding your child will
probably produce a more optimal result
than threatening punishment.

When you have your child's agreement, ask your child to read from any
textbook that was assigned to him or
her at school. The teacher will only
assign your child books that are the
proper grade level. A geography, history, or literature book will do fine.
Position yourself so you can follow
along as your child reads; or, with a little planning, you can photocopy a page
or two from the book you choose, and
follow along from your copy while the

child reads. This allows you to make
notes. Reassure the child that you will
not correct him or her and that you
love him or her. As the child reads, you
will want to watch for four things:

- **Mispronunciation,** which basically
  is saying the word incorrectly. This
  area also includes adding or omit-
  ting words in sentences. Your child
  should be able to read eight out of
  ten words accurately. If your child
  stumbles over more than half the
  words, he or she may have a problem.

- **Fluency,** or the smoothness with
  which your child reads. Does your
  child read with emphasis in the
  proper places so that you can easily
  understand what he or she is reading? Does your child read in a halt-
  ing, choppy manner? If your child
  struggles with too many words, his
  or her fluency will be poor, and this
  may indicate some underlying reading difficulties.

- **Skipping lines/Losing one's place**
  may also indicate some problems
  with reading. As your child reads,
  notice whether he or she skips
  words or whether he or she skips
  from one line to the next. While
  your child reads, ask him or her to
  look up at you, then ask your child a
  question, especially in the middle of
  a longer paragraph. Then ask your
  child to continue reading. Count
  how long it takes your child to find
  his or her place again. If the child
  takes longer than five seconds, he or
  she may have a reading problem.

- **Comprehension** is probably the

most important area of reading. As your child reads, write down at least seven questions to ask him or her when he or she is finished. Your child should get at least five right. If your child has a score of three or less, he or she most likely has a problem with comprehension.

How did your child do? Did your child have any difficulties? Did your child have a few difficulties in only one or two areas? Did your child have trouble in all the areas? Some children clearly have reading problems; some clearly do not. Some children read poorly but have good comprehension. Others read smoothly and accurately but have poor comprehension. Both could probably use some help. Most children fall somewhere in the middle.

If after doing the above evaluation you are still concerned about your child's reading ability, you should contact your child's teacher to see if he or she has noticed any problems. You will be better able to converse with your child's teacher about mispronunciations, fluency, skipping lines/losing one's place, and comprehension. If the teacher has not evaluated your child's reading skills, you can ask him or her to do so. You may or may not get a positive response. Be brave. Be kind. Be persistent. Many teachers I know are highly overworked. The teacher will either confirm or deny your suspicions. If you get an, I don't know. He seems OK, then you're back in the middle group with the rest of us, which means your child probably has enough skills to get by and will probably do

fine. If you have the financial means or health insurance to do so, you may want to seek out a more formal and detailed evaluation.

Would you like to help? The roles of parenting and teaching are quite different. If you would like to help teach your child to read better, first you have to determine whether your child will accept you in the role of teacher. Some children can accept the change; others cannot. If you have a child who refuses to have you as his or her teacher, please let someone else do the job. You are too important as your child's parent. If your child will accept you as a teacher, then you will do best to make it fun. The younger the child, the more fun and play will be required. Also, your teenager appreciates humor and fun; ask any high school teacher. As you begin, remember that compliments, charm, and rewards enhance the teaching process. If you have trouble in this area, turn to the section on motivation for ideas.

Here are some simple, easy steps:
1. Set up a regular time and place where the two of you can work or play. It should be free from interruption or distraction.
2. Pick material that is of high interest to the child. It can come from a book, magazine, brochure, recipe, food label, computer program, instructions for a video game, comic book, baseball card, and so on. Go for high interest and fun.
3. Pick material that is at your child's reading level. When a child can eas-

ily read and understand eight out of ten words in a sentence on a consistent basis, you have found your child's reading level. If your child can read only seventy percent or sixty percent of the words on a page, the material may be too challenging and your child may lose interest. When you succeed at something, you want to do it again. We want your child to experience success at reading.

Recommendations:
1. Make sure your child's vision is satisfactory. Have an evaluation by an optometrist or ophthalmologist.
2. The more they practice reading, the faster children progress. Set aside a time to read each day.
3. Everybody has interests. Let your child read material that interests him or her.

How do you know if your child has difficulties in speech and language development?

Another area of major development in a child's life has to do with speech and language development.

What do we mean by "speech"?
Speech and language are two different areas. Speech includes such areas as articulation, lisp, stuttering, mumbling, substitution, omission, distortion, and addition of speech sounds. Speech therapy includes many physical exercises to strengthen the tongue, lips, and vocal cords. Speech more formally concentrates on the pronunciation and articulation of words and the correct placement of those words in a sentence.

What do we mean by "language"?
Language development, as many people commonly describe it, has to do with how well the child understands and uses both the spoken and written word. One way to look at language development is to break it down into four major categories.

- **Receptive Language.** The first area describes how a child receives language. How does language get into the head? Either by what one hears or by what one sees, as in reading. This is referred to as "receptive language." When a word is spoken, for example, "apple," the child instantly creates an image of an apple, or immediately understands and can identify the object by its name. The child who has some delay in receptive language may hear the word "apple" and take extra milliseconds to link that word to the actual object. For example, when a parent says, Go to your room and get your tennis shoes, this child may not immediately understand what he or she is supposed to do. It may take the child a few extra milliseconds to understand first what the phrase, "Go to your room" means. Second, the child may not immediately be able to visualize what tennis shoes are. These children sometimes appear to not listen. They may ask, What room? or What are tennis shoes? Frequently a parent thinks that this is a bright child asking a dumb question. These kinds of conflicts between parent and child may suggest a receptive language delay.

- **Associative Language.** A second area of language development describes what happens to language when it gets into the head. Once a child can easily identify the meaning or idea of a word, the child must understand its relationship to other objects or ideas. For instance, if the child hears the word "apple," he or she may also immediately associate it to the color red. The child probably can compare it in size and shape to a ball. The child may group it in relationship to fruit. The child may understand it as a food.

    Telling your child to clean up his or her room could be a big challenge unless the child knows specifically that dirty clothes go in a certain place. Clean clothes, books, and toys must be put in certain places, and the bed has to be made. Often a child with this difficulty

goes to his or her room and does only one thing, saying, I'm done, or It's clean, or I'm finished.

When a child reads, he or she probably can tell you what was said in the story. The child may not be able to draw inferences or apply the information to other situations. Another example is when a parent tells a child not to hit his younger sister or brother. The child then hits the dog. The parent then tells the child not to hit the dog, and the child breaks his or her toys. The child is following directions, but he or she is not getting the general idea about not hitting, hurting, or being destructive. This could be an associative language weakness. Sometimes these problems appear in what a child hears, and other times in what a child sees or reads.

- **Expressive Language.** A third area of language development includes the entire expressive range. Once we understand language, how do we express ourselves so others will understand us? We do it through gesture language or expressive verbal language. When you ask a child a question, he or she may know what you are saying. The child may even have some ideas to express. The child may not be able to find the right words, or put them in the right order or context to give you a proper answer. The child may shrug his or her shoulders and say, I don't know, or simply give you a blank stare. Often these children like to give only one-word answers. How was school? Fine. What did you do? Nothing.

Many children can express themselves well verbally, but have great difficulty when it comes to writing or putting their ideas on paper. Usually this problem is discovered early in a child's education, as the child begins to write stories in second, third, and fourth grade. I can't think of anything to write, is a common comment of these children. It seems that each sentence is a difficult struggle. A child who seems to have difficulty in both areas most likely has expressive problems.

The cause of expressive language disturbances is varied. The problem may be developmental or genetic; it may appear from birth on. The problem may be neurological, as in an expressive aphasia that is a neurological disorder in the brain. It may be due to brain damage to the language area in the brain. It may be due to an emotional problem, as in the child who is very depressed and unable or unwilling to talk. Sometimes the difficulty may be caused by the environment in which the child is raised, wherein the child is not allowed to speak except under very restrictive circumstances. Dyslexia is often considered a language disorder.

- **Memory.** A fourth area of language development has to do with both short- and long-term memory through both hearing and seeing.

There is a growing body of evidence that suggests that language is also learned kinesthetically, or through body movement or touch. This is easily proven with riding a bicycle. Even if you haven't ridden a bicycle for some time, it can be easily relearned, because the body seems to have an inherent memory.

Memory is a key ingredient in the process of communication. It is the storehouse of information taken in visually or auditorially. There are two factors that are vital in this storehouse. The first is the capacity to store incoming information. The second is the capacity to retrieve or access that information as needed. People with poor memory functions need repeated exposure to store the information and/or have difficulty retrieving the information at will. Some people can retain information that they hear. If they listen to a lecture or tape, they may have better retention of what was said. Other people remember better if they can read or see what is being done. A third group of people do best if they hear an explanation, read the explanation, and write down the explanation, using all three sensory modalities. This is called a "multisensory approach" to learning, and is often used with poor spellers.

Short-term memory, long-term memory. Short-term memory and long-term memory are stored in different parts of the brain. Some theorists believe that all information comes into one part of the brain first (short-term memory), and is evaluated for its importance to the individual. It then is stored in another section of the brain that holds information long-term. Tasks that are frequently repeated will move from short-term to long-term memory regardless of their value. Commonly it appears in elderly people that the long-term memory begins to out-function the short-term memory.

Developmental stages. Generally between the ages of birth to eight, the child's perception and language develop. After about age eight, individuals use language and perception to learn and communicate at a more complex level. In early and middle adolescence, abstract concepts are integrated in the child's language development. Most basic perceptual development should be concluded by about age eight. A fully intact auditory and visual perceptual development must be in place to support language development. Language development continues throughout life.

Learning a new language. Language problems sometimes appear when an individual tries to learn a new language. Any problem in the child's language of origin will be highlighted as the child tries to learn a new language. Young children appear to learn new languages easily. These children learn because of exposure and necessity. They also have fewer preconditioned notions to undo.

What do you do about it? Usually speech problems are quickly and easily identified in preschool or kindergarten. If you suspect that your child has a problem with speech, or a delay in speech development, you might consult a professional speech therapist or speech pathologist. If you suspect a problem with your child's language development, you probably can help your child.

1. If you think the child has difficulty understanding the meaning of your words, use short sentences and make sure the child knows what you're saying by asking him or her to identify the key words in the sentence, for example, Please go brush your teeth. If it appears the child doesn't understand the direction, ask him or her to repeat it back to you.

2. If you suspect that your child has difficulty seeing the relationship between items, ask him or her questions. In the last example, you might ask, What do you need to do? Where do you brush your teeth? What do you use to brush your teeth? Where is that kept? When are you supposed to brush your teeth? These are the natural connections made by a child with good associative skills.

3. If the child has difficulty putting thoughts and feelings into words, encourage him or her to be specific. Many children will say, You know. Encourage the child to give you full-sentence answers to what you ask, for instance, Tell me one thing

you did today, and then wait for a complete sentence.

4. First it is important to find out if the child's memory is better for things that are heard or for things that are seen. A chart on the wall that gets checked off when chores are done might be best for the child who needs visual support. Telling instructions to a child who has a strong auditory memory will give good results. Showing a child, telling a child, and rehearsing with a child will often give you the best results.

5. If your efforts fail, or if the problems are severe, seek professional help from a speech and language therapist. Many public schools have speech therapists on staff to serve the district. You might also contact a child psychologist who has experience with language development.

Recommendations:

1. Parents are often used to interpreting their children's language. Consult a speech and language specialist if you have continuing doubts.

2. Children suffer when they are teased by other children about their speech problem. Take care of the problem as soon as possible.

How do you know if your child has a visual perceptual weakness?

What is visual perception? Vision and visual perception are not the same thing.

By vision we mean adequate visual clarity, good ability of both eyes to focus on things near and far, good ability to adjust to light and darkness, as well as other measures usually performed by an optometrist or ophthalmologist.

Visual perception refers to the organization and integration of visual patterns. The term usually comes into play with regard to a child's learning, especially in reading. The ability to see the pattern of the letter, wherever it is on the page, facing in the same direction is part of visual perception. For instance, a child who reads haltingly and makes many reading errors may have a visual perceptual weakness. If the child transposes letters, for example, says "was" for "saw," or "tops" for "spot"; if the child reverses letters, for example, says "bad" for "dad," or "dig" for "big"; if the child adds or leaves out letters in a word; or if the child frequently skips lines or loses his or her place while reading, most likely the child has a weakness in the area of visual perception.

Some researchers have subdivided

the area of visual perception into categories, such as visual tracking, visual closure, visual figure-ground, visual constancy of form, and visual spatial relations.

Visual Tracking is the ability to follow a line of words in a book, a ball flying through the air, a rabbit running on the ground, a person giving a visual demonstration, and so on.

Visual Closure is the ability to visually recognize an object that is only partially visible, such as your keys next to a lamp, your shoes under the chair, the remote control between the cushions, the orange juice partly behind the milk, and the like.

Visual Figure-Ground is the ability to pick out relevant forms from a confusing background, such as the right T-shirt from the laundry basket, your tennis shoes from the other shoes in the bottom of the closet, the jar of peanut butter from the other jars next to it, the flat-head screw driver from the other tools in the tool box, and so on.

Visual Form Constancy is the ability to recognize a certain form no matter what position it is in. An "A" is still an "A" if it is tilted at a forty-five-degree angle, or upside down, or sideways. A square is still a square even if it is balanced on one of its corners. A jar of jam is a jar of jam even if it comes in a different bottle than it did last week. Not being able to see similarities could be a visual perceptual problem.

Visual Spatial Relations is the ability to judge the distance between objects. Jamming too many objects into too small a space when there is more room nearby, sitting too close or standing too close when there is no real reason to do so, frequently bumping into objects in the environment, putting objects too close to the edge, etc., are all examples of some difficulty with visual spatial relations.

How does a visual perceptual weakness show itself at home?

- When you ask a child to get something that is plainly in view and the child can't find it.
- When you ask a child to find something that is partially in view and, even staring at it, the child can't recognize it.
- When you ask a child to get something from his or her room, the cupboard, the refrigerator, or the garage, and the child can't retrieve it.
- When you show a child how to do something and the child's eyes keep wandering off what you're doing, even though the child says he or she is concentrating.
- When the child constantly bumps into furniture, hits himself or herself on the corners of tables, chairs, or doorways.
- When the child frequently stands too close to other children and can't judge the distance between objects well.
- When the child frequently drops his or her food, spills and knocks things over.

- When the child constantly mixes up left and right directions.
- When the child can't throw, catch, hit, or kick a ball close to the level of his or her peers.
- When a child can't visually plan how to organize his or her toys or clothes.

The more categories your child falls into the greater the likelihood that your child has a visual perceptual weakness. If your child also has difficulty reading, then you can be pretty sure there is a problem.

What can you do about it? Visual perception improves naturally as a child matures, and most children are thought to have a fully mature visual perception system by about the age of eight or nine. If your child lags behind developmentally there are several things you can do. However, it is important to note that there is some difference of opinion regarding whether visual perception can be improved through remediation.

The first thing to keep in mind is that the child has to be motivated to learn or try something new. Pushing, forcing, criticizing, blaming, or getting angry at a child is not going to get the child to be open or trusting, which is what you want to achieve. Provide tasks that are well within the child's proven ability. Make it fun; make it play.

For example:

1. Board games are wonderful for developing visual perception because they incorporate a wide variety of perceptual skills. Games such as Candy Land, Chutes and Ladders, Sorry, Hi Ho Cherry-O, Monopoly, and Life are all good examples. Go to the store with your child and pick out a few games. See if you can play them two or three times a week.

2. Any type of art activities, such as drawing, tracing, pasting, cutting, playing with clay or Play Doh, coloring, or painting, is useful. Mazes, in particular, are especially good for visual organization and tracking. If you have a child who really likes mazes (and there are many who do) buy a book of them and let your child do one or two a day after homework.

3. Any kind of sport activity that involves throwing to a distant target, running and turning, kicking, or catching helps a child use his or her eyes and body at the same time. Remember, the object at this level is not to be the best but simply to have fun while strengthening the visual perceptual skills. If the child does not have a lot of fun or does not feel positive about himself or herself in the process, your child won't want to continue.

4. Make up any kind of game that requires visual perception. See who can find their tennis shoes first; who can get dressed the fastest; who can find the most square (round, rectangular, oval) objects in the room. Also, play driving games that require the use of visual perception. The game I Spy is a good car game.

If you haven't heard of it, ask your seven-, eight-, or nine-year-old. Educational bookstores are a good place to find some of these games.

5. Video and arcade games are also a very good way for children to improve their visual perception and their eye/hand coordination.

Recommendations:

1. If your child seems to have only a mild visual perceptual weakness, then any of the above suggestions will probably be sufficient.

2. If your child seems to fit most of these categories and is having difficulty reading, then you may have to consult with your child's teacher, or perhaps contact an educational or clinical psychologist to obtain a complete evaluation.

How do you know if your child has an auditory perceptual weakness?

What is auditory perception?

Auditory perception has to do with how the brain distinguishes and organizes sounds, rather than with the actual mechanics of hearing. Some experts in the field subdivide this area into auditory discrimination, auditory closure, auditory blending, and audito-ry figure-ground. The categories of auditory reception, association, and memory may belong with the area of language development rather than perception.

Auditory Discrimination is the ability to distinguish between sounds. For example, some children cannot tell the difference between words like "bin-pin," or "boy-box," or "tin-tan" if they are not looking at you. These children may not be able to distinguish between the "s" and "sh" sounds in speech.

Auditory Closure is the ability to fill in the missing sounds to make a whole word. For example, if a child with good auditory closure heard "gu to ur roo ight now," the child might fill in the missing blanks and hear "go to your room right now."

Auditory Blending is the ability to take two separate sounds and blend them together, for example, ap - pl = apple, goo - d ni - t = good night.

Auditory Figure-Ground is the ability to focus on the relevant auditory information in a confusing background. Being able to listen to a teacher while other children are talking in the background, or being able to listen to someone on the telephone while the television or radio is on in the background are two examples of auditory figure-ground.

How do I recognize an auditory perceptual weakness at home?

- Child frequently misunderstands or misinterprets what you say.
- Child frequently says Huh? or What? even though you know the child heard you.
- Child has great difficulty understanding people with accents or understanding young children who do not clearly articulate words.
- Child rarely can identify the lyrics to songs.
- Child has difficulty understanding you when there is background noise.
- Child complains that he or she can't hear in the classroom because others are talking.

What can you do about it? If you sense your child has an auditory perceptual weakness, probably the best thing you can do is to simply be aware that your child has this difficulty. This means that when you talk to your child be sure that you face him or her and that you clearly articulate your words. If you can do this inconspicuously, your child will understand you better. Also, for some children, you may have to speak more slowly and/or move to a quieter area. It's important to make subtle changes so the child won't feel that you are talking down to him or her or singling him or her out.

Recommendations: If you think your child has difficulty with auditory perception, you might suggest a speech and language evaluation by a specialist at your child's public school. Otherwise, you should consult an edu-

cational psychologist or a clinical psychologist in your area.

How do you know if your child has a sensory motor weakness?

Sensory motor development is often described in two categories:

Fine Motor, which has to do with the small muscle control needed to button a shirt, tie shoes, draw straight lines, and write.

Gross Motor, which has to do with the large muscle control needed to bend, run, throw a ball, kick, catch, and so on.

Some children are strong in one area and weak in the other. Some are strong in both, and some are weak in both. Oftentimes, in children between the ages of four and six, girls will develop fine motor skills earlier than boys, while boys will develop gross motor skills earlier than girls. If this is reversed for your child, do not be alarmed; there is a wide range of development during this time. If you think your child is behind in either gross motor or fine motor development, there are several things you can do.

A quick way to check your child's development is to ask a teacher in your child's preschool, kindergarten, or elementary school. Teachers can probably answer your questions quickly, and they will be familiar with the terms "fine motor" and "gross motor."

A second way is to observe your child's work during open house. Often the children's written work and drawings are displayed around the classroom. You should compare your child's writing or drawing to at least ten to twelve other children of the same age and sex. If you only compare your child's product to one or two others, or to a child of a different sex, you can easily get an unfair comparison. Also, remember that sometimes a teacher will exhibit only the best products, so be careful.

A third way to assess if there is a problem is to observe your child in his or her classroom or out on the playground. Again, remember to include your child in a sample of at least a dozen children. Do not compare your child to the best child and do not compare your child to your best friend's child. These samples are too small and will do a disservice to you and your child. These comparisons will either inflate or deflate your opinion in an unrealistic way.

A fourth way to evaluate your child's sensory motor development is to ask your pediatrician during one of your child's regular exams. With some simple tests, your child's doctor can tell you if your child is on track.

The best way to determine if your child has a sensory motor weakness is to evaluate a child using all four ways. If the child is behind in all four areas,

you can be reasonably sure that he or she has some problem with sensory motor development. If there is no lag in any of these areas, then you can relax and stop worrying. If there is some mix, then you might consider an evaluation by a professional psychologist.

It's important to remember that most of us have lags in one or two areas, so don't be alarmed. Every child has strengths and weaknesses. If you don't see them yet, you soon will.

What can you do about it? *Fine motor coordination* can be improved by playing many games with your child:
- Trace, color, or paint within the lines.
- Button, lace, thread a needle, or sew.
- Play Pick-up-Sticks, Lincoln Logs, or Legos.
- Screw, bolt, nail, or cut with a jigsaw.
- Play video games.
- Do anything that requires small, accurate movement of the fingers.

Gross motor coordination can be improved through the following activities:
- Run, jump, kick, throw, catch, or bend.
- Play Hop Scotch, obstacle course, or any physical sport.
- Dance, or do Yoga, Karate, or gymnastics.
- Roller Blade, skate, or play soccer.

Recommendations:
1. Ask teachers if they see a problem with sensory motor weaknesses in your child. If they do, consult your

pediatrician about specialists in your area.

2. If you cannot find a specialist who deals with sensory motor development, a good physical fitness instructor may be of help.

How do you know if your child reads enough?

The importance of reading. Of all the subjects your child learns in school, none is as important as reading and reading comprehension. The reason is clear. To learn all other subjects, such as history, geography, and even algebra and geometry, you must be able to read and understand the written word. As the child enters twelfth grade and college, reading speed and reading comprehension are the primary skills needed to succeed. Almost all college work is reading and understanding what is read.

Checking on reading skills. There are several ways to know if your child is reading both enough and at the correct level. Your child's teacher may be able to answer the question. Many schools have yearly tests that measure reading ability. Not all schools routinely give the information to parents, unless they ask.

Children who are of normal or above-normal intelligence should be able to read with adequate speed, accuracy, and comprehension. If not, there is a problem that has to be solved. To solve the reading problem, the parent, the teacher, and the child must be involved.

Your child's teacher can usually tell you about your child's reading level in comparison to other children of the same age and grade. A second possibility is to get an independent evaluation by a psychologist, who can test your child in reading.

If your child is above his or her grade level in all areas of reading, then your child is reading enough for basic purposes. If your child is not up to grade level, then parents must take action.

Parents should set good study habits for their child. If a child needs help in reading, then the child should read at home on a daily basis. How long depends on the child and the problems you want to solve. For example, a child who wants to improve reading skills should read at least half an hour to one hour a day. What the child reads depends on the child's level of reading. Sometimes, your child's teacher can help you select the proper books. Most public libraries have books arranged by grade level, which can be very helpful to parents.

Aside from the remedial aspects of reading, parents should consider whether their child is college bound. College students need excellent reading skills. Reading develops a child's vocabulary and spelling skills, as well as provides a fund of information for your child that cannot be learned in any other way.

Results of good study skills. Those parents who attend to the question of reading skills do a service to their children. Children need good study skills to survive in school, and one way to help with reading and other school subjects is to teach children to read at home on a daily basis. Since entrance exams to fine schools and colleges always involve reading skills, parents can start with young children to help them learn good study and reading skills.

Recommendations:
1. Children will be more inclined to read if they are reading materials they find interesting. Ask your child what he or she would like to read about.
2. There is no substitute for daily reading practice. Set up a schedule for your child to follow.
3. Ask your child questions about the material. This helps with reading comprehension.

How do you know if your child is bright or gifted?

All parents believe their child is bright. Sometimes, however, we either have doubts, or we have to know exactly how bright our child is to get him or her into a special program, such as school gifted programs. Sometimes we need the information so we can plan sensibly for the child's future.

What is intelligence? Psychologists are experts in intelligence testing. These tests reveal a number—the IQ, or intelligence quotient—that is a statistical measure. This measure allows us to compare our child with all others of the same age and background. By background we mean that children must be raised in this country, where the test was standardized. With a number such as one hundred being average, psychologists can measure how much above or below average your child is, depending on the child's score. Unfortunately, for children born in other countries or children with special problems, it is difficult to get an accurate measure.

Intelligence tests measure a variety of information and skills. Some measures of intelligence focus on developmental levels, some focus primarily on verbal levels, and some are oriented toward performance or perceptual motor tasks.

For example, the test may measure the range of information a person gets from books, travel, conversation, movies, television, or general exposure. Another area that is often measured are the words or vocabulary a child can use. Reasoning skills, the ability to use abstractions, the ability to compute oral arithmetic, short-term memory and remembering things in order, analyzing and planning skills, and spatial ability—all contribute to the measure of intellectual ability. We give all these tests to children at their appropriate ages, so there are different tests for different ages. There are many kinds of intelligence, and tests measure only some of them.

How parents can determine intelligence. As parents, there are many ways to measure how bright your child is. Sometimes teachers will tell you. Sometimes, other people will be impressed with how well your child performs certain tasks. However, you can get a measure of how bright your child is by comparing him or her with other children of the same age. Grades are one measure of how your child performs compared to other children. How wide a range of information about his or her surroundings does your child have compared to other children? How good is your child's practical judgment? How well does your child do with numbers? How good is your child with his or her hands? Can your child remember a series of numbers—say, five or six in a sequence? How is your child's reading

ability compared to other children his or her age? When your child talks, how wide is his or her vocabulary compared to same-age friends?

If your child is ahead of his or her peers in many of these areas, you have a bright child. If it is important for school purposes, you may want to have your child tested for intelligence by a psychologist. A psychologist may use such tests as the Wechsler Pre School and Primary Scales of Intelligence, Revised, or the Wechsler Intelligence Scale for Children III, or another equally valid and reliable instrument.

What can you do about it? Contrary to some opinions, intelligence can be increased or improved. That is, you can raise your child's intelligence or ability to do better in a school setting.

1. One of the most effective ways is to increase your child's vocabulary by reading more to your child, by having more adult-like conversations with your child, or by directly exposing your child to more words.

2. Expose your child to other cultures, other traditions, and other areas of interest. What does your child know about foreign countries? What does your child know about the history of people?

3. Expose your child to other ideas. What does your child know about politics, economics, philosophy, anthropology, religions, photography, classical music, the arts, athletics, science, and the like?

4. Improve your child's arithmetic skills. Learning to calculate will

improve your child's concentration, as well as his or her reasoning skills.

5. Be aware of your child's exposure to toxic chemicals. There is evidence that exposure to toxic chemicals, such as lead, may lower intelligence.

6. Monitor your child's diet. Nutrition plays an important role in intelligence. Consult your pediatrician regarding your child's diet.

Enhancement: Many studies suggest that early stimulation of a child's brain and body can enhance general intelligence. When the child's natural curiosity is encouraged and fostered, and learning is made fun, intelligence is enhanced.

Recommendations:
1. Children who work at their level of intelligence do not become bored in school. Find out at what level your child is functioning and then find the appropriate class.

2. Many public schools have gifted classes. Find out if your school does.

3. Gifted children are still children. Raise your child in as normal an environment as possible.

How do you know if your child is ready to separate from parents and attend college?

Parents' problems and children's problems. As we grow up, there are many rites of passage, or stages, we go through. One of the last and most traumatic rites of adolescence is graduating from high school and leaving home for college. Before they make final decisions, parents must consider various factors, such as availability of money, feelings about separation, responsibility and maturity of the child, appropriateness of the college chosen for the child, and, finally, consideration of the continuing relationship with the child as he or she changes from child to young adult.

The twelfth grader also has some serious issues to confront. How does the child feel about leaving home, about leaving friends, about taking responsibility for money, about taking responsibility for studying and maintaining grades, about handling private chores, such as laundry, and, most importantly, about managing time? Each of these areas can cause and have caused grief to many first-year college students.

Money considerations. Parents trying to be generous will sometimes agree to their child's college of choice without being aware of the enormous cost of each semester or quarter. College costs have risen dramatically. There is the cost of tuition, books, special equipment for some courses, room and board, daily expenses, health care, transportation several times a year—or the cost of a car, insurance and gas, and so on. Even for state universities, which were once almost free, the costs may reach as high as $15,000 per year; double that for private universities. What can you, as parents, afford? Your child may not be able to work because of school pressure or the inability to find a job close to school.

Feelings about separation. This major separation that parents and children undergo creates mixed feelings in both. There is pain, anxiety, and fears of the future, as well as visions of great success and independence. These mixed feelings raise conflict within each party. Parents want their children to grow up happy and become independent, successful adults who can care for their own families and themselves. Yet, it is hard to break old patterns. Your baby may be seen as your "baby." There may be doubts whether your child can do it. We may begin to miss our children before they are gone. All these conflicting feelings may arise at the same time and make us wonder if the child should leave.

For children, the break may be even greater. The child may feel as if he or she is being thrust out into the world unready. The conflict may have to do with the child's desire to be independent, which is healthy, and the child's desire to remain dependent and cared for. Some children handle this conflict by deciding to stay home and attend a local college.

Responsibility and maturity. These areas involve your child making decisions for himself or herself. Maybe, for the first time, your child has to handle large sums of money. Your child has to make money last for a month or more at a time, and possibly account to you for how the money was spent. This is a difficult task if you are not used to it or ready for it. Maturity is the ability to act in an age-appropriate manner. An eighteen-year-old should be able to act like other eighteen-year-olds. You can expect mistakes in handling money, managing personal affairs, and managing new and difficult personal relationships. Many times, for the first time in their lives, children have to share a room in college with two or three other students. The child has to handle such areas as eating properly, going to bed on time, and organizing and managing time, as well as studying enough. Finally, parents will know they chose the right college when at the end of the first semester there are no major complications. Colleges do not expect the first semester, or indeed the first year, to be necessarily representative of what the child can do.

Contact with parents. Children vary.

Some children will call almost daily or certainly weekly. As time progresses, the need to call becomes less and less. Parents also vary. Some call more often than others, and feel rejected as their child calls less often. Remember, the normal child is trying to become independent. As the child makes friends, he or she doesn't *love* you less, the child *needs* you less. The child begins to develop friends and grows very close to them as he or she reaches the next stage of life.

Recommendations:
1. Get assistance from public schools or private help from college placement specialists. Make sure your child has adequate information about what is available.
2. Take your cues from your child about how often to call. This way, you will not let your anxiety spill over to your child.

How do you know if you should help your child with homework?

The purpose of homework. Theoretically, homework helps the child reinforce what he or she learns in school and teaches the child to work independently. Some teachers believe that children must do their own homework, so the teacher can see what the child can do independently. Some teachers want parents to help, especially if the child needs help to complete the work. Unless parents contact their child's teacher, the purpose of the homework may be unclear.

The role of the parent. The role of the parent is twofold. First, the parent should support the teacher's purpose for homework. The teacher will guide you regarding how much to help. Second, the parent should determine if the child is functioning well under the homework system. This can sometimes be tricky.

Determining how well your child is doing. Here are some things you can do:
1. Call the teacher and ask if your child completes and turns in all of his or her homework on time.
2. Check progress reports or report cards for "cooperation" or "work habits." Any low marks in these areas usually indicate incomplete or late assignments.
3. Low test scores, and especially inconsistent test scores (low, high, low), usually indicate poor preparation, which is often the result of inadequate homework habits.

Determining where the problem lies. If the child is functioning well under the system, then simply continue doing whatever it is you have been doing. If, on the other hand, the child is not doing well, you will have to determine the following:

1. Is the child capable of the work and able to work independently, but not applying himself or herself?
2. Is the child able to work independently, but not understanding the work?
3. Does the child understand the work, but is unable to work independently?
4. Does the child neither understand the work nor is able to work independently?

To determine if the work is too hard, take one evening and ask the child to bring home all of his or her books. Ask the child to read aloud one or two paragraphs from each book. If the child can pronounce eight out of ten words easily and knows the meaning of those words, he or she is at a good reading level. Let the child read a page or two silently, then ask him or her five comprehension questions about the material. If the child can answer at least four out of the five questions, the material is at the right level for him or her. If the child's performance falls below this standard, the material may be too difficult, which will mean more effort on his or her part. More effort may require more motivation or more help. If the child scores above this level, the material may be too easy and perhaps too boring. The same applies for math. Have the child do five math problems. If the child can do them without any help from you, he or she gets at least four out of five right, the child is working at the right level.

To determine if the child can work independently, ask the child to do his or her normal homework within your view, but not with you sitting right next to him or her. Make sure the child has enough work to keep busy for twenty minutes. Use your watch or a clock to keep time. Get a piece of paper and a pencil. Observe the child every two minutes exactly, and place a (+) sign if the child is on task and a (-) sign if the child is off task. Off task means the child's eyes are wandering, or the child is doing something to distract from the work. At the end of twenty minutes, you should have ten marks. Of the ten marks, the child should have at least seven plus signs. If the child has five or less, it means he or she has some difficulty staying on task.

Now you have determined if the child is capable of doing the work, is motivated, and is able to attend sufficiently to work independently. If there are problems in any of these areas, you can consult other chapters in this book, consult with the child's teacher, or seek outside help.

How much time should my child spend on homework? Current trends seem to be running as follows:

Grades 1 to 3	30 minutes to 1 hour
Grades 4 to 6	1 to 2 hours
Grades 7 to 8	2 to 3 hours
Grades 9 to 12	2 to 4 hours

If the child spends less than the minimum amount of time, and he or she gets excellent grades, count your blessings. If the child spends more than the maximum amount of time, determine if your child is highly motivated to learn or if he or she is having a great deal of difficulty with the work. You will know because the child will complain a lot. Either the work is too difficult, or the child is distractable. In either case, the child may need your help. Give the child sufficient help so that he or she can complete homework within an average amount of time. Remember, if you make it pleasant, the child will accept the help.

The dangers of helping too much. It is generally a good idea to establish a regular study period, every school night, regardless of whether the child has homework. You should make it as consistent as possible, and start it in the first grade. If you do this, the child will develop a powerful tool that can last a lifetime. If the child doesn't have homework or finishes early, have him or her use the time to review, prepare, do extra credit, or pursue a personal area of interest. If you can model a study time by having the whole household do some kind of quiet activity, you can strengthen the habit. It may take one or two years of enforcing this behavior before it becomes ingrained in the child's behavior. You will also get less resistance as the child gets into more difficult homework.

Some traps to avoid. The You Do It trap. Here, children do not want help with problem solving, they want their parents to do the work.

The Grandiose trap. Here, the child embarks on a project that is clearly

beyond the child's capabilities and time limits.

What to do when the homework is too much. When the work load is too heavy, consult with the teacher. If you get no help from the teacher, then your child may simply have to work a little harder, or you may be able to help the child with some of the work. Sometimes, if the work is completely unreasonable and the teacher is unwilling to compromise, you or a tutor may be able to help research or summarize some of the material. However, the child has to be able to get the necessary information, understand it, and repeat it on a test, if necessary.

Recommendations:
1. Allow your child to do homework alone unless he or she needs help.
2. Make sure your child is spending the minimum time mentioned doing homework and reviewing.
3. Homework is the child's responsibility, not the parent's. Make sure you do not take over the problem as your own.

How do you know how to help your child develop study skills?

The benefits of early training. From infancy onward, anything you do consistently will enhance your child's study skills. Helping a child make transitions, such as getting up in the morning, going to bed at regular times, learning how to brush his or her teeth, taking a bath, doing chores, and so on, all help to build good study skills. Doing a set activity at a certain time each day sets the basis for good study habits.

Here are some basic skills that have to be learned:

- **Previewing.** Before starting any activity, take a few minutes to overview what has to be accomplished. If it's math, see what problems have to be solved. What is the paper supposed to look like when it is done? What kind of problems are involved? What materials do you need to do the job? How long will it take to complete? Whether doing the dishes, cleaning a room, mowing the lawn, or fixing a bicycle, if you see the end before you begin, it can keep you on track.

- **Getting started** is often the hardest part of studying. Some people like to start at the beginning and progress in a logical order, taking things in sequence. You can start with the hardest, the easiest, the shortest, the longest, the most interesting, the least interesting, the middle, or the end. It probably doesn't make much difference as long as you find out what works best for your child. Most children don't know they have that many options. You may have to experi-

ment for the child to become convinced of what works best. "Best" is defined by a combination of speed and accuracy. If either one is sacrificed too much, studying won't be effective.

- **Sustaining concentration and attention.** This is a discipline that usually comes with practice, lots of practice. For children younger than seven, fifteen to twenty minutes may be the longest they can hold their attention on a particular task. For older children thirty to ninety minutes or more, depending on their age, is the usual attention span. An undisciplined or highly distractable older child may only be able to handle twenty-minute study intervals, with a five-minute distraction. By taking short breaks, some children can attend to a task for longer periods. For some kids, having an adult supervisor or a peer study with them helps them concentrate and keep their attention focused. For others, it provides a distraction. You will have to see what works best for your child.

- **Providing the right environment** is crucial for many kids. A well-lit, quiet room, free of distractions, with fresh air is highly beneficial for most kids. Some children, especially some teenagers, like to have background music when they study because it helps them concentrate and keeps their energy up. For some, the music acts as "white noise," which they actively use to block out, thereby forcing themselves to concentrate. You might try a study period with and without music to determine if music helps or hinders your child's study habit.

You should consider your child's internal environment. On the physical level, the child shouldn't be too tired, too hungry, or too full. On the emotional level, the child should not be concerned with personal, family, or social issues while he or she is studying. If you think these issues are interfering, listen to your child's concerns before he or she begins to study. This may take an hour or more. (pages 181-85 for more information on communicating with children.)

- **Reviewing** is possibly the final basic step in developing good study skills. For the child who chooses speed over accuracy, reviewing can be excruciatingly painful. When children are done studying, they feel they are done. Reviewing helps pick up any errors that might have occurred, and also helps commit information to memory. After all, this is where we want the information.

Recommendations: It takes time to learn study skills; be aware of your frustration over your child's slow development of these skills.

How do you know when to intervene with teachers at school?

All children may have problems at school. The question often comes up for parents about whether to let a child solve his or her own problems at school, or to set up a meeting with the teacher. Knowing when to step in or to let the child deal with a problem can sometimes be a delicate issue.

The risks of intervening too soon.
- The child becomes dependent on the parent's strength and doesn't learn how to express his or her needs to an authority figure.
- The child doesn't develop the internal coping mechanisms necessary to deal with a difficult situation.
- The child becomes embarrassed by the parent's action.
- The teacher begins to view the parent as overprotective and may subsequently develop negative attitudes toward the parent or the child.

The risks of intervening too late.
- The child suffers or fails unnecessarily.
- The child feels unsupported and develops negative behaviors as a result.

How to determine when and when not to intervene. Because every child and every teacher is different, what you do one year may be different than what you do another year. Some teachers welcome parental input, others do not. Sometimes a teacher may have one attitude and a principal may have another, which means you may have to deal with both.

Communication is the shortest and easiest route to find out what is best. Meetings with the teacher either before school begins or within the first few weeks of school are common in most schools. This is a good time to share your concerns and raise any questions you might have. The teachers are prepared to listen at this time. Some teachers need the first few weeks to get into a routine and to get to know your child a little bit. *At this time, you should ask the teacher how he or she best likes to communicate should you have any questions down the road. Does the teacher prefer a phone call, a note sent to school with your child, or a personal meeting? Most teachers have a definite preference.*

The approach. The way you approach your child's teacher may hold the key to success or failure. If your child tells you that the teacher is unfair, or that other children are bullying him or her, or that there is some other problem that has to be resolved, how you approach the teacher may greatly influence the outcome. People do not like to be confronted or attacked. To approach the teacher and say, My child says you are unfair, or some equivalent, may not help resolve the problem. Rather, to approach the teacher with, My child has a problem. Can you help us solve this problem? may work better.

When you meet with the teacher, express your desire to do what's best for your child. Ask the teacher for his or her opinion about what your child needs and how you can assist in that effort. Remember, the teacher will want to do what he or she thinks is best for your child, too. If you suggest that the teacher should change his or her way of dealing with your child, you will most likely create an opponent rather than an ally. You may have better luck reassuring the teacher that the two of you are headed toward the same goal—namely, the education of your child—and giving the teacher some examples of what has worked well with your child in the past. You might ask why your child did so well in a specific class. Also, be prepared to hear some negative information, without reacting defensively. Remember, you are there to listen as well as to speak.

If this approach does not work, you at least get to hear the teacher's side of the story, which is sometimes helpful in clarifying why your child is having a problem. You should only become forceful in first asking for a change if it is clear to you that the teacher is being unfair. If this second approach is not successful, there may be other avenues to a solution, such as talking to other parents with similar problems and then setting up a meeting with the principal. A parent representing a significant number of other parents with a complaint is in a far stronger position to bring about changes.

In many cases, it is a good idea before you intervene to ask your child whether he or she wants your assistance. Sometimes children past the fourth grade will complain, but they really don't want their parents to solve the problem. You can reassure yourself that the child is OK if the child can give you some ideas about how he or she plans to deal with the problem. However, as the parent, you should make the final decision.

When should you definitely get involved?

- When your child's physical safety is at stake.
- When your child is continually harassed and you've tried working with him or her on it at home and there is no progress.
- When your child refuses to go to school.
- When there is a drastic change in your child's performance or attitude from the previous years.

Learning from the situation. After the situation is resolved, parents should talk to their child about what happened. Let the child review what happened and how the problem was resolved. This then becomes a teaching situation for the child. He or she learns how to deal with this kind of problem. The child may learn something about how to work with a teacher or person in authority or about how to solve a problem with another child. You, as

parent, also learn how to deal with your child more effectively. You may also teach your child's teacher that you are an interested and involved parent who is willing to spend the time to help your child.

Recommendations:

1. It is never wrong to ask a teacher about your child. To ensure the teacher's cooperation, make sure your approach is not a hostile one.
2. If you are unhappy with the teacher's response, discuss the problem with the principal.
3. If you feel the situation is out of control and your teacher and principal are not helpful, you may get some assistance by contacting the school district or a child advocate.

How do you know if you should volunteer in your child's classroom?

One of the first questions you should ask yourself is, Will my child benefit from my presence in the classroom? If the answer to that question is no, then you should not volunteer. If your child would like you there, and/or need you there, and if the teacher approves, then you should volunteer. We assume you have the time and interest to do so.

How do I know if I shouldn't volunteer?

- If the child directly requests that you not volunteer because he or she feels embarrassed (feels like a baby in front of friends or is worried other kids will make fun of him or her) or the child feels inhibited (is afraid of taking risks, failing, and looking bad in front of the parent).
- If the teacher doesn't want you there. We want to lighten a teacher's load, not add to it.
- If after trying it for a few days or weeks, you notice a drop in your child's performance or attitude. If this happens, you should ask the child directly whether your presence is the cause.
- If it means more to you than to your child. You may have trouble separating from your child or giving up control to the teacher. Ask the teacher, your friends, or your spouse. They'll tell you.

How do I know if I should volunteer?

- The child asks you to be there, and the teacher thinks it is a great idea.
- The child needs the extra academic help and will accept it from you.
- The child needs additional behavioral supervision, and the teacher likes having you there. Remember, the teacher is the boss. You take directions from him or her.

Recommendations:

1. Before you volunteer, consider whether or not you are the kind of person who is willing to take directions from the teacher.
2. Before you volunteer, consider whether or not your child will benefit.

How do you know when is the best time to move when your children are in school?

Sometimes moving can be a problem. For a family, moving is one of the most disruptive and upsetting phenomena there is. The accumulation of sometimes years of possessions, the packing, the arrangements, the search for a new home, the enrollment in a new school for the children, and so on, can be overwhelming. When you add to this the psychological and educational needs of your children, the potential for stress is enormous.

What does the move mean to you and to your child? Sometimes parents look forward to a move with joy and excitement for a new beginning. Sometimes, however, the focus is on losing old friends and acquaintances and looking anxiously to the unknown. These feelings communicate to your child, and you should deal with them. How does the child look at the move? What does the move mean to the child? Is the child's reaction one of depression or sadness, or does the child look forward to the move? Is the child giving up old friends that he or she will miss terribly, or is the child looking forward to new situations and new friends?

Decide when it is a good time to move. Families move often to better their economic condition or to hold onto a good job. This means that one person, often the father, is going to work in a different city. If it can be arranged, summer vacation is usually the best time to move. Friends may also move during the summer. Friends may go away on summer vacations. Children expect change during the summer, and a switch to a new school is the least stressful change possible. If the move is calculated close to the summer, it is best to wait to move the entire family, even if one parent has to move one or two months ahead of the rest. The next best time to move is between two semesters. In this way, the child does not lose any time in school. Specific subjects usually begin and end within each semester. A third possibility is to move over the extended Christmas vacation. This break is usually a two-week vacation, and a move during this time may be less disruptive than at other times of the school year.

Consider your child's age when you decide to move. A move can be less stressful if parents take the time to discuss moving with their children. Talking about feelings may help par-

ents clarify what they should do. Clearly, a young child may make a move with less distress than an adolescent who has many ties to the community. If you have to move during your child's high school years, do not move during the last two years if possible. This is an important time for most teens.

Are there other solutions to the problem? Other arrangements can sometimes be made if a family has to move during the school year. Sometimes, a child can stay with grandparents, other family, or close friends for a few months until a semester is over. These arrangements may help overcome a child's negative feelings toward a move.

Recommendations: Discuss any possible move with your child. Your child's reaction should tell you how much emotional disturbance there will be.

How do you know what to do if your child is being teased or bullied?

The results of being teased or bullied can be severe. Some children are harassed in school by other children or groups of children. Some children seem to sense vulnerability in others, and they pick on those children. The question is, when is it appropriate for the parent to take action? Not all children tell their parents when they are bullied. They (particularly young boys) feel that such a declaration is not acceptable. Other children do tell their parents, but then stop telling them when parents do nothing about it. The teasing or bullying may be occasional or often. It may be mild or severe. The result of teasing and bullying sometimes is only mildly disruptive, but other times it leads to severe consequences, such as suicide in children. Parents have to evaluate how severe the impact is on their child, and this is sometimes difficult to do. Fathers, in particular, who want their sons to be manly and stand up for themselves often ignore reports of being bullied.

You need to know how socially developed your child is. Teasing probably is prevalent in all grades, even kindergarten. However, teasing and bullying begins in earnest around the third grade and increases steadily until it peaks in sixth through tenth grade. After tenth grade, children begin to gain some maturity and realize when teasing is inappropriate.

For boys, most teasing has to do with pointing out some weakness—real or imagined—to which they are vulnerable. They could be teased about being too short, too tall, too fat, too skinny, too weak, too babyish, too dumb, or too uncoordinated. They may also be teased about red hair, freckles, big ears,

big nose, braces, glasses, or having a name that rhymes in an unflattering way. Anything could be used to provoke a response. The teaser usually is trying to gain social dominance.

For girls, teasing is quite different. While girls certainly name-call and ridicule, the main dynamic is who decides who is included or excluded among a group of peers. Gossiping, spreading rumors, or telling outright lies are only a few tricks of the trade. Manipulating and intimidating peers to control friendships is frequent among the power girls. Loyalty and betrayal become key concepts.

Is there a purpose to teasing? Yes. Teasing is designed unconsciously to help children cover their vulnerabilities before they enter adulthood. The only problem is, this vulnerability has to be uncovered later to achieve real intimacy. No vulnerability, no intimacy.

Is the teasing destructive? Yes, especially if it goes too far, or if it lands on a particularly sensitive individual, which it usually does. Too much teasing can weaken an individual and leave scars on a self-image that can remain throughout life. It is important to bring teasing under control.

Things your child can do.
1. Ignore the comments made by certain individuals. What the teaser wants is a big reaction of any kind. If there is no reaction, some people will leave you alone. A big reaction only invites more provocation. This

doesn't work in every case, but it is a good place to start.

2. Walk away from the individual or individuals who are teasing you. If you are on the playground or someplace where you can walk away and join a different group, doing so can sometimes successfully stop the teasing.

3. In a strong voice tell the individual to stop calling you names or to stop doing whatever is offensive. Sometimes even this little bit of resistance is sufficient.

4. Change the subject and engage in play with the person who is teasing you. Sometimes a child teases not to be malicious but simply to get your attention. You might suggest an activity that you both could enjoy, and make a friend out of a potential enemy. Sometimes young boys and girls tease the very children they like.

5. Tell the child who is teasing to stop, and warn the child that if he or she does not stop, you will tell the teacher or yard duty person that he or she is bothering you. You run the risk of being a tattletale, but if you tell a person whom the teaser fears, the teasing they will probably stop.

   When a child goes to an adult to complain about teasing, most adults do very little on the first complaint. The adult either suggests ignoring the child or avoiding the child. If your child, however, goes to an adult after trying several things and says something like, Mrs. Jones, Bobby is teasing me. I tried to

ignore him, but he kept it up. I walked away, but he followed me. I offered to play with him, but he just laughed at me. I warned him I was going to tell you, but he didn't stop. I really need your help, the adult will almost always get involved. With practice, almost any child can learn this, and it will separate serious teasing from not-so-serious teasing.

6. Try teasing the teaser. If you can say something that embarrasses the teaser to a significant degree, he or she may leave you alone. Sometimes you can find the teaser's weakness. While not always recommended (it can escalate teasing to a physical level), it does work on many occasions.

7. Perhaps the most effective way to deal with teasing is to *make it funny.* When you make it funny, the positive attention goes to you without directly embarrassing the teaser. This method doesn't usually escalate the problem. What the teaser discovers rather quickly is that he or she is helping you become more popular. It is very effective. Comments like, I know you are, but what am I? repeated after each insult only frustrates the teaser. If a teaser calls you stupid and you then act like a stupid person in a funny way, the teaser may not get the desired result. When a teaser does not get the desired result, he or she finds other kids to pick on.

8. If your child has tried the previous seven steps with no success (trying

them will make your child stronger) then it may be time for you to step in and either talk with the teacher, the principal, or, if necessary, with the parents of the offending child. Sometimes the other child's parents are not aware that their child is a bully. However, don't be surprised if you run into another bully, only in adult form.

How to help your child who has a problem with fighting. Many teachers and parents make a conscious or unconscious distinction between verbal fighting and physical fighting. Verbal fighting may not get you into trouble in school, but physical fighting certainly will. It is important to teach children that there is a significant difference. While it is effective in the short run for a child to respond physically to a verbal insult, it only hinders the child in the long run. However, if the other child initiates a physical confrontation, it can be effective to respond physically, although not always.

Enrolling more sensitive children in a physical sport such as karate can give them physical confidence (especially during grade school). Sports focus on self-control. There is a good deal of peer support to ignore teasing, and the child will feel good about himself or herself in the process.

Recommendations:
1. Make sure your involvement does not make the situation worse for your child.
2. Try to get your child to agree to your plan, so that he or she is forewarned.

SOCIAL DEVELOPMENT

How do you know if your child has the right friends?

How children pick friends. Children usually pick friends in one of two categories: similar or different. Children choose friends who are very similar to reinforce who they are, build their confidence, and make them feel secure. When children choose friends who are very different, they want to learn new behaviors and develop new skills. These friends often stretch and test a child's viewpoint, values, etc. A child may not feel as secure with these friends, but he or she may feel more excited.

Oftentimes, children will pick friends from both groups, although the two groups don't usually get along with each other. Sometimes children will be drawn to younger children. This is usually a sign that a child is a little immature for his or her age or that the child needs to feel superiority in a relationship. Just like adults, children strive to balance power with love, independence with security, and excitement with predictability. Friends become a major avenue for learning and support.

Why children pick the friends they do. To determine whether your child has the "right" friends, you have to know what your child needs. You can determine what your child needs by the friends he or she chooses. If your child is weak, he or she may choose strong friends. If your child comes from a restrictive home, he or she may find friends that come from a different environment. Take a moment to examine the personalities of your child's friends. Ask yourself, What's attractive about so and so? Why would my son or daughter be drawn to this child? Oftentimes, a child will seek out another child with very different

147

moral, ethical, social, or religious values. Try to see what your child needs, and see if that quality can be integrated into the family. This will often reduce the child's need to go outside the family to get it. Is your family too loose? Is it too formal? Is it too rebellious? Is it too conforming? Is it oriented too tightly to achievement? Is the child seeking greater connectedness, or is the child seeking greater power and control?

Oftentimes the friends will offer certain qualities, but in an unbalanced form, and this is what usually worries parents. See if you, as a family, can offer the same quality of energy, but in a more mature and balanced form.

Preventing problems. There is a trap that parents have to avoid. Although we are talking about your child, this child spends many hours a day away from you. As the child grows older, it is more and more difficulty to decide whom he or she should have as friends. Those parents who try to use a heavy hand—especially with adolescents—and forbid association with other children stand a chance of both failing and reducing their credibility with their children. There are better ways to deal with the problem, such as getting the child interested in new activities that do not involve these friends, etc.

Recommendations:

1. Children change friends very quickly. Do not get discouraged if your child does not want to play with the friends that you have chosen.

2. As your child gets older, he or she increasingly resists parents' help in choosing friends. You may only be able to arrange situations and introductions.

How do you know how to help your child make friends?

Does your child have enough friends? The personalities of children, like adults, differ dramatically. As adults, we can be very social or tend to stay alone with few friends. However, children require social activity for their development. They learn by observation. They learn by copying others' behavior. They need the social interaction to develop. Since we live in a society that thrives on both cooperation and competition, children must learn these skills at an early age. A good way for parents to decide if their child has enough friends is to compare their child's socialization skills with others of the same age. From a young age we can see whether a child is sought out by other children or whether the child is a loner.

How do you know if your child feels socially unaccepted? Children will let you know how they feel through their behavior. The child who feels rejected by others will usually play alone. The child may give up trying to join social groups, such as playing with other children at recess or after school, or going to school socials if the child is older. There is a feeling of sadness or mild depression about these children. They usually resist parents' attempts to help them socialize, although they desperately need help.

On the other hand, the child who is socially accepted is regularly asked to play by other children.

What can you do to help your child socially? When parents observe that their child tends to be less social and more alone than they should, there are a number of interventions they can make. Children can be gently pushed to join groups for special purposes, such as karate classes, music or art classes, social dancing classes, etc. They can be urged to join such groups as Boy Scouts or Girl Scouts. They can be urged to join religious social groups of their own faith. They can be urged to join special interest groups, such as computer clubs, stamp clubs, etc. They can be urged to join sports clubs for soccer, hockey, tennis, etc. Parents can urge children to invite other children to their home for sleep overs, or let their children go to other children's homes.

Check on your child at different ages. Clearly, the approach you use depends on the age and personality of the child. The child who has one or two good friends may be very happy and fulfilled socially. Other children have many friends, but no one particularly close. Most children have at least one best friend. If you can say that your child is very happy and has some friends, there may be no reason to worry.

Recommendations:
1. Encourage, but do not force friends on your child.
2. If your child has no friends and complains about it, you may need to find a child counselor.

How do you know if your child is socially mature or immature?

What is maturity? Maturity refers to the child's age-appropriate development and the child's ability to take age-appropriate responsibility. We say a child is mature when the child acts his or her age. Although this idea sounds fine, all of us—child and adult alike—vary in our maturity level. The child who likes to play games may be a normal, mature child. The adult who plays games excessively may be immature. The second measure, responsibility, is a good way to check on the first description. If the child or adult completes all the work for which he or she is responsible, he or she may elect to play or relax for the balance of the day, and that behavior is not considered immature.

How does immaturity show itself? The child shows immaturity in social situations in two ways. The child may decide to play only with younger children. The child may not be able to maintain a relationship with age-appropriate or same-age children. The socially mature child chooses friends of about the same age. Some may be older and some younger, but most will be about the same age when possible. Secondly, the mature child chooses activities that are appropriate for his or her age. Although we may all at times play games or exhibit behavior that is typical of a younger age, the majority of what we do is age appropriate.

How do you prevent immaturity from becoming a problem? You can help your child develop an appropriate maturity level in several ways. First, see how your child compares to other children of the same age. Does your child fit in? Does your child like to play the same games these children do, or does your child play games typical of younger children? If your child plays with younger children, is it by choice or by circumstance? That is, does your child have the availability of children the same age? If not, then you, as parent, may be able to help.

Remember, we all regress as adults and children at times. We may play baseball as a child, but we may also enjoy it as an adult. Maturity depends

not on one bit of behavior, but on the overall behavior an individual shows.

Recommendations: The more social events your child attends with children of the same age, the faster socialization skills will improve. Look for social situations your child may be interested in, for example, Boy Scouts, Girl Scouts, clubs, or athletic activities.

How do you know if your child is overly shy or overly aggressive?

What does it mean to be overly shy? Most children have one or more friends and can enjoy being both alone and with a group. There are children that avoid most social contacts. These children may only want to spend time with themselves or a few select people, and they cannot seem to relate to others in a social situation. They may stay alone, on the sidelines at a party or a dance. They may not be able to have a conversation if someone talks to them. They seem to be painfully alone and at times lonely. We are not talking about the child who prefers to be alone most of the time, but one who cannot relate easily and comfortably when he or she prefers. We are talking about the child who lacks social skills and who seems painfully afraid to relate to others.

What does it mean to be socially aggressive? The previous picture is in contrast to the child who hates to be alone. A socially aggressive child only likes to be with others. The child is often socially assertive, aggressive, and controlling. Often this child is not aware of his or her impact on others. The child may dominate social situations, and may, at times, be rejected by others because of this attempt to control.

How children show social unease. While no judgment is made on the preference to be alone or with others, it is important that children have the social skills necessary to function in our complex society. When they do not, children tend to display some exaggerated behavior that shows they feel uncomfortable. Children can become very quiet and withdrawn. They can show their discomfort by their inability to communicate and their withdrawal in a group where all others are participating. Another child may be loud and attention-seeking, to the detriment of the group function, as a way of showing unease.

What can you do to prevent this problem? From a very young age, a child's social development is under parental control. The most important step a parent can take is to let a child play with other children. The more a child plays with other children, the

more socialization skills are learned. This may be before nursery school. It may involve playing on the playground, or it may be pushing a child to join social groups, such as church or temple groups, Boy Scouts or Girls Scouts, or sports groups. What is important is that you, as parent, feel your child can function with children of the same age, as well as younger and older children.

Recommendations:
1. Children learn appropriate behavior in social situations. Have your child interact as much as possible in social groups, such as clubs, athletic activities, and so on.
2. Give the aggressive child an outlet such as athletics or karate.

How do you know if your child is socially overextended?

How does being socially overextended show itself? Parents sometimes have difficulty understanding how much time their child should spend with friends. With younger children, it is easier for parents to control social relationships. If a child makes too many appointments, it shows up in possible school problems, and with the child constantly asking to be driven places. With teenagers and even ten- and eleven-year-olds, social overextension often shows itself by constant overuse of the phone and preoccupation with friends and social events.

The behavior of social overextension. Although having friends and a good social life is essential to a child's mental health, there are excessive behaviors that lead to other problems in the child's life. It is the clear preoccupation with social activities to the detriment of other activities that creates problems. The urge to be accepted as part of a group or groups is normal. Satisfying that urge to the extent it interferes with family functioning or school functioning clearly becomes a problem.

Preventing and correcting social overextension. When parents become aware that a child's social life is becoming a problem, some action must be taken. Ideally, you can discuss the problem with the child and look forward to some changes. Some children are almost mesmerized by the phone, and see it as an essential part of their daily life for hours every afternoon and evening. If requests do not work, then parents must take more direct action and either limit phone time or remove the phone entirely. If a child is involved in too many activities, then the parent must act to limit those activities. This is often a painful process for the child and the parent; however, some balance of the child's time must be made.

Recommendations:
1. Limit the days your child can socialize, if there is too much going on.
2. Limit time for phone contacts if the child spends too much time on it.
3. Set up schedules for homework and other activities so the child's time is taken up by more solitary activities.

EMOTIONAL DEVELOPMENT

How do you know if your child has an emotional problem?

What is an emotional problem? An emotional problem is basically some unresolved feeling that leads to useless or destructive behavior.

All of us have emotional problems from time to time. The difference is with normal support most of us solve these problems and return to our normal level of functioning.

An emotional problem becomes more serious when it interrupts our capacity for work, school, or relationships. The longer and more severe the interruption, the more serious the emotional problem.

How does a child show emotional distress? Children show emotional problems either through the expression or repression of certain feelings or behavior.

Feelings. An emotionally healthy child is able to express fear, anger, hurt, guilt, and happiness, and love at the appropriate times. This means they have access to a full range of emotions that enable them to communicate with adults. A healthy child has a relative balance of these emotions. In other words, a child may get angry, express it, and get over it. A sad child may cry, be comforted, and get over it. A fearful child may be reassured and regain confidence. Any child who frequently and consistently stays in one emotional area may be demonstrating an emotional problem.

A child who seems to be angry about everything; a child who is afraid of everything; a child who gets hurt at the slightest incident; or a child who feels guilty for no real reason shows signs of emotional imbalance. A child who is always unrealistically happy or loving is also a child with an emotional imbalance.

In the reverse, any child who completely closes off a particular emotional area over a prolonged period of time may indicate an emotional problem. A child who never shows fear, even when it is appropriate, anger, guilt, hurt, or affection is not balanced emotionally, and is limiting his or her ability to communicate effectively.

Behavior. The clearest sign of a developing emotional problem is a change in the child's behavior. Some children hide their feelings, or sometimes parents are too busy to notice the child's feelings, in which case the child's emotional problem may transfer into the child's behavior. These changes may show in the following areas of home, school, and with friends:

- Changes in sleeping habits. Sleeping a lot more or a lot less. Difficulty going to sleep. Restless sleep. Nightmares. Using sleep to avoid responsibilities.
- Changes in appetite. Eating too much. Eating too little. Excessive, unexplained weight loss or gain. Eating alone rather than with the family. Eating only unusual foods.
- Changes in health. Increased and unexplained medical problems. Frequent accidents.
- Changes in personal hygiene and dress. Dressing in an unusual manner, along with neglecting cleanliness.
- Changes in personality. Excessive anger, depression, anxiety. Sudden mood swings, irritability, explosive behavior. Preoccupation with one particular idea or behavior. Lying or stealing.
- Changes in time spent with the family. Withdrawal from family members, isolation, violation of family rules.
- Changes in school behavior. Skipping school. Failing grades. Learning difficulties. Disciplinary problems in school.
- Changes in social relationships. Withdrawal from previous social relationships at school, church, or other group. Changing friends. Giving up all current friends. Getting new, but unsatisfactory, friends.
- Changes in attitudes toward life, *e.g.,* life is meaningless, why go on? What does it all mean? Excessive reactions to changes in life, such as family moving or some family crisis.
- Enough changes in the child that parents feel uneasy or friends ask what's going on with the child.

What can parents do about the child's emotional distress? If you think your child has an emotional problem, you might try some of the following:

1. Set aside a time and place where neither you nor your child is likely to be interrupted.
2. Tell the child that you are concerned about some of his or her behavior, for example, I've noticed that you've been really angry a lot lately.
3. Reassure the child that you care about him or her and that he or she is safe with you, for example, I real-

ly care about you and you won't be in trouble by talking with me.

4. Ask the child to give you some specific information, *e.g.*, Tell me some things you've been angry about lately. (Substitute afraid, disappointed, sad, annoyed, guilty, or whatever you think the child has been feeling.) Also, ask the child what things have gone well lately, or what he or she is happy about.

5. If the child doesn't want to tell you what's wrong right away, it's because the child doesn't trust that he or she will be OK if he or she tells you. Ask the child if there is something bothering him or her that he or she just wants to keep private? If you get a "yes" on this one, ask the child why he or she is afraid to tell you. If the child says he or she is afraid of punishment, or that you'll get mad, you can tell the child that it is better if he or she tells you, than if you find it out for yourself.

   If you get a "no," reassure the child that you care about him or her and remind the child that if something is wrong you would prefer to hear it directly from him or her rather than from some other source.

6. After this conversation, see if the child's behavior or feelings begin to return to normal in the next few days.

7. If you have no luck with a conversation, you might ask some of the child's friends, siblings, or teachers if they have noticed a difference in your child. You might also ask if they have any idea what the problem is. Usually one of the child's friends will know, or at least confirm, that the child is having difficulties.

8. If you have no luck at all and the condition persists, you should contact a psychologist or therapist in your area.

Recommendations:

1. The most important skills a parent can use with their children are listening to the child and observing their child's behavior.

2. All emotional problems have a direction. They either are getting better or worse. If your child's behavior is worsening, seek professional help.

How do you know if your child is overanxious?

What is anxiety? Anxiety, or fear, is one of the few basic feelings that all of us experience on a daily basis. In smaller amounts anxiety might appear as tension in trying to get everything done on time, or worrying that things will not work out according to plan. In moderate amounts—which is healthy—anxiety might express itself as caution, reserve, concern, etc. We become overly anxious when our fear seems out of line with the cause of that fear, or when the fear is based on some irrational or unrealistic belief.

Sometimes children worry too much about their performance, their looks, or their acceptance. Sometimes children worry about their parents dying, about being alone, or being hurt. Sometimes children are afraid of monsters and the dark. All of these, to some extent, are normal fears that are overcome as the child gains self-confidence. In this age of anxiety, parents have to know that both their children's anxiety and their own anxiety may be perfectly normal, if it is not persistent.

Symptoms of anxiety. Anxiety shows itself in a number of ways in both children and adults.

Muscle or Motor Tension.

- Tension in our muscles, which may show as trembling, twitching, or feeling shaky.
- Feeling restless and unable to settle down and do your work.
- Feeling tired when there is no obvious reason to be tired.

Internal Feelings.

- Feeling short of breath, smothered, or that your heart is beating too fast.
- Having dry mouth, feeling dizzy or lightheaded, having trouble swallowing or feeling a lump in your throat.
- Feelings of nausea, diarrhea, or other stomach upset; experiencing hot flashes or chills.
- Urinating more often than usual.

Exaggerated Feelings of Awareness.

- Feeling keyed up or on edge, feeling irritable, being excessively startled by sounds.
- Difficulty concentrating, as in school. Having your mind "go blank" on tests.
- Difficulty falling asleep or staying asleep; being excessively irritable.

What parents can do about persistent anxiety. If at least six of these symptoms are often present for six months or more, then parents should seek professional help to deal with a serious anxiety problem. Some children seem to be more chronically fearful or anxious than others. Parents can assist their children by giving them additional encouragement and security. Some children need help to get over their initial fear, then they do well, as in going to camp for the first time, joining a soccer team, or taking music lessons. Going to school for the first time is a typical event in which children and parents feel anxious, both from the separation and the new situation.

One of the first places children look for encouragement and security is from their parents. Where there is an overanxious child, you probably will find an overanxious parent. Is this the case with you? If it is, then you must get your anxiety under control before you can help your child. Whenever possible, have the relaxed parent deal with the anxious child. When a child is fearful, he or she looks to the parent for both confidence and protection. If a parent is anxious, it reinforces fear in the child. There are many times as a parent when we are afraid or unsure of what to do, but it is important to reassure any children in your presence. The younger the child, usually the more reassurance he or she needs. It is important to remember that even older children, who may appear to have an air of confidence, need reassurance.

Firm, warm, and consistent structure is usually the best approach for an anxious child. These children need predictability in their lives. Anything you can do to create this predictability, through preparation and rehearsal, benefits the child.

Recommendations: If you are an anxious parent with an anxious child, and you do not have a relaxed, available spouse, you may have to rely on a friend or relative to help you and your child over certain obstacles. An anxious parent only makes an anxious child worse. A word of advice, get some professional help for yourself, your child, or both of you. It will save you a lot of grief later.

How do you know if your child is depressed?

What is depression and how does it show itself? Depression is a psychological disorder that shows itself in children in a number of ways, such as an irritable mood that persists throughout the day and for at least a year. In contrast, we all feel depressed, or down, at various times in our life for good and sufficient reasons. These feelings of depression may last minutes, hours, or days, but we soon recover from them. Children who are depressed or "dysthymic" may show us how they feel by exhibiting several symptoms.

Symptoms of depression.

- Depressed children may show a disturbance in how they eat, either by losing their appetite or by overeating, with a subsequent change in weight. This change may require some medical assistance.
- There may be a change in how your child sleeps. The child may have trouble going to sleep, or difficulty waking up in the morning. The child may sleep too little or too much, and this change persists.
- Some children show low energy and seem tired all the time, even though they appear to get enough sleep.
- The child may show low self-esteem. The child may put himself or herself down, or not try because he or she expects to fail. The child may compare himself or herself unfavorably to others.
- The child may demonstrate poor concentration in school or at home, and may have difficulty making decisions about how to spend his or her time.
- The child may demonstrate feelings

of hopelessness about the future or about trying anything new in life. The child may act as if he or she has given up totally.

If your child shows at least two of these symptoms for a year or more, then he or she is definitely depressed and is in need of psychological assistance.

What can you do about it? Because depression takes many forms, it is at times difficult for parents to help their children. If the child seems sad, withdrawn, argumentative, and unwilling to talk, parents may have difficulty opening up a dialogue. If you ask such a child if anything is wrong, if he or she feels depressed, the child may not be able to identify any specific feeling and will say, "No." It may be better to ask a child, What kinds of thing are you worried about today? or What kinds of things are making you angry lately? or What kinds of sad things have happened to you lately? These types of questions tend to elicit more specific answers.

Ask yourself, When did my child's behavior begin to change? If you are not sure, ask your spouse. Ask another child in the family, or one of your child's close friends. You may be able to identify a particular time when things began to change.

Depending on your child's age, pick a time (at least thirty to sixty minutes of uninterrupted time) when you can talk with the child about his or her feelings. Your approach should be caring. You should create a listening attitude of nonjudgment. Allow the child to feel

angry, sad, worried, or guilty, depending on what's behind the depression. Remember, listening is more important than talking or asking questions, and you may need more than one session to get the information you want.

If some talking has been done, then spending more time with the child, making him or her feel more loved and closer to you, may help the child come out of the depression. Also, encourage the child to reengage in activities to help overcome feelings of depression.

Recommendations: If you have made several efforts to find out what is bothering your child and there is no observable change, you might want to take the child for a psychological checkup to get a professional opinion. Sometimes this approach will resolve the problem quickly and efficiently. If the child's depressive feelings are complicated by other psychological problems, such as anxiety, then it is even more important that he or she see a mental health specialist.

How do you know if your child is overwhelmed or suicidal?

How do children become overwhelmed? Any system that carries too much weight will crack at its weakest point. What is your child's weakest point? Does the child's grades start to slip? Does the child start to withdraw? Does the child have more arguments and fights? Do the child's eating or sleeping patterns change? What happens to lots of children from birth through adolescence is that they get sick when they feel overwhelmed. Getting sick or injured takes us out of our daily routine and responsibilities. It may also get us some sympathy or attention. If we do not get sick or injured consciously, then we may do it unconsciously. Older children who are overwhelmed may get into trouble to get attention and, perhaps, get grounded. Getting grounded is a convenient way for some children to take time out from social obligations. As pressure builds, something happens. In certain cases, children, especially adolescents, will even attempt suicide.

How do you know if your child is suicidal? Suicide is one of the major causes of death in adolescence, and younger children can also commit suicide. Although suicide appears to be a sudden, impulsive act, there are usually signs, sometimes for a long period of time, when the child or adolescent is depressed and appears ready to do something drastic. Unfortunately, parents often believe adolescents have no major problems comparable to the problems they have. Whether this is true, children feel as deeply as and become as depressed as grown-ups do.

A child may consider suicide if he or she feels unloved. The child may feel he or she can never satisfy a very demanding parent. The child may feel depressed due to loss of a loved one in the family, or the death of a friend. Sometimes the child is depressed just because a best friend has moved away. The child may feel alone and friendless. The child may say, Nobody loves me, and really mean it.

Beginning in infancy, we all have different developmental tasks to accomplish. As we grow older, these tasks become more complex and difficult. It is fair to say that adolescence holds some of the most difficult tasks to accomplish—that of learning responsibility, learning independence and yet remaining part of a group or groups, such as family and friends. We may remember our first "crush," or falling in love. Although adults smile at children going through this stage, the inevitable end of this kind of relationship can be devastating. Suicide may represent a solution to a situation that is interpreted as intolerable by the child. The adolescent may see no adequate way out or solution to the problem. The child may feel that parents and others couldn't possibly accept him or her as is.

What can parents do? If you notice that your child shows signs of being overwhelmed with life or possibly feeling suicidal you can help. Early detection is always a positive step. If the child begins to be accident prone, shows a poor self-image, seems anxious and disturbed about his or her body or developing sexuality, or becomes depressed, you should note these symptoms. You can help by listening to your child. Sometimes asking questions helps. If you listen often enough, you will know what concerns your child. If this does not work, then you must seek professional psychological help quickly. It is better to have your child evaluated than be too late to help him or her.

Recommendations: It is better to be safe than to suffer the consequences of suicide. If in doubt, contact a child counselor immediately.

How do you know when your child shows signs of being sexually molested?

What does it mean to be molested? In the last few years, child molestation has clearly come to the forefront. Children can be molested physically, emotionally, and/or sexually. By *molested* we usually mean that a child has been approached by either another child, adolescent, or adult, who has touched the child's genitals or made clear, sexual advances toward the child.

These approaches can leave a child devastated, especially as is often true, the molester is a family member or friend whom the child trusted.

What are the symptoms of sexual molestation? Behavior is so variable in our society that we cannot predict with certainty what fears or feelings each molested child will develop. Many molested children become depressed or anxious, or both. Parents have to know what to look for in their own children. Although each child is born with tendencies toward different personality structures, most young children usually present a happy appearance and are active, curious, and friendly. Along the way developmentally, children may develop some short-term fears. For example, they may be afraid of the dark, afraid of some animals, or afraid of natural disasters, such as earthquakes and the like. These are usually short-lived fears that children learn to overcome.

When a child is molested, he or she may exhibit certain signs that suggest the child is in trouble. These may differ for each child, but some universal symptoms exist. In general, question any significant change in the child's behavior. Look specifically for any of the following changes:

- The child may withdraw from friends and family.
- The child may become uncommunicative.
- The child suddenly may not want to be with a particular friend or family member.
- The child may begin to cry more easily, or become moody and clearly depressed.
- The child may become agitated and nervous or very anxious.

- The child's school grades and school performance may suffer, and the child may not want to go to school.

What can parents do about it? Parents face a difficult task. Children may not want to discuss molestation with parents because they are afraid of being punished for doing something wrong, or they are afraid to involve the person who perpetrated the behavior, or they are afraid that the person who molested them will harm them or their parents if they tell someone what happened.

Depending on the child's age and verbal skills, sometimes it is best to simply ask the child what's wrong. If the child who usually communicates openly to a parent suddenly becomes reticent, it is significant. The danger is in interpreting that significance. Our legal system is overwhelmed with molestation cases, which are difficult to prove. However, there are now child abuse phone lines that parents can call to locate agencies that will take care of all the details. It is important to report molestation and prevent the offender from doing it again.

For the child, the proof of molestation is not as important as the acceptance and love he or she receives from the parents. Parents may never learn the actual facts, but they can help the child by being supportive and loving. Many mental health workers who specialize in this area are available should you decide to seek their help.

Recommendations: Even with the best of intentions and awareness, parents may not be able to prevent an incident of molestation from occurring with their child. What is important is that the child get professional help. Too many individuals have carried the memory of molestation with them all of their lives and have never resolved it. The sooner help is given, the sooner the problem can be dealt with, and the child returned to a previous state of mind.

How do you know if your child is on drugs?

What is a drug? One definition of a drug is anything that alters your mood. Does this mean that music, movies, sports, exercise, and food are drugs? What about cigarettes, coffee, and alcohol? Are they drugs? What if we limit our discussion to chemicals that alter our mood? Then certainly coffee, cigarettes, alcohol, marijuana, cocaine, heroin, amphetamines, sedatives, and hallucinogens would all come under that category. For the most part, we are talking about drugs that are classified as *illegal* because of their potential danger to humans: drugs such as marijuana, cocaine, heroin, LSD, mushrooms, and so on. However, there are many variations and new additions to this list on a regular basis.

Why do people take illegal drugs? The basic reason that people take drugs is because they alter their mood, at least for a time, into a perceived better state. People stop taking drugs when the pain of taking the drug is higher than the pleasure of the drug. In working with teenagers who use drugs illegally, experts have found other motivations.

- Some children have hormonal or biochemical imbalances that draw them to certain drugs. A child who is somewhat "hyper" or always rushing may be drawn to a calming drug. A child who feels slow or sluggish might be drawn to a stimulating drug.

- Some children have emotional weaknesses and immaturities. They have emotional pain that drugs help them forget. A shy or insecure child may use drugs to provide a sense of confidence. A lonely child may use drugs to feel more connected to others. A tense child may use drugs to loosen up or relax. Basically, from an emotional standpoint many children use drugs to feel more powerful and connected. As children mature and learn useful ways to manage their feelings, they have less use for drugs.

- Some children use drugs to have new experiences. For them, it is something of an adventure or an experiment. These children have heard of certain "amazing" experiences, and they want to try them for themselves. For these children the use of drugs is like exploring another world or reality. For many of

these children, there isn't a meaningful religious or spiritual alternative in their life.

How can I find out if my child is on drugs?

1. Perhaps one of the first steps is to sit down with your child and ask about his or her feelings and values regarding to drugs. Does the child think some drugs are OK and some are not? Ask your child which, if any, drugs make him or her curious. Ask your child if he or she has tried any drugs or has a desire to try some. You might ask your child how prevalent drug use is in school, or among friends, or at parties. See if you can get an initial picture of the world your child lives in and where your child stands in it. If you can't have this kind of conversation with your child, then you better think of how you can develop a better relationship with your child.

2. If you happen to come across any drugs or drug-related equipment in your child's possession, such as pipes, bottles, cans, seeds, pills, small glass vials, glassine bags, etc., this is a good indication that he or she is involved with drugs. If you are not sure what some of the more frequently used drug paraphernalia looks like, a quick trip to the library, the local public high school, or the local police station will give you all the information you need. Ask and you shall receive!

3. Your child's personality begins to change. Oftentimes, as children

become involved in more frequent drug use, they begin to have mood swings. They become more irritable, more hyper, more lethargic, more paranoid, more withdrawn, more touchy and/or more defensive. Some of this behavior may be a normal part of adolescent growth, but, in combination with other signs, it could also be part of some drug use.

4. Behavior also changes with drug use. Children may sleep more. They may stay out later. Lying and stealing often increase to hide the drug use. Grades or attendance at school slips. The child may drop sports or other outside interests.

5. The child changes friends. The child may shift to a new group of friends. Children who use drugs often lose old friends who are not users and make new friends who are users. As mentioned in other sections, take the time to meet your child's friends.

How can parents help?

1. If you have suspicions, evidence, or direct knowledge of the child doing drugs you have to talk to him or her to find out just what the child's been doing, with whom, where, and for how long. If you're lucky you may get eighty percent of the truth. The child may refuse to talk to you, or the child may open up. You won't know until you try.

2. Some parents restrict their child's activity after discovering some drug use. The parents forbid them to go places after school, in the evenings, or on weekends. Some parents restrict their child's association with certain friends or forbid them to go to certain places where drug use is more prevalent.

3. Some parents take away privileges, such as driving the car, going to concerts and movies, using the telephone, watching television, or listening to the stereo.

4. Some parents take the child to see a counselor who specializes in drug problems, or, if it is serious enough, they enroll the child in a drug rehabilitation program.

What you decide to do about your child's drug use depends on your value system. Some parents suspect that their child is experimenting with drugs or suspect they will and consider that a normal part of growing through adolescence. These parents basically stay out of their child's life and hope the child comes through all right. Some parents took drugs as adolescents and will only get involved if the child gets arrested or if his or her grades drop to alarming levels. It's up to you.

Recommendations: Consult local drug education programs for more information. You can usually find them in the newspaper, the library, the police station, or your public high school.

How do you know if your child is in a gang?

Why would your child join a gang?
Children join gangs for a variety of reasons. For example, to have more friends, to have more power, to be part of the "in group," to protect themselves from other gangs and, to have some control over their lives. Children move into gangs when they feel alienated from their family, their friends, or the adult society at large. Some children move into gangs because their peer group is largely affiliated with gangs, and they have few alternatives. Gangs are attractive if they represent closeness, identity, protection and power for our children. Does my child know I believe in him or her? Am I someone my child can trust? Am I someone my child believes will give him or her a fair hearing? Does my child believe I am someone who can protect him or her? Does my child actually *feel* loved and accepted by me? If you are not sure, you should discuss these questions with your child. If the answers are negative, then you have some work to do. You will have to build a new relationship with that child. As children move through adolescence they often withhold information from parents because they want to be independent and take more control over their lives.

Some signs that your child is moving into a gang.

•   **The child begins to change dress style.** Dress is one way that children show their affiliation. Sometimes it is colors, and sometimes it is the type of clothing. The colors of red, blue, black, and khaki are related to various gangs. Bandannas, hats, jackets, pants, and shoes are frequent identifiers for various gangs. Some children try to emulate gang wear even though they are not actual gang members.

•   **The child changes hair styles.** Hair may be short, or heads may be shaved. Hair can be long or cut into styles, but, currently, many gang members prefer the short look. Hair also might be colored. The more children look like their friends, the more they identify themselves as a group.

•   **The child gets tattoos and body piercing.** These are sometimes part of gang initiation rites. Oftentimes tattoos are on the face or the hand. These are used to signal gang affiliation.

•   **The child exhibits change in attitude, which is usually more defiant.** What is "cool" differs in each gang. Again, attitude is used to show machismo and membership.

•   **The child makes new friends and gives up old friends.** These usually are individuals whom parents do not know or have not met. Sometimes these friends are older. Often, they may be from another school.

- **The child has new hand gestures, handshakes, or hand signals that are exchanged between your child and friends.** A number of gangs have special, sometimes secret, hand signals, which they use to show affiliation.
- **The child has a supply of spray paint cans, large marking pens, drugs and drug paraphernalia.** "Tagging" is a term for writing one's initials on walls, walkways, buildings, and so on, and it is usually part of gang or pregang activities. As children move into gangs, parents may begin to notice some of these materials accumulating in the child's bedroom or car.
- **The child begins to stay out late or stays out all night.** When there is poor adult supervision, or the child is not where the child says he or she will be, there is greater likelihood for getting into trouble. The reason that children do not tell parents where they are going, or lie about where they have been, is because the children know that their parents will not approve. Otherwise, why not tell the truth?
- **The child begins to withdraw from school, family, or work activities.** This behavior indicates that the child is identifying with, or has more interest in, activities that do not mesh with school, family, or work. This is a significant symptom that calls for some direct parental action.

A note of caution. As mentioned, it certainly is possible for children to demonstrate some or all of these behaviors without being a gang member. However, if you see some of these behaviors, it would be wise for you to get more involved in your child's life. You also may have to seek professional help to change your child's behavior.

What can you, as a parent, do? Many parents have mixed feelings about interfering with their adolescent's social life. We want our children to have a sense of freedom and independence while at the same time we want to have some connection with them. Children who are in middle or late adolescence cannot be absolutely controlled, nor can they be abandoned. As parents, we must work to find a solution somewhere between these two extremes. There are some approaches that may work.

1. **At least meet, if not get to know, your child's friends.** Have a party at your house and be present. Ask your child to invite the friends that he or she hangs out with to come over for a barbecue. Take your child and a few friends to a sports event, or on a short vacation. Tell your child you want to meet his or her friends—one at a time, if necessary—before you will feel comfortable letting them go places unsupervised. Gather phone numbers, addresses, and names of the friends' parents.
2. **Make contact with the parents of your child's closest friends.** By

simply introducing yourself to the parents of your child's friends, you open a line of communication that may be needed down the road. Most parents are too shy to do this, but it could be the single best protection you provide for your child. Getting to know the parents of your child's friends will tell you which situations are safer than others. It will tell you who you can rely on for help and who you can't. If parents can work together, they can form a net before the children fall too far. Before contacting the parents of your child's friends reassure you child that you will respect his or her privacy and keep that privacy (except in an emergency), or the child will move further away from you.

Recommendations:
1. Meet your child's friends.
2. Make contact with the parents of your child's friends.
3. Contact your local police agency for information about gangs in your area.

How do you know if your child is gay or lesbian?

Is there a problem? Some parents become terrified or hysterical if they

suspect that their child is gay or lesbian. Other parents feel that they love their children and will accept them no matter what their later sexual orientation. Society seems to be moving toward a more accepting attitude about homosexual lifestyles. Some children clearly make a commitment to a certain lifestyle at a young age. Sexual orientation is often clear by puberty, about twelve or thirteen years of age. Some children do not make a commitment until late in their adolescence, and some even later. As society becomes more accepting it is likely that children who feel ambiguous about their sexual orientation will experiment. More and more children confront the issue of sexual orientation at least by their teens. Most resolve the issue by remaining heterosexual, but a greater number than ever before opt for like-sex, or homosexual, orientation.

How does homosexuality show itself?
The question of homosexuality, be it gay or lesbian, usually comes up when a young boy seems sensitive or effeminate, or when a young girl seems particularly masculine, even though there are many cases in which neither feminine boys nor masculine girls have any homosexual interests. There are also many situations in which very masculine men and very feminine women are homosexual in orientation. The difficulty in discussing this complex area is that many children experiment with gay or lesbian behavior for a short time as they reach adolescence . Parents can do irreparable harm to children by try-

ing to force the issue with threats or punishment of the child.

What causes homosexuality? Is it nature or nurture? Is it biological in origin or is it learned behavior? The answer is unclear. Recent research has focused on a region of the hypothalamus as a possible biological determinate of homosexual attraction. At the moment, there is no clear biological determining factor for sexual orientation. An interest in homosexuality can be psychologically induced in children from households in which the roles of men and women are too narrowly defined and the expression of certain needs and interests is not allowed within the roles. As the child matures or gains distance from the family environment, the child may seek to fulfill the expression of those needs and interests in a same-sex relationship.

Can you prevent homosexuality? Historically and at present so many creative people are homosexual that we must be extremely careful in tampering with nature. Homosexuality like many other human attributes cannot be prevented. It can be pushed to the background by force or social pressure, but at great cost. If this is an issue that causes you, as a parent, pain, you should discuss it with a professional, such as your pediatrician or a clinical psychologist.

Recommendations:
1. Create an environment in which you can discuss the topic.

2. Consult with a professional psychologist or medical doctor if you have questions.

How do you know if your child has a weight problem?

The problem of weight. The simple question of whether your child is too fat, too thin, or just right causes an inordinate amount of confusion and stress in our society. With an abundance of food and drink, we are plagued with poor nutrition, with children eating the wrong foods, and with personal and cultural definitions of what the right weight is for both ourselves and our children.

Fat is often in the eyes of the beholder. Different times have viewed weight in different ways. Some cultures value children whom others might call overweight. Part of the problem is that many Americans are overweight, due to lack of knowledge about nutrition, due to genetics, or simply due to poor eating habits. Many adolescent girls suffer from either being overweight or obese, while others suffer from being too thin, which may be called anorexia. An interesting experiment is to ask ten people how they feel about their body. Most will answer they are too fat or too thin. Many of us cannot accept the body that was given to us; we want to follow the current attitude toward what we should weigh. The woman of today was considered unfashionably thin eighty years ago. More important in some ways than weight is nutrition.

Body build and weight. There are at least three or more body builds that retain weight in different ways. There probably are other body builds that can be considered, but let us look at just three. Some children are slender and always remain that way. They exercise a great deal and seem to have no problem being very healthy despite being thin. A second body build is chubby. Some children seem to retain fat more easily. These children are usually less athletic and seem to gain weight very easily. A third child is athletic. These children tend to weigh more than slender children, but because they are athletic they have more muscle development than most. There are endless variations of these three body builds, but parents should be aware of what type of build their child has.

What did your child inherit? It is a truism that most children look like their parents, and are built like them. Often parents will discuss their child, whom they feel is overweight or underweight, and say that they were exactly like him or her when they were the same age. We must be aware of genetic factors in children. If a child is following the same pattern of development as the parent, that must be taken into consideration.

What should you do?

1. Talk to your pediatrician or family doctor. Your doctor has statistics for ideal height and weight measurements for the average child and your child in particular.

2. Look at your family and its history. In some families, children shoot up at an earlier or later age, and this may affect your child's size and weight.

3. Check your family's size. Does your family have a large or small bone structure? Does your family tend to be tall or short? How does your family shed weight?

4. Look at your child. Compared to other children of the same age and height, does your child appear overweight or underweight?

5. Remember that sex plays a difference. Girls tend to store weight differently than boys. Although girls tend to put on weight more easily, there is greater pressure, by far, for girls to be slender.

6. Speak to a nutritionist. Sometimes weight control is not just a matter of more or less, but of eating different foods. We have come a long way in our knowledge of nutrition, but many families never take advantage of that knowledge. The best information may not come from a magazine. Consult someone knowledgeable.

When you have the information. Finally, when you have expert opinions, you are ready to set up a plan. The plan may range from doing nothing, since everything is fine, to starting a new nutrition plan. Do not forget to enlist you child's help when changing his or her eating habits and diet.

What about exercise? No good nutrition plan is complete without exercise. The two go hand in hand. If your child is very athletic, the question is resolved. If not, you may have to plan a better exercise program for your child, or have someone more knowledgeable help you do so.

Recommendations:
1. Look to the larger picture first: healthy lifestyle, proper food choices, family history, genetic patterns.
2. If you still think there is a problem, consult a physician or a nutritionist.

How do you know if your child has an eating disorder?

What is an eating disorder?
In a nation obsessed with food and weight it is not surprising that we have so many eating disorders, ranging from anorexia to obesity. *Anorexia* is a disorder that affects many female adolescents who try to lose weight to be fashionable. Anorexic children literally starve themselves to death if they are not helped. The other prevalent extreme are children who weigh more

than their pediatricians say they should weigh. The "ideal weights," as measured by insurance companies, may or may not fit your child exactly. There is a wide range of body types that tend to have more or less fat or muscle, just as we all tend to vary in height from a supposed average.

How does an eating disorder show itself? Excessive weight gain or loss in your child may be the first clue that something is wrong. Any gain or loss of ten to fifteen pounds in three to six weeks should get your attention. Ask yourself if there is any logical reason for the change in weight, such as an illness, or forced lack of physical activity. Or, for example, is the child an adolescent who has recently taken up body building for football, or gone on a special diet that you, as parents, should know about? Sometimes children go through growth spurts in which there is noticeable weight gain or loss, but usually it is not as dramatic as what is described here. If there is no clear motive for your child's change in weight, then you should make an appointment with your family physician for a checkup.

Emotional factors, such as depression, may also affect eating habits. If weight gain or loss is not very noticeable, but the child seems to be "obsessed" with food—either the eating of it, or the *not* eating of it—this may be another clue.

If your child expresses a great fear of being fat, even when the child loses weight or has normal or below-normal weight, this may be another clue. This is particularly important if the child is obviously thin, but expresses the feeling that he or she is fat. This may indicate the first stages of the eating disorder called *anorexia nervosa*.

Another serious sign that your child might have an eating disorder is if your child goes on frequent eating binges, which the child feels he or she cannot control. The child may feel self-critical and discouraged, followed at some length by trying to quickly lose the weight through drastic dieting, throwing up, and using laxatives and diuretics. This cycle of bingeing, depression, and purging is related to the eating disorder called *bulimia*. You should bring this behavior to the attention of your family physician and a mental health specialist who deals with eating disorders.

How can you help the child who has an eating disorder? Look and listen. Parents have to listen to what their children say and be aware of their child's behavior. While a gain or loss of a few pounds may not have any significant psychological meaning, more than that may be both meaningful and possibly life threatening. Young adolescent girls, especially, have died from eating disorders, due to starvation or suicide. Do not wait too long before consulting your pediatrician or family physician. Your doctor's reassurance that all is well may put your mind at rest.

Recommendations:
1. Excessive weight gain or loss in your child should be noticed.
2. Excessive and unrealistic concern about being too fat should be noticed.
3. Consult a professional psychologist or counselor.

How do you know how to help your child and yourself when there is a disaster?

Although we all face minor, and sometimes major, upsetting situations, when we face a disaster, both parents and children often have trouble coping or dealing with each other and with what to do. The way in which you, as parent, respond to your child following a disaster can affect how the child behaves and how quickly he or she recovers.

Parental behavior. When there has been an accident, a fire, a flood, or some other calamity, each of us tries to get along in a different way. Some of us tend to hold feelings within. Others become hysterical, cry, or use other ways to show we are upset. At these times, all we can think about is the tragedy and the possible loss we have suffered. If we are injured, we turn inward even more. However, it is during these times, when we are involved with our own problems, that we tend to neglect the feelings, and sometimes the needs, of our children.

Children's needs. It is at those times when we are most vulnerable that our children are also most vulnerable. It is easy to overlook the psychological needs of our children when we are looking after the physical needs or our children and ourselves. There are ways to help children in stressful situations. Since there will always be stress in our children's lives, as well as our own, we must be aware of these coping strategies in advance.

1. Teach children in advance what to expect in upsetting situations.
2. Teach ourselves to look for behavior that can lead to problems after a disaster and learn how to avoid those later problems.

Teaching children in advance what to expect.

Places: In school, children are taught where to go and what to do in case of fire, earthquake, hurricane, or tornado. Parents have to teach children where to go and what to do if they are at home or in the neighborhood during these disasters. Children also should be taught what to do if a parent is hurt or upset or away from home. If there is a car accident and a parent is hurt, children should have a plan of action. If there is a plane crash or other disaster, children have to know what to do and where to go.

People: Although children often gravitate to the responsible adult in a crisis, they have to know what people they can trust away from home. Children must learn to trust the police, firefighter, or other emergency personnel until a relative or friend can be contacted.

Personal reactions: Children sometimes react to disasters like adults, but sometimes they react in their own unique ways. Children often need special attention to meet their needs, which are, at times, difficult to see. A child's reaction to disaster is often dependent on the child's age, although some reactions are common to all children. There are immediate reactions that happen at the time of the disaster, and there are delayed reactions that might not happen for a few hours, days, or weeks.

Immediate reactions possible for all children:

- Anxiety and fearfulness of what might happen right now.
- Fear of anything related to the disaster.
- Fear of the future, including future disasters.
- Sleep disturbance and nightmares.
- Indifference about things like school or their favorite toys.
- Loss of security and loss of the feeling that everything is will work out all right.

Reactions of different age groups and what to do: Because children of different ages have different levels of understanding and different levels of vulnerability, their responses differ to disaster situations.

Reactions of ages one to five, the preschool group: In this group, the major fears are loss of parent or abandonment, as well as fear of physical pain. The younger the child, the more he or she is affected by changes in the parents and the adults in their world. Since this group does not understand intellectually what is happening, they pick up the fears and anxieties of the adults around them.

Some major responses for this age group are listed below:
- Anxiety and fears.
- Inability to express in words what they fear.
- Loss of appetite.
- Falling back on old habits, such as thumb-sucking.
- Losing control of bladder or bowels, or experiencing constipation.
- Clinging and increased dependence on parents.
- Fear of darkness, animals, people.
- Fear of being alone.

How to help children one to five after a disaster:
1. Touch and hold your child to help your child feel secure.
2. Listen and talk to your child.
3. Give your child additional attention.
4. Let your child talk about what happened, again and again.
5. Let your child express feelings through play, especially going over the disaster again and again.
6. Help your child get back into a comfortable routine for him or her.
7. Allow, for a limited period of time

only, special privileges, such as sleeping in the same room as parents.

Reactions of children ages five to eleven, early childhood: During a disaster, older children tend to fall back on outgrown behaviors.

They might show any of the following behaviors:
- Babyish behavior.
- Dependency on and clinging to parents.
- Whining.
- Irritability.
- Nightmares.
- Avoidance of friends.
- Aggressive behavior with friends at school or in the neighborhood.
- Fighting with brothers and sisters to get parental attention.
- Inability to focus and attend at school.
- Avoidance of school.
- Anger at parents.

How to help children ages five to eleven after a disaster: Children at this age are more verbal and parents can help them a great deal by talking to them.
1. Listen and talk to children; answer questions.
2. Play with the children.
3. Touch and hold the children, if the children allow it.
4. Be less demanding about chores, or school, or the usual routines.
5. Resume the usual routines at home if it seems advisable.
6. Explain to your child that you are

upset and may act differently than usual, particularly if you are irritable.

7. Discuss with your child what the family plans will be for the near future.

Reactions of children ages eleven and above: After age eleven, some children continue to react much like a younger child, and some tend to respond more like adults. Of course, some responses are universal at any age. There is often what is called a "ripple" effect throughout the family. Dealing with these feelings helps ease the fear and discomfort, and helps with recovery.

Older children and adults may experience the following reactions:

- Difficulty with sleeping.
- Depression.
- Denial of feelings, such as, It doesn't bother me.
- Loss of the feeling of security.
- Feelings of guilt that others were hurt more than they were.
- Anger or irritability.
- Feelings of numbness, or not allowing themselves feel anything.
- Being acutely vigilant for danger signs.
- Flashbacks, or the tendency to relive the incident.
- Other changes in feelings or behavior that are unusual for the individual.

After the disaster: Parents can be most helpful to their children after a disaster by being aware of the changes within themselves. These feelings are often of short-term duration, but as the shock wears off and we put our lives back together again, these common responses may occur:

- Irritability and anger.
- Difficulty sleeping, with possible nightmares.
- Feeling tired and unable to concentrate.
- Feeling shock and fear of the disaster.
- Excessive use of medication, such as pain relievers, sleeping pills, alcohol, or drugs.
- Depression.

As parents feel some of these reactions, it affects their responses to their children. Parents can help themselves and their children by doing some of the same things they would normally do for their children:

1. Talk about the experience.
2. Take care of yourself: get adequate sleep and exercise.
3. Reestablish personal relationships that you may have taken for granted.
4. Spend time with your children and loved ones.

A final note to parents. A few basic rules are helpful to us all:

1. Remember that physical contact, such as touching, hugging, and loving affection are important to both children and adults.
2. Normalize your routines and be supportive.
3. Talk about the present and the future. Clearly you should talk about your feelings about the disas-

ter, but remember to talk about the good things to come.

4. Nurture yourself as well as your loved ones. Parents are at the core of the family.

5. Finally, if symptoms persist, talk to a professional.

Recommendations:

1. Teach children in advance what to expect in a disaster; rehearse it.

2. Keep people together as much as possible during and immediately after a disaster. There is safety and comfort in numbers.

3. Listen and talk to your children about their feelings after a disaster.

4. Put children back on their routines as soon as possible.

5. If emotional or behavioral changes occur that were not present before the disaster, consult a professional psychologist or counselor.

How do you know if your child is suffering the results of a trauma?

What is a trauma for a child? Traumas are different for children and adults. The results or symptoms may be the same or different. What is a big trauma for a child may be a little trauma for an adult. A traumatic loss of a loved one

for an adult might elicit very little response in a child. Most children who are confronted with a feeling or experience that is too painful, fearful, or overwhelming will tend to regress to childish behaviors and into a more-secure and well-defended attitude. Remember, what is traumatic for a child may or may not be traumatic to a parent. Even adults differ dramatically in their response to trauma. Some holocaust victims committed suicide, while others used their energies to deal with their day-to-day situation and survived. More recently, the California earthquake of January 1994 that terrified many people, left some saying, It was nothing. Some of us will not become afraid, or we will deny feelings almost completely.

How does the child show symptoms of trauma? Children show the effects of trauma and an illness called *Post Traumatic Stress Syndrome* in a variety of ways. Some of the symptoms appear internally and some appear externally. Oftentimes, children who have suffered from a trauma will complain that they can't stop thinking about what happened. They may have recurring dreams, nightmares, or memories of the event. Sometimes they begin to fear things associated with the trauma. A child who was bitten by a dog may become abnormally afraid when a dog barks in the neighborhood. A child caught in a flood may become extremely fearful or very anxious on a cloudy day. A child involved in a car accident may become extremely tense riding in a car. In all these cases, the child is in no immediate danger, but feels the anxiety intensely, as if he or she were. Children can become overly alert and tense, or "hypervigilant." They show adult reactions in addition to being more dependent or withdrawn.

What can a parent do to help a traumatized child? The most important response a parent can have is awareness that the child has been traumatized. Listen to the child and give parental reassurance. Following the California earthquake of January 1994, many children of all ages began to sleep in their parents' beds again. Although this response is usually frowned on by professionals, in this circumstance the comfort of the child, as well as the parent, was of paramount importance; therefore, the behavior was allowable for a short period of time. However, if several months pass and the child still shows the signs of trauma, as described in the initial part of this chapter, parents might be wise to consult a professional to evaluate the situation.

What is essential in parents' behavior? A child or adult who has been traumatized needs comforting. For a child, it may mean cuddling and reassuring him or her that all will be well and that he or she will be fine. These simple behaviors are sometimes overlooked with children who are very quiet. Sometimes just being there or sitting with a child is what counts. Try to be aware of the messages your child sends to you.

Recommendations:

1. Look for any emotional or behavioral changes that were not present before the trauma.
2. Be aware that some reactions are delayed as much as six months after the trauma.
3. If the emotional and behavioral changes do not subside on their own, consult a professional counselor.

How do you know when your child needs psychological testing?

Why have your child tested?
Psychological testing is used to answer questions or to help solve problems. Often when problems with children are evident, psychological testing can refine and clarify what problem should be worked on first with what emphasis.

As professionals, we believe every child should have a yearly physical examination, if only to avoid the possibility of any illness. Similarly, we advocate that every child be psychologically evaluated by first grade to help determine the child's strengths and weaknesses, so as to better plan for the child's future.

Additionally, if there is a problem,

the evaluation helps both parents and teachers know how to best help the child. Psychological testing is also helpful when parents and teachers disagree on what the problem is. An independent evaluation answers questions and gives parents perhaps new directions to pursue in the child's development.

What does psychological testing cover? Psychological testing can cover numerous areas. A thorough testing should cover the following areas:

1. A developmental history: Usually a form filled out by parents. Records are obtained also from the pediatrician and other professionals involved with the child.

2. An intellectual evaluation: To determine how bright the child is, what is the child's intellectual potential, and where is the child functioning now.

3. Evaluation of language development: A measure of receiving language, associating language, expressing language. Evaluating short-term memory for visual sequences, such as spelling, and auditory sequences, such as listening to the teacher's directions.

4. Evaluation of perceptual development: Measures of the child's ability to distinguish sounds as in speech-sound discrimination. Measures of visual perception, such as eye-hand coordination, seeing figures against their background, seeing figures in a constant fashion, seeing letters and words in their correction orienta-

tion in space, such as b and d, or m and w, and seeing items in space as they relate to each other and to one's body.

5. Evaluation of sensory-motor development: Making sure the child's ability to hear and see and feel are within normal limits. Measures of eye, hand, and foot preferences. Measures of dexterity, gross and fine motor coordination.

6. Measures of emotional-social development: How has the child developed in relation to other children of the same age? How does the child handle anger? How does the child relate to other children? Does the child have friends? Is the child a leader or a follower? What is lacking if anything in the child's development? What should be strengthened? Does the child need help in any area?

7. Evaluation of academic development and progress: How does the child measure compared to other children the same age in reading, writing, arithmetic, spelling, study skills, ability to attend and focus, maturity of work skills.

8. Evaluation of the child in special areas: Some children need a more in-depth neuropsychological evaluation, because of possible brain damage. Other children need special testing because English is their second language.

Where can you get your child evaluated? There are both public and private agencies and individuals who perform diagnostic psychological testing. Public schools may provide partial evaluations of children free of charge, although the waiting period may be long. There are many private clinical psychologists who specialize in evaluating children.

Is the information confidential?

When evaluations are performed by a private psychologist, the information is always confidential. If an evaluation is performed at school, the information may not be confidential, but put in the child's cumulative file. In special situations where an evaluation is ordered by the court, say in a divorce, the information is available to the judge and attorneys and may not be confidential.

How is an evaluation paid for? Often parents' health insurance covers some or all of a psychological evaluation. Read your health policy or call your insurance department or agent.

Recommendations:

1. If a child is struggling with an emotional, social, or academic problem and you have not been successful in remedying the problem, you should consider psychological testing to get more information.
2. If you want information about proper school placement, have your child tested.

How do you know when your child needs psychotherapy?

Parents sometimes wonder whether their child's or adolescent's problems are severe enough to warrant psychotherapy. There is no question that children have problems. In fact, adolescents are at the greatest risk for suicide. On the other hand, rushing into psychotherapy is not warranted if the problems are fleeting or minimal. How is a parent to know?

What is psychotherapy?

Psychotherapy is basically a "talking technique" that addresses the belief systems, the feelings, and the behavior of an individual in an effort to create a positive change in the individual's way of functioning. Some therapists focus on identifying how and why the problems arose. Some focus on identifying, expressing, and managing feelings. Others focus on the behavior itself.

How do you know if your child should be in therapy? Children are referred for therapy when others suspect they have an emotional or behavioral problem. (See pages 153-55.) Sometimes children are brought into therapy as preparation for some high-risk situation, such as a divorce, a move to another area, an operation, parents planning to put a pet to sleep, a relative dying, and so on.

In most cases, however, parents or teachers may recommend a child for therapy after they have tried unsuccessfully to solve some problem with a child.

How to find the right therapist for your child and yourself. The "right" therapist is someone who is fully licensed and qualified, someone whom your child likes, and someone who can also relate well with you. (You may have to interview at least three different therapists to get some perspective.) In one to three sessions, the therapist should be able to give you a clear picture of what is bothering your child. In addition, the therapist should be able to explain how he or she will approach the issue. The therapist should be able to explain how his or her techniques, *e.g.*, play therapy, art therapy, sand play therapy, etc., will help create change.

What is the parents' role? Most therapists who work with children also work with parents, for the two go hand in hand. Ask the therapist. Some therapists include one parent or both parents in a session from time to time. Some therapists have parent meetings every few weeks. Some call between sessions to check on the child's progress at home or school.

To find a good therapist, ask your friends whom they know; ask your child's pediatrician, or contact your child's school. Schools and pediatricians usually have a list of successful

therapists with whom they have worked in the past.

How do you know if your child is making progress? Averages for therapeutic progress have been established by examining completed cases across the United States:

* A crisis situation should be under control between one and six sessions.
* Symptoms should be reduced by about session twelve.
* Permanent personality changes should come about in one to two years of weekly therapy.

Because children's problems are less ingrained than an adult's, you may see progress at a quicker rate. If you do not see the kinds of changes that you expect, ask the therapist why. He or she should be able to explain where your child is at the moment, and why there hasn't been more progress. The therapist may be able to set your expectations in proper balance. If your child doesn't progress, and you don't have a good explanation, then you should consider changing therapists.

What are the signs that your child's psychotherapy is completed? When you, the child, the therapist, and the teacher all agree the child is ready to terminate, that's the best time to end psychotherapy. However, it is rare for that to happen. Sometimes progress is seen in the therapy before it transfers to home or school. Sometimes progress is seen at home before it shows up at school, and sometimes it's the reverse.

In most cases, it is the child or the therapist who begins to feel that the child has gone about as far as he or she can go for the time being, assuming that the behaviors and feelings that were problematic are no longer present. Sometimes therapy is terminated because of money or scheduling difficulties or some other unexpected cause. If this happens, then therapy should be resumed as soon as possible. Because the child can form a strong relationship with the therapist, any abrupt termination can seriously hurt the child. For most terminations, a good rule of thumb is to have one ending session for every four therapy sessions. For example, if a child has come weekly for six months, you should allow approximately six sessions to work through the "saying good-bye" process.

What are the probabilities of success?
In the hands of a competent therapist the probabilities for improvement are high. Some children make quick progress, and others work slowly. It depends on the child's level of trust in the therapist and the therapist's skill. As a parent, you should have some sense of success after the first six therapy sessions.

Recommendations:
1. Consider psychotherapy when your child is having an emotional, social, or behavioral problem that persists.
2. Consider psychotherapy as preparation for high-risk situations, such as divorce or the death of a loved one.

How do you know if your child has good self-esteem?

What is self-esteem? Self-esteem in children is feelings, both positive and negative, about themselves. When children think and talk about themselves, these feelings are happy, satisfied feelings, or unhappy feelings of dissatisfaction with themselves. These feelings are shaped and molded in childhood by children themselves, or by parents, siblings, friends, relatives, teachers, other individuals, and by society. The younger the child, the more self-esteem is influenced by parents.

How parents influence self-esteem.
Parents are a child's most essential teacher, especially in the child's younger years, and they can influence children in many ways. Parent's can "put down" or negatively influence children in the following ways:
1. Name-calling: calling the child "bad" or "stupid" or any derogatory name when the child makes an error.
2. Proving that the parent is superior and the child is inferior in areas that are completely parent-dominated so that the child cannot compete fairly, such as in a game.
3. Rejecting the child as he or she is, and continually putting the child

down, especially in front of friends or others that are important to him or her.

4. Comparing the child to brothers, sisters, or other children unfavorably, and indicating the child will never be good enough.

5. Requiring that your love be contingent on the child's perfect performance. That is, the child must be the best, or the child is nothing at all.

Equally, parents can be instrumental in positively helping children develop a healthy self-esteem by demonstrating the following behaviors:

1. Accepting the child as is, that is as a child in the process of learning and growing.

2. Allowing the child to love himself or herself and to be satisfied with his or her performance.

3. Allowing the child to make choices on his or her own that are appropriate to the child's age and maturity level.

4. Making it clear that the child is loved for himself or herself and not for what he or she produces.

How society can influence self-esteem.

Parents alone cannot determine a child's self-esteem. Friends and society as a whole plays a major part in self-esteem, especially as children grow older. The totality of one's experience determines how we feel about ourselves.

- Any devaluing by society, such as prejudice based on race, sex, physical characteristics or behavioral characteristics can influence self-esteem.

- Any devaluing by society of what a child produces, if it does not meet some predetermined standard.

- Unfair criticism or unreasonable comments about how a child looks or any group the child has joined.

- Any physical, sexual, or emotional abuse by a peer group or older child.

What can you do about it? Parents often do a good job protecting their children physically, but they neglect the all-important psychological side of the child. Not only do children feel pain and sadness at rejection, child and adolescent suicide is more frequent than adult suicide. Parents can especially let their children know that they are loved and accepted—not that they will change and grow in good ways, but that they are satisfactory at this moment and special to you. Children who grow up with a positive self-esteem instilled by parents usually both like themselves better and perform better than those children who do not have this benefit. We are all hurt by events or by unhappy people. Parents can help children get over these situations so that there is less damage to the child's self-esteem.

Recommendations:

1. Minimize overly critical comments made by the parent or the child.

2. Do not make acceptance and love conditional upon performance.

3. Help the child to establish competence in areas of his or her interest.

How do you know how to get a child to discuss feelings?

What are feelings? Feelings are energies that oftentimes precede humans actions. Thoughts can create feelings that prepare us for actions. For example, some thoughts can create angry feelings that might encourage us to shout or get physically involved. Feelings could be described as "fluid" in that they seem to pass through us. They rise and fall; they increase and decrease. Feelings sometimes build up when they are not expressed, and that can create tension or stress that can result in unhealthy actions. Being able to identify and appropriately express feelings can prevent a build up of stress and can help us communicate effectively.

Why do we have feelings? Human beings have the most evolved language system of all the species on earth. Humans also have the most highly evolved social system. Feelings play an important role in social communication. Just as the body has a built-in balancing system, called sensation, that tells us when things are too hot, too cold, too rough, too soft, too sharp, or too smooth, feelings tell us when we have to confront, wait, be alone, or join a social relationship. Feelings are the natural energies for balancing relationships. By communicating our feelings, we can develop healthy relationships.

The four major feeling groups need to be considered. There are basically four major feeling groups; they are characterized by the words anger, fear, sadness, and happiness. These are considered primary feelings in that they appear to be prevalent in all cultures and they have existed since the beginning of humanity. Another set of feelings, secondary feelings, are made up of various combinations of primary feelings. Also, there are many degrees and intensities of feelings. For instance, the "anger" group might include everything from simple annoyance to irritation, determination, frustration, anger, and rage. The "fear" group might include everything from caution to worry, fear, dread, and panic. The "sad" group might include everything from aloneness to disappointment, hurt, rejection, abandonment, and isolation. The "happiness" group might include everything from happiness, joy, love, bliss, excitement, and humor.

The four major feeling groups are each of great importance. Each of these feeling groups plays a different role in how we communicate and behave. The energies from the anger group tend to direct us to move ahead, try harder, and confront situations. The energies from the fear group tend to direct us to wait and observe our surroundings. The energies from the sad group tend to remove us from our activities. The energies from the happiness group tend to make us share or join with someone or something. If we are closed off to any one of these feeling groups, we will be handicapped in both relating and communicating.

The place to begin in understanding the four major feeling groups. We begin, as always, with the basis of trust and acceptance. We trust that we won't be hurt by what we say. We accept that there is freedom to say it as we see it. (See related sections for more information on creating good communication between parents and children.)

By about age five, most children can distinguish between feeling sad, mad, happy, and afraid. To test this, simply ask your child to name things that make him or her mad, sad, happy, or afraid. If you ask the child about just one category at a time, you will see that he or she can pretty well identify the categories. The child may need a little help with mixed feelings. For example, I'm mad that my brother broke my favorite toy, and I'm sad that I don't have it anymore.

Asking a child, teenager, or adult, for that matter, how he or she feels can sometimes make a person feel confused or overwhelmed. A rush of mixed feelings can be difficult to express. So, you might get an, I don't know or an OK response. If you get this type of response, break it down into smaller responses. You might ask, Are you frustrated or mad about anything in this situation? Are you worried or afraid of anything in this situation? Are

you disappointed, hurt, or sad about anything in this situation? Are you pleased, happy, or proud of anything in this situation? These questions will help sort out a host of feelings, and you will get a better overall picture of the child's feelings. In addition, the child will feel better because he or she will feel more completely understood.

For example: Billy borrowed Matthew's new bicycle without permission and had an accident in which Billy broke his collarbone and ruined the bicycle. Billy was rushed to the hospital for X rays, bandages, and an arm sling. Because the front wheel and the frame were bent, the bicycle was pretty much a loss. Fortunately, the parents were in the position to buy Matthew a new bicycle, even though it was quite expensive; but Matthew seemed down. The parents asked Matthew what was wrong. His response was, "I don't know." The parents replied, "How can you be so unhappy? We bought you a new bicycle." Matthew's response was, "I don't know."

Later that evening, Matthew's father went into Matthew's room and said he wanted to talk about what happened. He told Matthew that he loved him very much and that he knew that it was sometimes difficult to have a younger brother. He asked him, "What's the most frustrating thing for you about Billy?" This time Matthew's response was, "He comes into my room all the time without permission. He takes my things without asking, and he either breaks them or loses them. And you guys don't even punish him!" Matthew was angry not only with Billy but also with his parents. His father responded, "I guess you have a right to be mad. I'd probably be mad, too, if someone broke something very special to me." Matthew continued, "Yeah, I was watching that bike for months, hoping nobody would buy it before my birthday. I really loved that bike." (Matthew started to tear up.) His father replied "Didn't you like the new one we bought you? It's just like the other one." Matthew responded, "The new one's OK, but I really liked the other one." Giving Matthew a hug the father said, "I'm really sorry, too, that your bike got broken."

"What did you think when you heard Billy screaming?" the father continued. Matthew said, "At first, I was scared because I didn't know what happened. Then, when I saw him with my bike, I was mad and I was glad that he hurt himself. I even started calling him names. But then, when I saw the bone sticking out of his collar, I got really scared. That's when I ran to get Mom. It was gross." His father asked, "What were you thinking while you waited in the emergency room?" Matthew said, "I was wondering if Billy was going to die, and I was feeling bad because I yelled at him while he was on the ground." The father reassured Matthew of his love for him. He reminded Matthew that he wanted the boys to share, but that he and Matthew's mother would try to help protect Matthew's space and possessions in the future. Matthew's somber mood disappeared.

This is an example of an effective way to get a child to discuss his or her feelings. Pay special attention to how the father in this case didn't judge the goodness or badness of Matthew's feelings, but simply allowed him to go through a process. It is also very important to notice that, when discussing feelings, one sufficiently expressed feeling naturally flows into the next feeling. After expressing his initial feelings of anger, Matthew naturally moved to his feelings of sadness. In the course of the discussion, Matthew expressed a full range of emotions, including some guilt for wishing pain onto his brother.

Not every discussion will go this smoothly, but, with practice, both you and your child will be better able to identify and discuss feelings.

How to help your child get rid of negative feelings. All feelings are natural and normal. Some feelings are labeled "negative" because when they are not understood or dealt with appropriately, they can lead to destructive or unhealthy behaviors. Frustrations that build to the boiling point, hurts that are not healed, fear that is not overcome, guilt that is unforgiven all lead to destructive behaviors. Identifying and expressing these feelings is the first step in transforming them. The second step is understanding the causes of these feelings.

What causes your child to have these feelings? It is not always easy to find the source of a feeling. Sometimes feelings are caused by thoughts. The thought might include images that come into our head, things we say to ourselves, or memories that are evoked. Daily we are bombarded by sights and sounds that can evoke feelings. If we succeed in our achievements on any given day, or if we fail to meet some expectation, we might provoke certain feelings. Since feelings are related to various biochemical actions in the body, eating foods, doing exercises, feeling tired, getting sick, or doing any variety of physical activities, can affect our feelings.

A good way to discover where a feeling originated is to ask, When did I first start to feel this way? Frequently, this can help us pinpoint where a feeling began. By asking what happened and how the person perceived what happened, you usually can get a good idea of how the feeling got started. You can also examine the validity of the adopted perception.

How do I change my child's feelings?
Step three is changing an unwanted feeling. Thoughts, feelings, and actions are not the same things, but they are all intimately related. The simplest way to change your feelings is to change either your thoughts or your actions. If you put different thoughts in your head, if you develop a new perspective, or if you change your thoughts, you will begin to feel differently. On the other hand, if you change your activities, such as listening to the radio, watching television, reading a book, exercising, going for a walk, you will also begin to

change your feelings.

If a feeling is persistent, then talking to someone else about it can help you get a new perspective on the matter. In addition, when we talk about feelings we allow them to pass, because feelings are naturally fluid.

Children show individual differences in expressing feelings. We know that there are wide differences between the sexes, between age groups, and between individuals when it comes to discussing feelings. In general, women are more open and willing to discuss feelings than men. For this reason it is sometimes better, especially with boys, to ask them specific questions rather than general, open-ended questions like, How do you feel?

Adolescents in particular can be very closed to sharing feelings with adults, especially if the children have not built up a good rapport with at least one parent during the growing years. However, the same rule applies to teenagers as to younger children: trust and acceptance are key.

By the time many children reach adolescence they have already learned to avoid certain subjects with their parents. During adolescence there is a natural drive toward independence that makes sharing feelings with parents a difficult task. Adolescents yearn to make their own decisions, regardless of whether they are able. However, adolescents who come from families that encourage discussion with parents will often do so as they grow up.

It is also important to respect the

seriousness of an adolescent's feelings. If a child of twelve says he or she is in love, a parent might smile and joke about it. To the child, however, this may be a very serious relationship and if you do not take it seriously, you may alienate your child. Keep your child's confidence; that is, do not tell somebody else about what happens in your child's personal life. Some parents feel free to discuss their child's personal problems with others. This leads to feelings of betrayal and hurt in your child. Your child has to feel secure that you understand him or her and confident that you will treat his or her feelings like you want your feelings treated.

Recommendations:

1. Remember that when your child discusses feelings, your own unexpected feelings may emerge.
2. All feelings do not have to be dealt with or resolved immediately. Be careful of taking some action before it is necessary.

How do you know what do you do when a child threatens suicide?

Some facts parents should know about suicide. In our society, unfortunately, suicide by children occurs too frequently. The highest rate of suicide in our society is among adolescents. Parents have to be aware of the signs and symptoms of suicide as well as other emotional distress.

Parents need to be aware of signs and symptoms of suicide. Most potential suicides in children and adolescents are betrayed by behavior. The key is to recognize these signs and follow up this recognition with appropriate action.

Some children will tell parents, I feel like committing suicide, or I am going to kill myself.

Although this may clearly be an attempt to gain attention with no real intention of carrying through the threat, parents must be aware of the underlying message. The message is, I'm in trouble and I'm hurting. Whether parents feel there is or is not a possible plan to carry out the threat, they have to pay attention to their child's behavior.

Signs of possible suicide or severe distress may be one of the following:

- The child shows a definite change in behavior.
- The child seems depressed or withdrawn.
- The child interacts differently with friends or parents.
- The child seems apathetic.
- The child gives away prized possessions because he or she won't have further need of them.
- The child seems hopeless and sees no future for himself or herself.

The key here is the feelings of hopelessness and the idea that there is no future out there for the child. There are other individual signs for each child. Suicidal children often cannot discuss feelings with their parents because they fear rejection or lack of acceptance.

Action parents can take. When parents interpret these overt or covert signs, they have to decide how serious the possibility of suicide is. Parents can start by taking the extra time to listen when the child is able to talk. The more a child talks about a problem, often the less final it becomes. Other possibilities open up, and frequently the child begins to feel better. Some children get the message from parents that everything they do is wrong. Parents have to cease criticizing and become more accepting during these trying times.

If parents believe the situation is serious, there are a series of things to do. Have your child see a therapist, such as psychologist, psychiatrist, social worker, or child counselor, as quickly as possible. These professionals are trained to assess how serious the situation is. If the situation is critical, then short-term hospitalization may be indicated. A call to a suicide center, the local police, or your pediatrician should quickly put you in touch with somebody who can offer your child a protected environment. Parents have to take action to protect the child, because they are often the first and only ones to see some of these behavioral changes and the possible threat to the child.

Recommendations:

1. It is dangerous to ignore threats of suicide. See whether your child's behavior is consistent with his or her words concerning depressive feelings.
2. If you are concerned, consult a professional psychologist or counselor.

How do you know how to handle an aggressive child?

How do I know if my child is aggressive? An aggressive child is one who not only initiates what he or she wants and pursues it relentlessly, but who also will physically and verbally intimidate others to get what he or she wants. A child who does not respect the boundaries of others physically or verbally, but who is quick to protect his or her own boundaries, might be considered an aggressive child. An aggressive child may be quick to anger; argue loudly when asked to do something he or she doesn't want to do; become verbally or physically destructive when angry; use insults, ridicule, guilt, criticism, and other forms of intimidation with adults in his or her environment.

Oftentimes, aggressive children will seek out aggressive play. You might see it in their choice of video games and television shows. Their play may include war games with guns and other weapons. They may choose activities that are more dangerous and active, such as motorcycle or car racing or sky-diving. They seem to take things just a little further than other kids their age. They might be in frequent trouble at school or in other public places.

Is it bad to be aggressive? It is not bad to be very active, outgoing, creative, or assertive. It is also not bad to be deter-mined and focused to get what you want. The difference lies in the areas of boundaries and respect. Aggressive individuals have a tendency to domi-nate their environment. An aggressive child tries to dominate his or her envi-ronment by determining what will happen and who will do it. Because of this, rules usually have to be set up to protect the rights and freedoms of other individuals.

What should I do when my child is aggressive?
1. Determine if the aggressive behav-ior results from a recent occurrence or if it is a long-standing attitude.
2. Determine if the aggressive behav-ior is a general attitude, or if it is apparent only with one situation or one individual, for example, only at school, only with a sibling.
3. If the behavior is more situational and specific, you may be able to talk to the child about what hurt his or her feelings or what he or she fears that promotes the aggression. If the child's vulnerable feelings can be resolved, the aggressive behavior will usually cease.
4. If the aggressive behavior seems to be related to the child's general person-

ality, then a longer training period is needed. In most cases, as a parent, you will help the child respect limits, have consideration for the rights and feel-ings of others, and develop patience and waiting skills. This cannot be done overnight. It usually takes consistent limit-setting, consistent and effective consequences (positive and negative), repeated explanation, and lots of repe-tition.
5. If you want a child to do some-thing, here are several things to do:
a. Tell the child clearly what, how, when, and where you want some-thing done. Suggesting to a child, It's dinner time! can elicit many responses, such as, What are we having? or I'm not hungry. A clearer message is, Turn off the television and come to the dinner table now. Messages that are clear, complete, and time-specific leave less room for negotiation, misinterpretation, and argument. An indirect state-ment often invites resistance.
b. Follow through effectively:
• Do not give a direction when you are unable to follow through, for example, while you are on the phone, talking to someone else, cooking dinner, and so on, unless you are willing to stop what you're doing immediately and make the child do what you asked.
• Do not tell a child to do some-thing two, three, or four times, because the child learns that he or she doesn't have to do what you said the first time. The child learns that he or she only has to do what you

say one-half, one-third, or one-fourth of the time. And the child only has to do it when your voice reaches "that pitch" or when he or she hears you come down the hall, because then the child knows something is going to happen.

• Do not answer the question, Why? until after the child has done what you have asked. Tell the child, When you have (washed your hands, put your toys away, put your pajamas on, finished your homework) I'll tell you why. Children rarely ask why after they have done something. In ninety-nine percent of the cases, Why is simply asked to get out of whatever was requested.

• Do not get into an argument with the child. Use argument deflectors, such as, Nevertheless . . . ; regardless of that . . . ; or, be that as it may. . . . For example, as you peel the child off the television and get him or her ready for bed, the child might ask you why he or she has to go to bed when a sibling is still up; or the child might tell you how mean you are and how much he or she loves the other parent more than you; or the child might point out your flaws so that he or she can get you angry and possibly engage you in an activity or discussion other than going to bed. The child is trying to avoid the request. If you don't get into an argument, the child will have no choice but to follow through.

c. Be consistent! If every time you went one mile per hour over the posted speed limit on your local highway you automatically received a ticket for $100 or more, no one would even approach the speed limit. However, because you only get caught and punished once in awhile, you probably push past the limits. The same is true for our children. If we set rules with clear consequences, but we only enforce them periodically, we make our children test us twenty-four hours a day. If we don't follow through consistently because we are tired, happy, having company over, or we are at the supermarket, on the telephone, etc., children will test us at each point. They also learn within the first four or five years of life that they can manipulate us by pleasing us; arguing with us; out reasoning us; guilting us; intimidating us, withdrawing from us, and more.

d. Show appreciation verbally and physically for completing an assignment quickly and well. Skip excessive praise for some children, because it sends a message that the behavior is more important to the parent than to the child. However, if your child beams when you give him or her praise, then by all means give plenty when he or she does the right thing.

e. Use "logical consequences." Logical consequences are different from illogical consequences. Illogical consequences result when a parent is fed up with a certain behavior, such as leaving dirty dishes where they don't belong; leaving book bags, shoes, and clothing in the wrong room; or leaving dirty towels in the bathroom. When a parent reaches his or her limit, he or she might blow up, giving the culprits various punishments. This type of discipline makes children view their parent as unpredictable (She didn't complain about it the last three times we did it.), overreactive, and responsible for the bad feelings that result. This type of discipline breaks down the trust between parent and child, does not encourage responsibility on the part of the child, and lowers the child's self-esteem.

Logical consequences occur when a parent identifies the behavior he or she wants the child to display or the behavior that he or she doesn't want the child to display. Second, a consequence is assigned to that behavior. The consequence has to be significant to get and keep the child's attention. You have to find something that will motivate the child, whether it is the loss of certain privileges, like television, sports, friends, phone, desserts, etc., or the gain of certain privileges, like praise, money, allowances, treats, movie rentals, video games, toys, etc. Everybody is motivated by something. Third, you have to enforce the consequence quickly and consistently. The younger the child, the sooner the consequence should be applied so the child makes the association. One caution about setting consequences: Never set a consequence when you are

angry. Express your anger, but don't set a consequence until you have calmed down, because you will usually have to stay at that level of intensity to enforce the consequence. Grounding a child for the rest of his or her life probably won't work.

Whenever possible, have the consequence relate to the value that was missed by the infraction. For example, a child who leaves clothes in the wrong room may be asked to pick up all the clothes in every room, including the towels in the bathroom, every day for a week before he or she is allowed to play or watch television (depending on the child's age). Or the child may be asked to neatly fold and arrange clothes in his or her closet or dresser drawers with daily inspection for a week.

f. Set up a chart and a reward system. Some children are motivated to work for stars, stickers, points, or allowances. The stars and points add up for special treats or privileges. Usually it is best to keep a written chart posted where the parent and child can see it easily. One rule of thumb is to require one chore or behavior for every year of the child's age. Usually with a reward system, the parent has to consistently notice if the child is actually doing what he or she is supposed to be doing. In addition, the rewards will have to be renegotiated from time to time. A reward system does require some parental attention, but if it is done right, it can be a very effective way to manage an aggressive child's behavior.

What if none of these work? If you have run up against a brick wall, and you have tried the above suggestions, it is probably time to seek professional help. Ask the child's teacher or the school principal for suggestions. They usually have worked with a number of child therapists and know who is effective. You might also ask your child's pediatrician. There are usually many nonprofit organizations in the phone book that might be able to help. Don't give up.

Recommendations:
1. It takes time to change aggressive behavior. Try not to move too quickly.
2. Consider where your child learned this aggressive behavior.

How do you know how to handle a fearful child?

Is the fear general or specific? Some fears are specific. They refer to one or two things. A child may be afraid of dogs, snakes, or spiders. A child may be afraid of the dark. However, the child is just fine when it comes to the rest of his or her life. Some fears are more generalized. The child is fearful about every new situation; is not assertive about his or her needs or opinions; or is shy in almost all interactions with siblings, friends, relatives, as well as new people. These children generally have trouble separating from parents.

How to deal with specific fears. Specific fears are the easiest to undo if you want to undo them. (Fear of poisonous snakes, spiders, and dangerous situations may be useful and healthy.) Fear of driving on the highway, fear of flying, fear of the dark, are common fears that people regularly seek help for. The most effective process is called systematic desensitization. Basically, you have to do two things: learn to relax your mind and body; and practice going from a situation that is not scary to one that is a little scary to one that is a little more scary, learning to relax at each stage.

A child who is afraid of the dark might start off with all the lights on in his or her room, while learning to relax. After a few days or weeks, you may be able to reduce the lighting to one or two lights. After more time, you may be able to reduce the lighting to a simple night-light. If you wish to go further, you might spend several nights sleeping in the room with the child with all the lights off.

When the child is comfortable with this, you might move to the doorway, waiting for the child to go to sleep; then outside the doorway; and, eventually, out in the hall, outside of the child's view. If the child has successfully learned how to relax, he or she will be able, at some point, to sleep in his or her room with the lights off.

How to deal with general fearfulness. When the child's fearfulness is more general and is part of the child's personality, the training can take longer. Here are a few things you can do:

1. Determine if your child is the kind of child who, when going swimming, frets before going into some cold water either by: A) worrying and complaining for a while, then taking a running start; or B) going in slowly, starting with the toes and working his or her way up. If your child is more like example A, then there might be many situations in which he or she initially expresses fear, but in which he or she can be persuaded past the fear by adults, without experiencing negative consequences. Going to camp, going to a new school, joining an after-school sports program, sleeping alone, going for sleepovers, etc., are likely to be enjoyable activities once the child gets over his or her initial fear. As the child gets older, he or she will recognize this usual feeling pattern, and he or she may be able to "encourage" himself or herself more frequently.

   If your child is more like example B, it might be harmful to try to push the child past the fear too quickly. Oftentimes, you may first have to get the child used to the environment by: taking the child to visit a camp; introducing the child to the counselors; repeating visits until the child begins to feel comfortable; or joining with a sibling or friend at first. The same may be true if such a child joins an after-school activity. He or she may have to be coached slowly into an activity. This approach, even on a good day, can try the patience of a saint. Pushing the child too soon, however, can create even greater resistance down the road.

2. You can accept the fact that a fearful child simply may not take advantage of all the opportunities that you could provide. He or she may not have as many friends as other children, and you, as a parent, may feel sad, disappointed, or guilty.

3. Many children who are fearful are also quite bright. Their fear is a result of very sensitive feelings. They may be very judgmental or critical of others, or they may be very sensitive to the criticism or judgment of others. When these children are introduced to new situations or new people, they may first exhibit initial shyness, but then they might get bossy, controlling, or critical. This usually creates conflict followed by rejection and the child's subsequent desire to leave. By addressing the child's need to share and the child's judgment of others and self, the child's social skills will improve and his or her confidence can return.

4. If the problem becomes too great a concern for you, you might seek professional help. Sometimes therapy alone or in conjunction with medication can be an effective way to create a change in attitude. While we don't immediately recommend medication, there are newer medications available with fewer side effects that can boost a child's confidence and sense of well-being until he or she establishes new habits. When the new behaviors are well in place, you may be able to reduce or remove the medication with no ill effects.

Recommendations:
1. Techniques for getting rid of fears are dependent on the meaning and the depth of fear the child has. Some children can only resolve these problems very slowly.
2. Fear and anxiety are there to protect the child. The child may not be ready to give up the fear until he or she feels safe.

How do you know what's serious for your child?

Children who are quiet, unexpressive, or dramatic are sometimes difficult to read when something serious is hap-

pening. As a parent, you will usually have to approach these children if you think there is a problem. If the child doesn't come to you with a problem, or if the child is very dramatic, you will usually have to take the lead.

What does it mean when your child is quiet? The quiet child usually doesn't like to be noticed, may be a "pleaser," and is sometimes passive. When there is a problem, quiet children may retreat further into themselves and get quieter or even depressed. In a busy household, these children can get overlooked, as the squeaky wheel usually gets the oil! A quiet child who injures himself or herself or breaks things around the house, or possibly fails in school, may be trying to get your attention in a passive way.

What does it mean when your child is unexpressive? The unexpressive child may be either loud or quiet but may have difficulty putting thoughts or feelings into words that accurately communicate. Because expressing things in words is difficult for these children they can build a lot of inner tension which might be expressed in fighting, nail-biting, hair-pulling, overeating, and so on. Because using words is difficult, these children give up trying to communicate.

What does it mean when your child is dramatic? There are some children for whom life is very dramatic. They sometimes go from crisis to crisis. Things are either incredibly great or terribly wrong. They don't really seem to have a middle range. Everything to them is important. Consequently, parents tend to minimize the child's reactions. You remember the story about the boy who cried wolf.

Here are some suggestions for parents.

1. It is a good idea for all children to have a scheduled maintenance program, but specifically with unexpressive children it is a must. A little time alone with the child each day, every few days, once a week, or once a month, should allow you some time to ask him or her some basic questions. *Scheduling consistent, regular time together is crucial for getting these kids to open up.* This is also true for dramatic children, because when they are around other children, they get more dramatic, not less. When dramatic children are alone with you, they have a chance to settle down.

2. During these special times have the child answer a few basic questions. For example: What kinds of things made you *angry* this week (day, month)? Let the child name one, two, or three things. If the child has more, let him or her go on. What kinds of things are you *worried* about (things you are afraid of)? What kinds of things made you *sad* (hurt your feelings)? What kinds of things made you *happy?* These four questions will cover the four basic feeling groups, and you will be able to get a fairly good picture of how

your child is doing. Remember: If you want your child to open up, you have to be nonjudgmental about what he or she says. If you are listening, you are not criticizing, explaining, or defending. You are just listening.

Recommendations: Although it is good to explore your child's feelings, it is necessary to respect the child's vulnerability. Don't push if the child is resistant.

How do you know how to recognize and help your child deal with stress?

Be aware of signs of stress. Any system that gets overloaded will begin first to bend and then break at its weakest point. An increase in your child's fighting, arguing, and irritability, whiny and clinging behavior, tiredness and depression, anxiousness and fearfulness, hyperactivity, illness, and injuries are all common signs of stress. While all of these may be present to some degree on a daily basis, we usually notice an increase when a child is under stress. As you get to know your child, pick out the symptoms that he or she most often exhibits when under stress. Each child has a different way to let you know when he or she is at the limit. A noisy child may get noisier or quieter. A quiet child may get quieter or noisier. See if you can discover which way your child goes. If you can find a pattern with your child, he or she will most likely use that pattern for the rest of his or her life, unless it is brought to his or her attention.

How parents can deal with signs of stress. There are several important things to do:

1. **Identify the signs** of your child's stress, and you have to discover how the child usually deals with it.
2. **Help the child begin to identify when he or she is stressed.** Over time, the child will be able to recognize the early signs.
3. **Rest** is probably the single best approach to reduce stress. Rest is especially important for young children who overdo it.
4. **Exercise** is also a necessary component for many people to reduce stress. It not only releases pent up physical tension, but it also releases calming chemicals during the relaxation phase.
5. **Recreation** is also a vital and frequently overlooked ingredient to reduce stress in children. Although children hardly ever have to be encouraged to play, as they get older, children may become more involved in other activities. Play is not the same as sports. Play is freeing. You are able to imagine and act out imagination. There are not necessarily any rules. You don't necessarily have to perform at any level, so there isn't any pressure. True recreation truly recreates the individual.

Recommendations: Learn the kinds of situations or combinations of situations that relax your child. These may be different than what relaxes you.

PHYSICAL DEVELOPMENT

How do you know if your child is ill?

What are some common signs? Very young children become cranky, whiny, or tired when they get ill. They may have trouble sleeping or eating. Sick children may be extra thirsty or feel hot to the touch. They may complain of aches and pains in various parts of their body. More obvious clues are coughing, vomiting, and complaining of headaches, earaches, and stomachaches.

As we grow up, we become more aware of the early signs of illness. It is sometimes hard to tell when young children with high energy levels are sick because they don't complain.

What should a parent do? Look at the child's color, touch his or her face and head, and take the child's temperature to determine if the child is getting sick.

If you have any questions about your child's physical health, you should contact your family doctor.

Recommendations:
1. Take notice of any persistent physical complaints
2. Check color of skin for redness or whiteness and take the child's temperature.
3. If you're not sure, consult a physician.

How do you know what to say to your child who is bed-wetting?

Whose problem is it? Toilet training seems to generate a lot of feeling in our society. Views differ on when to begin

195

training, but the child usually wins the debate because he or she becomes trained when he or she is ready. Many children are toilet trained sometime around the third year of life. Most children are able to sleep through the night without wetting the bed by the age of four, five, or six, with occasional lapses. A five- or six-year-old might wet the bed if he or she is particularly tired; stays out too late; is sick; has too much junk food or soda the night before; etc. If the child at five or six still wets the bed every night or most nights, then the child may have a bed-wetting problem that can be either emotional or physical. As a parent, you have to know the source of the problem before trying to solve this difficulty.

Before saying anything to the child, investigate whether there is a history of bed-wetting on either the mother's or father's side of the family. Is the problem inherited? If so, there is some history that will tell you approximately when the bed-wetting will stop. In some cases, the bed-wetting, or *enuresis,* will not stop until early or middle adolescence. It is rare to have bed-wetting continue into late adolescence or adulthood. By discovering if there is a family history of bed-wetting you will be able to help your child recognize there are other children and family members like him or her.

What can you do about it? It is important to mention bed-wetting to the physician when the child goes in for the four-year-old and five-year-old checkups. If your child's pediatrician is unaware that the child is still bed-wetting, the doctor should be told. Should you tell the physician with the child present? The answer to this question depends on how open you and the child are with each other and how comfortable the child feels around the doctor. If the child is easily embarrassed, especially about the subject of bed-wetting, you may have to find a way to notify the doctor ahead of time. The doctor may prescribe certain medication that helps some children stop bed-wetting, or the doctor may recommend the child see a psychologist for counseling if there is no physiological basis for the problem.

Can you prevent bed-wetting? All infants are born without bladder control. Only as they mature do children learn to gain control over bladder functions. Many parents feel embarrassed, frustrated, and guilty when their child doesn't meet what they consider the norms of development for the child's age. Oftentimes, the parent's hurt, fear, and anger is vented on the child, who is not capable of handling the adult's anger. It is better for the parents to express their negative feelings to other adults.

Talking to the child about bed-wetting. Parents can talk to their child about bed-wetting when the child is relatively happy and calm. Some parents use a little bit of quiet time just before bed, or just after waking up, but before getting out of bed. Ask the child how he or she feels about the bed-wetting. If you get a response that indicates the child is not very happy about it, then there may be some motivation to try new things. For example, the child could drink less liquid for several hours before bedtime. Or, you could try waking the child to urinate before you retire to bed. If, on the other hand, you get a response that indicates that the child does not really care about the bed-wetting, or worse, the child refuses to even discuss the problem, you may have to wait until the child is ready.

Recommendations: If the child constitutionally or genetically is not ready to do anything about the bed-wetting, parents may have to wait until a later time. Do not make this issue a battleground. Relatively few college students are known to be bed wetters. No president of the United States has been a bed-wetter as far as we know. There is hope for your child.

How do you know what to say to a child who is soiling his or her pants?

Is this a parent problem or a child problem? Even more so than bed-wetting, soiling, or *encopresis,* can become a major battleground between parent and child. Some children use soiling as a

way to fight back or gain control over their parents. These children sense from their parents that bowel control is an important issue of control, and because children can control so little, they use this area as a battleground.

Through positive rewards and encouragement, most children can be potty-trained by about the age of three or four. Occasionally, there may be lapses, perhaps when the child is sick or has diarrhea. A child who still soils his or her pants on a regular basis by the age of four, five, or six is considered to have a problem.

What can you do about it? One of the first things a parent can do about soiling is to consult with the child's pediatrician to determine if there are any physical problems that may be causing some of the difficulties. Second, it is important to know if there is any family history of a similar pattern. Third, if your child's pediatrician agrees that the soiling is a problem, medical intervention may be helpful. Finally, if these approaches are not successful, it may prove worthwhile to consult a child psychologist who has experience in solving soiling problems.

Other approaches. Parents of children who soil their pants often recommend downplaying the problem. These parents teach their child how to change his or her clothes and how to wash up. A positive approach is most often recommended: offer rewards and warm encouragement. Getting angry, punishing the child, or shaming the child is usually not very effective, because a strong-willed child can easily use soiling as a way to punish the parent. Oftentimes, what happens in these cases is that a power struggle ensues. This is one issue that is difficult for a parent to win by force, because the parent does not have power over the child's bowel function.

It is encouraging to remember that, as the child grows older, the social stigma of soiling becomes so strong that the child usually learns to control his or her bowels and function in an age-appropriate fashion.

Another approach, called *positive reinforcement,* or rewards, for children ages three to six, may help motivate a child to change. Rewards may be of several types:

- **Material Objects,** such as food, toys, or stickers that can be turned in for toys.
- **Privileges,** such as going places or doing things that are highly desired.
- **Praise,** for being such a big boy or girl, or for pleasing Mommy or Daddy.
- **Charts,** for providing a visual measure of the child's success. The desire to be powerful or successful may be rewarding for some children.

Recommendations: Parents must think ahead before they criticize or punish a child for soiling. This issue may not be within a parent's control. Instilling feelings of shame and guilt may be exactly the wrong approach to solve this problem.

How do you know if your child has a hearing impairment?

What is a hearing impairment?
Although it is obvious if a child is unable to hear anything at all, a mild hearing impairment, or *tonal gaps* is often undiagnosed. At home and at school your child may not be able to follow directions and, therefore, may be deemed oppositional, difficult, or uncooperative.

Sometimes children can hear fairly well, but have difficulty with speech sound discrimination, *i.e.,* they are unable to distinguish between beginning or ending consonants or middle vowel sounds, so language is unclear to them.

Sometimes children whose native language is one other than English have difficulty hearing the sounds used in English. This is not a hearing problem, but a mimics problem.

How does a child with a hearing impairment behave?
- Children who don't hear don't respond. Adults and teachers can get angry because they believe the children are ignoring them.
- Children with a mild hearing impairment may hear incorrectly or misinterpret what is said. Adults can get angry because they believe

the children are not paying attention.

- Children with a mild hearing impairment may not follow directions, such as doing their homework, because they cannot hear the directions given.
- Children with a mild hearing impairment can become social outcasts because other children won't explain or take the time to clarify game instructions.
- Children with a mild hearing impairment may be thought rude or not interested in other people and become isolated from other children.

How do you help a hearing-impaired child? A hearing-impaired child needs a parent advocate to ensure that he or she gets the educational, social, financial, and emotional services and supports that are available to him or her. There are many public and private organizations that can be helpful.

When the child is young, parents and teachers alike must help other children accept and understand the hearing-impaired child.

Recommendations:
1. A child who consistently misinterprets what you say or asks you to repeat yourself may have hearing loss.
2. Consult a hearing specialist.

How do you know if your child has a visual impairment?

What is a visual impairment? A visual impairment means that a child has difficulty seeing, usually because of some structural difficulty with the eyes or supporting visual system. A visual impairment may lie anywhere along the visual system, such as the eyeball, corneas, lens, or muscles.

How do you know if your child has visual problems?
- Child complains that his or her eyes hurt.
- Child constantly rubs his or her eyes.
- Child holds the paper or book too close to his or her eyes.
- Child sits too close to the television.
- Child squints while looking at objects that others can see clearly.
- Child complains that his or her eyes are tired after reading only a few minutes.
- Child complains about seeing double.
- Child's teacher suggests he or she may be having difficulty seeing.

What to do. The first thing a parent should do is make an appointment with an eye doctor. Ophthalmologists, or eye physicians, and optometrists can help your child with an eye problem. Ophthalmologists tend to deal with eye diseases, while optometrists both examine eyes and prescribe corrective lenses.

Recommendations: Consult either an ophthalmologist or an optometrist.

How do you know if your child has a sleep disorder?

What is a sleep disorder? Sleep allows the body to repair itself physically, as well as mentally. The result is that the person starts the new day with renewed energy to handle the day's activities. Children usually need more sleep than adults. There is some variation in a person's need for sleep, ranging from six or seven hours to ten hours each night. A person who needs too much or too little sleep may have a sleep disorder. If we work too hard and sleep too little, it isn't long before our bodies send us a message. This message indicates the body is breaking down and functioning poorly. We may feel tired, sluggish, or cranky, or we may develop one illness or another with seemingly little immunity to these illnesses.

Causes and symptoms of a sleep disorder. A child has a sleep disorder if he

or she routinely cannot sleep through the night after the age of one. (Bedtimes and routines are covered on pages 1-3.) This chapter deals with the causes and symptoms of a sleep disorder. Sleeping too much may also signal a problem of withdrawal or depression, and a child who sleeps excessively should be examined carefully. Sleeping too little may mean the child is anxious.

What can you do about it? If the child wakes up in the middle of the night ask yourself these questions:
1. Did the child have a scary dream?
2. Did a noise, pet, or sibling wake the child?
3. Is the child sick? Does the child feel hot? Does the child have a stuffy nose, sore throat, upset stomach, or possible ear infection?
4. Did the child have any stimulating foods, drinks, or medications too close to bedtime?
5. Is there some special event that the child is eagerly looking forward to or worried about?
6. Does the child have to go to the bathroom?

For most of the above occurrences, simply taking care of the physical needs and giving the child some reassurance will help the child to go back to sleep. Putting the child back into bed and waiting for a few minutes for the child to go back to sleep is usually sufficient.

A child who has nightmares on a regular basis past the age of three may be exhibiting signs of a sleep disorder.

See if you, as the parent, can get the child to describe the dream or any part of the dream. Describing the dream and discussing it with parents, or drawing images from the dream can give a child some sense of control over the scary images. Ask the child if there is anything that he or she is afraid of during the day; this can help bring out any past, present, or future events that the child is worrying about, but keeping to himself or herself.

In many cases, children have terrifying dreams and cannot recall any images from the dream. In fact, in the morning children often don't recall that they had a nightmare and woke up during the night (not to mention that they woke up the whole household). Also, some children who have nightmares are very hard to wake up; even though they are crying or screaming, they remain in a semisleep state. For these children, simply hold them and stay with them until they fall back to sleep. If the child continues to have nightmares you should contact your pediatrician and possibly a child psychologist.

A special type of sleep disorder. A special type of sleep disorder is sleepwalking. Sleepwalking occurs in a very small portion of the population on a regular basis, although it may occur in a larger portion of the population on an occasional basis. Usually the child who sleepwalks has a blank stare on his or her face, is unresponsive to communication, is hard to wake up, and does not remember where he or she went or what he or she did while sleepwalking. While sleepwalking itself is not dangerous, it can put a person in a dangerous situation.

One child in a sleepwalking state left his house about one o'clock in the morning. He unlocked and walked out the front door, climbed a tree near the house, and began to walk on the roof. His parents heard a noise on the roof and went out to investigate. Guess who they found! The father was able to get a ladder and get the boy down, but the boy did not wake up and had no memory of the incident in the morning.

Another child left his home about three o'clock in the morning and went to a neighbor's house. After ringing the front doorbell repeatedly until the neighbors answered, he asked if their son, who was about his age, could play. Needless to say he was escorted home. Like the first boy, he had no recollection of the incident in the morning. If your child has repeated sleepwalking episodes, it is best to consult your pediatrician and a child psychologist.

How do you prevent sleep disorders?
It may not be possible to totally prevent sleep disorders, but there is no question that a parent can help prevent most sleep disorders by following some sensible rules.

1. Your child should have a sensible bedtime which should become a routine. When a child goes to bed at a set time, a child learns to become sleepy at that time.

2. Watch what your child eats or drinks after dinnertime. Some chil-

dren have nightmares or disturbed sleep if they eat certain foods.

3. Some children benefit from taking a bath or shower just before bedtime, some do not. How does your child react?

4. Some children should not watch scary movies on TV because it disturbs their sleep.

Recommendations:

1. Consult your pediatrician. A pediatrician may be able to answer your questions about sleep problems.

2. If the problem is not a medical one and does not improve, consult a child counselor or psychologist for assistance.

How do you know if your child is eating the right foods?

What is the right diet for your child? America is famous for its preoccupation with food and diets. The right diet for your child may be influenced by several factors. The family history and culture play a very important part. Is your child underweight or overweight? These answers may depend on how you believe your child should look. Insurance companies may have one recommendation based on statistical values. Your child's unique needs, based on weight, family history, allergies, special

needs, and the like, will all influence what a healthy diet is for him or her.

We have to be careful when we talk about the "right" diet, when eating is a main concern of so many. Who among us does not eat some junk food? However, we might agree on several points. The first is that the child's diet has to be nutritious and satisfy the child's basic requirements. Your pediatrician or family doctor is the best source of answers here. Your doctor can tell you if your child is healthy and has an appropriate weight.

Second, the main purpose of a child's diet is to help him or her grow up healthy. The proper diet can affect all areas of a child's life and should be examined very carefully. With a wholesome diet, your child's physical, social, emotional, and academic life may be satisfactory. But what happens if a child's diet is not wholesome and adequate?

What are the symptoms of an improper diet? In preschool or kindergarten your child's teacher may say your child is hard to control and will not sit still and listen. The teacher may say your child has a behavior problem, and that he or she may be learning disabled or hyperactive. Although there are many causes of behavior problems in and out of school, we now know that inadequate diet is one possible cause of the problem.

How does food affect the learning-disabled child? The results are in and we know what to do. Although the exact foods may differ from child to child, there are certain basic foods that appear to affect behavior in many children. For example, we know that simple carbohydrates, such as sugar found in pastries, candies, soft drinks, and so on, create many difficulties for some children. These are foods many children love. Although poor diet does not affect all children, there is evidence that a faulty diet can affect not only learning, but also emotional development.

If your pediatrician says your child is healthy and weighs the right amount, and if your child is doing well socially, and functioning at maximum potential educationally, then he or she probably is eating the right food. On the other hand, if the child is too thin or too fat, and there are problems emotionally, socially, or educationally, then you should look at diet as one possible factor in the problem.

An experiment that parents can do with food. We have helped many parents by having them run their own experiment with food. It is an easy approach to a complex problem. The experiment does not cost anything, and it does not hurt. Of major importance, the results come very quickly. If diet is a factor in your child's overactivity or other negative behavior, you will quickly learn the answer. However, the experiment does require your attention, and you will have to read food labels.

The experiment: Put your child on a healthy diet of chicken and/or fish, as well as fresh vegetables and a little fruit, for four days. There is to be no sugar, fructose, or sucrose. Try to eliminate processed foods with other chemicals during this period. On the fifth day give your child sugar, candy, junk food and anything else he or she wants to eat. Then you decide whether there is a change in your child's behavior. You may also use this experiment to identify foods to which your child might be allergic.

Another source of information. We would be remiss if we did not mention the excellent work of licensed and credentialed nutritionists. If you want help to plan a diet, ask your pediatrician for a referral to a professional nutritionist.

Recommendations:

1. Learn about nutrition yourself so you can be aware of what nutrients, calories, and fats your child takes in every day, and what is needed.
2. Discuss the problem with your pediatrician or a nutritionist.
3. Examine your food cupboards. You may have to change your buying habits.

How do you know if your child has an Attention Deficit Hyperactivity Disorder?

Attention Deficit Hyperactivity Disorder (ADHD) is currently the correct clinical term used to describe individuals with attention deficit problems, who may or may not be hyperactive. The initials ADD were previously used to identify the same disorder. ADHD affects an individual's ability to sustain and control age-appropriate attention, impulsiveness, and activity level. Individuals who have this problem may show it in one situation, such as school, or in many situations, such as school, home, and with friends. At times, some of these individuals can show good control for short periods, but then worsen in situations requiring sustained attention.

When an outside source, such as the school or a teacher, says your child has an Attention Deficit Hyperactivity Disorder, it is time to take notice and to take action.

How do you know if your child has ADHD? Symptoms of ADHD are usually present from early in the child's life and most often noticed by age

seven. In young infants, the symptoms may include the following:
• Colic
• An inability to quiet down
• Frequent crying
• Less need for sleep
• A high activity level

In toddlers, we often see the following symptoms:
• A low sense of danger
• An unusual amount of energy
• A tendency to move from one activity to another very quickly

Parents may notice that the child wears out shoes, clothing, and toys faster than other children. The problem becomes important by school age, when the child may show a combination of the following behaviors:
• Easily distracted by outside activities
• Disorganized with room, clothes, papers, pencils, toys, and so on.
• Impulsive with words and actions
• Difficulty listening
• Difficulty following directions
• Difficulty staying on task
• Difficulty finishing tasks
• Messy and careless work
• Frequent daydreaming
• Difficulty doing things independently
• Difficulty accepting limits set by parents or teachers
• Constantly active
• Difficulty remaining in one place, unless watching TV or playing video games
• Often interrupts
• Sometimes talks excessively
• Difficulty changing activities

- Easily overstimulated
- Sometimes shows aggressive behavior
- Low frustration level
- Low self-esteem
- Socially immature

All children show some of these signs at various ages and various times. A few children show many of these behaviors compared to other children their age. These children are most at risk for having ADHD. A child who has an emotional problem or a child who is bored may show some of these signs, particularly in the classroom. If you suspect that your child has ADHD, you should have him or her evaluated to eliminate other possible causes of the behavior.

The cause of ADHD is often genetic; that is, it is inherited. It can also be due to environmental factors. For example, minute amounts of lead in the child's system, or some disease, such as encephalitis, or mothers who drink alcohol or use drugs while pregnant can cause the same behavior. Certain groups of children appear to have more Attention Deficit Hyperactivity Disorders in their populations. For example, children diagnosed with a learning disability are often also inattentive, impulsive, and overactive.

ADHD children have difficulty regulating their own behavior, or organizing and processing the information they are given. They seem unable to voluntarily control what they are doing and seem unable to recognize when they behave inappropriately. It is this behavior that we hear about, that gets these children into trouble in the classroom and often at home.

What can you do about it? Treating these children is often complicated. The earlier ADHD is recognized, the easier it is to help. If your child seems to fit many of the above descriptions, you should consider a formal evaluation. This disorder is too complicated for most parents to address without professional guidance.

1. The first step is to contact a clinical psychologist or an educational psychologist who is equipped to evaluate the child's overall learning, behavioral, and emotional development.

2. The second step is to receive counseling and education about ADHD and to learn how to handle the child who has this disorder. Parents usually need more specific information about behavior modification than they receive through general education. What the parents have and have not tried has to be reviewed by an expert in this area.

3. The third step is to provide educational and emotional support for the child, so he or she can avoid three major side effects of ADHD: academic underachievement, negative social relations, and low self-esteem.

4. Along with the psychological evaluation, the child should be evaluated for the potential use of medication. Three types of medication have proven successful with ADHD children. They are stimulants

(Ritalin), trycyclic antidepressants (Prozac), and tranquilizers (Phenobarbital). None of these should be used routinely. Although medication appears to be a quick and easy answer, the side effects of these drugs have to be considered carefully.

5. There must be good communication between the parents, the pediatrician and the school if a program to treat ADHD is to succeed. If an educational therapist is used, he or she must be part of the communication loop as well.

Recommendations:

1. Consult the child's teacher to see whether he or she confirms your observations about your child's behavior.
2. Consult a clinical or educational psychologist for a comprehensive evaluation.
3. Consult your pediatrician or a child psychiatrist for possible medical treatment.
4. Contact the Association for ADHD and seek support groups in your area.

How do you know if you should put your child on Attention Deficit Hyperactivity Disorder medication?

Parents need to educate themselves about the problem. Children with Attention Deficit Hyperactivity Disorder (ADHD) are identified by psychologists and physicians in conjunction with parents, teachers, school principals, etc. Over the years, various medications have been prescribed as one effective approach to reduce hyperactivity and help children focus and concentrate. When used successfully, medication results in improved learning and improved ability to maintain social relationships. Medications have included anti-anxiety, antidepressant, and anticonvulsant drugs, with Ritalin, Dexedrine and Cylert topping the list. Since ADHD has been identified, the number of children found with this syndrome has increased dramatically. Because medications have had a dramatic effect on some children (and adults with this disorder), professionals and parents are quick to recommend the drugs. However, these drugs are powerful and many parents are reluctant to use them on their children. Will the child experience serious side effects? Will the child become dependent on the drug? Will this lead to drug abuse later in life? How long will the child be on the drug? Will it cure him or her? Are there any effective drug-free alternatives? These are just a few of the questions that parents ask.

Learn how ADHD affects your child. ADHD shows itself in the child who is often disruptive to himself or herself or others. Lack of the ability to focus, concentrate, and sit still may occur. Children's grades may suffer. Their overactivity may disrupt the class or interfere with their ability to maintain social relationships. This not only upsets the children, but their parents as well. The task of the child is to go to school and learn academics, as well as to develop social relationships. If these goals are jeopardized, parents become very concerned.

In the home there may be similar disruptive behavior. Not following rules, increased fighting with siblings, repeated reminders to stay on task, and the inability to sit still are frequent complaints of parents with ADHD children. While all children exhibit some of these behaviors, ADHD children stand out among others.

Is there a cure? There are many people who claim success using medical approaches, behavioral approaches, nutritional approaches, and aging approaches—simply letting the child grow out of the ADHD behaviors.

Unfortunately there is no simple test to determine which, if any, of the current approaches would be effective for your child. However, in almost all cases, you can find something from each of these areas that is helpful. You might start where you feel most comfortable and learn what that approach has to offer. Remember, many different approaches and techniques have had success, but there is no single approach that works for everyone. Statistically, the combination of appropriate medication, behavioral training, parental counseling, and socialization training has proven the most successful.

Will my child become dependent on the drug? There are two kinds of dependency. First, there is a physical dependency, in which the body cannot function normally without a drug. Parents fear that their children will require larger and larger dosages and become so hooked on a drug that they cannot function at all without it. Parents fear that the medication will eventually weaken the child. Depending on the type of medication used, the effects are relatively short-lived. Medications pass out of the system within a few hours to a few days in most cases. There may be some irritability or crankiness until the child returns to the premedicated behavior.

The second kind of dependency is a psychological dependency, in which the child believes he or she cannot function without the medication. It is one thing to know that something helps you and another thing to feel inadequate without it. In most cases, when children know they take medication to help them concentrate in school, they do not become psychologically dependent. In fact, when medication is properly adjusted, many children report feeling the same as they did when they were not on medication, although everyone around them might notice a difference. However, parents fear that the child will not develop normal feelings of independence, confidence, and competence without the medication.

Will using this medication lead to drug abuse later? Using drugs of any type to feel better or to get better can later lead toward drug abuse. For the most part, medications are positively reinforcing. They either give us pleasure or take away pain. Drug abusers, however, are people who have not yet learned how to take care of themselves without drugs. They lack the knowledge and skill to make themselves feel powerful and connected while reducing their stress or pain without drugs. Medications for ADHD are usually used in conjunction with parent and/or parent-child counseling to help both the child and the parents use the drug correctly. In the vast majority of cases, children learn to distinguish between a medication and an illegal, unsafe drug. Drug abuse and drug addiction have more to do with psychological weaknesses than any medications used for ADHD.

Are there serious side effects? In the majority of cases, the answer is no.

However, these prescribed medications are more powerful than many over-the-counter medications. Because they are more powerful, these drugs have to be monitored by a physician. There are possible side effects to all drugs and there are side effects to the drugs used for ADHD. However, not everyone experiences the side effects. Your child may experience headaches, stomachaches, increased or decreased appetite, nervousness, tiredness, etc., as side effects of the ADHD drugs, or the child might not experience any of these side effects. The only way to find out is to go on a supervised trial of the drug with your physician. Usually the dosage is started very low, and it is slowly increased until there is some sign of effectiveness, either positive or negative. The drug dosage is then adjusted at this point. Only a few children who meet the criteria for ADHD have a negative experience with the drugs. Some have a neutral effect or no effect. The majority have a positive effect.

How long will my child be on the medication? This depends on the severity of the child's ADHD and the effectiveness of the medication. If there is a dramatic difference when the child is on the medication, he or she may need the medication more strongly than some other children, and, therefore, be on the drug longer. If there is only a very subtle difference when the child is on the medication, then there may be greater opportunity to use less of the drug and for a shorter duration. There is some evidence that suggests children moving into middle and late adolescence develop the skills to concentrate and control themselves without medication. In more severe or chronic cases of ADHD, medication may be recommended into adult life. For many years, ADHD was diagnosed only in children. Only in the past several years have more studies been done to determine how prevalent this condition is in the adult population.

In any good treatment program, it is a good idea to periodically check a medication's effectiveness by withdrawing it during specific times under the direction of a physician. Weekends, vacations, and the summertime are times when parents might take their child off medication, so the child can learn to manage without it. All of this, however, should be done with a physician's approval.

Are there effective alternatives to medication? Most parents are initially against the idea of using prescription drugs to alter their child's behavior. They will look for any noninvasive technique or natural way to resolve the problem. And this is healthy. For others, the medication is not effective, and they must seek out other alternatives. Some of these alternatives follow:

- **Diet.** For some ADHD children, diet control has proved very effective. It seems that sugars, such as fructose, sucrose, or ordinary table sugar, which are found in candies, cakes, ice cream, catsup, some breads, and many other packaged foods, clearly act to make children hyperactive, lowering their ability to focus and to concentrate. Even though some studies suggest that foods high in sugar do not affect concentration, behavior, and learning, ask any experienced teacher or parent. Also, there are now some claims (unsubstantiated) that certain herbs and dietary practices can help.

- **Allergy treatment.** Children who have allergies to specific foods, animals, or environmental items can exhibit many of the symptoms of ADHD. These children have to be thoroughly examined. Removing the allergic items or treating the child for allergies can sometimes reduce or eliminate the symptoms.

- **Biofeedback, relaxation, and meditation.** Children can often be taught to concentrate and control their hyperactivity through relaxation techniques, biofeedback machines, and meditation. For some, this has proven very successful.

- **Behavior modification and structured environments.** Children can be taught to become aware of their behavior in environments where there is effective and consistent structure. With the proper balance of rewards and consequences, children can learn to control their behavior.

Parents have to make the final decision about the use of medication. Parents should take all these factors into consideration and make their own decision. It is not an easy decision. Because there are so many variables, parents have to find an approach that will work for both the child and the parents. If you are patient and you persevere, you will find plenty of support for both you and your child.

Recommendations:
1. The recommendations for using medication should come only from your pediatrician.
2. Medication should only be used if behavioral methods have failed.
3. Remember there are side effects to all medication. Consider all these factors carefully.

How do you know when your daughter should go for her first gynecological examination?

Parents need to know when they should take some action. This is an area in which parents have difficulty making a decision. They don't want to traumatize the child. They want to protect the child's virginity. Finally, they lack information on what should be done and when it should be done.

What to do if your child is ill. When there is a medical necessity, your pediatrician or physician will suggest that your daughter go for her first gynecological examination, regardless of her age. The child's welfare is always of primary importance.

Consider the need for medical help if your daughter is beginning menstruation. If your daughter experiences any problems with her first cycle, it may be wise to contact a gynecologist. This may not necessarily require an examination.

Take your child to a gynecologist if she is beginning sexual activity. If your daughter is sexually active, she should have a gynecological examination. The time has come for parents and/or your physician to discuss with her both safe sex and the prevention of pregnancy. Parents may feel they are condoning premarital sexual activity by having this discussion. This is not accurate. Adolescents have to have information to protect themselves. Parents can clearly state their beliefs and values to their daughter at this time.

Age eighteen brings about important changes in a girl's life. As your daughter reaches this age, she becomes a young adult. Hopefully, she has reached a mature level of psychological and social maturity and is able to handle information about sex and sexuality.

If there was no reason for a gynecological examination before your daughter turned eighteen, most gynecologists recommend this as a good starting age. Because most girls become sexually active around age eighteen, if not before, your daughter needs both the information and the protection IN ADVANCE to protect herself.

Recommendations: Avoid traumatizing your daughter; rather, help her. Gaining her consent to an examination is very important.

INDEX

213